Family History, Historical Consciousness and Citizenship

New Directions in Social and Cultural History

Series Editors: Sasha Handley (University of Manchester, UK), Rohan McWilliam (Anglia Ruskin University, UK) and Lucy Noakes (University of Brighton, UK)

Editorial Board:

Robert Aldrich, University of Sydney, Australia
James W. Cook, University of Michigan, USA
John H. Arnold, University of Cambridge, UK
Alison Rowlands, University of Essex, UK
Penny Summerfield, University of Manchester, UK
Mrinalini Sinha, University of Michigan, USA

The *New Directions in Social and Cultural History* series brings together the leading research in social and cultural history, one of the most exciting and current areas for history teaching and research, contributing innovative new perspectives to a range of historical events and issues. Books in the series engage with developments in the field since the post-cultural turn, showing how new theoretical approaches have impacted on research within both history and other related disciplines. Each volume will cover both theoretical and methodological developments on the particular topic, as well as combine this with an analysis of primary source materials.

Published:

Art, Propaganda and Aerial Warfare in Britain during the Second World War,
Rebecca Searle (2020)
Family History, Historical Consciousness and Citizenship: A New Social History,
Tanya Evans (2022)
New Directions in Social and Cultural History, ed. Sasha Handley,
Rohan McWilliam and Lucy Noakes (2018)
Welfare State Generation: Women, Agency and Class in Britain since 1945,
Eve Worth (2022)

Forthcoming:

British Humour and the Second World War: 'Keep Smiling Through',
edited by Juliette Pattinson and Lindsey Robb
Capital Labour in Victorian England: Manufacturing Consensus, Donna Loftus
Captive Fathers, Captive Children: Legacies of the War in the Far East,
Terry Smyth
Intersectional Encounters in the Nineteenth Century Archive: Power and Discourse, edited by Rachel Bryant-Davies and Erin Johnson-Williams

Family History, Historical Consciousness and Citizenship

A New Social History

Tanya Evans

BLOOMSBURY ACADEMIC
LONDON • NEW YORK • OXFORD • NEW DELHI • SYDNEY

BLOOMSBURY ACADEMIC
Bloomsbury Publishing Plc
50 Bedford Square, London, WC1B 3DP, UK
1385 Broadway, New York, NY 10018, USA
29 Earlsfort Terrace, Dublin 2, Ireland

BLOOMSBURY, BLOOMSBURY ACADEMIC and the Diana logo
are trademarks of Bloomsbury Publishing Plc

First published in Great Britain 2022
This paperback edition published 2023

A catalogue record for this book is available from the British Library.

Library of Congress Cataloging-in-Publication Data
Names: Evans, Tanya, 1972- author.
Title: Family history, historical consciousness and citizenship : a new
social history / Tanya Evans.
Description: London ; New York, NY : Bloomsbury Academic, 2022. |
Series: New directions in social and cultural history |
Includes bibliographical references and index.
Identifiers: LCCN 2021038575 (print) | LCCN 2021038576 (ebook) |
ISBN 9781350212060 (hardback) | ISBN 9781350212114 (pdf) |
ISBN 9781350212107 (ebook)
Subjects: LCSH: Genealogy. | Australia–Genealogy. |
Great Britain–Genealogy. | Canada–Genealogy.
Classification: LCC CS9 .E93 2022 (print) | LCC CS9 (ebook) | DDC 929.1–dc23
LC record available at https://lccn.loc.gov/2021038575
LC ebook record available at https://lccn.loc.gov/2021038576

ISBN: HB: 978-1-3502-1206-0
         PB: 978-1-3502-1207-7
         ePDF: 978-1-3502-1211-4
         eBook: 978-1-3502-1210-7

Series: New Directions in Social and Cultural History

Typeset by Integra Software Services Pvt. Ltd.

To find out more about our authors and books visit www.bloomsbury.com
and sign up for our newsletters.

Contents

Illustrations

Acknowledgements

I want to begin by thanking the many wonderful family historians who dedicated their time to answering my questions in their surveys, interviews and focus groups in Australia, Britain and Canada. I loved communicating with you all. I have learned so much about the meanings of history in your lives and what historians might do with that knowledge. You are an inspiration. I hope thousands of others can learn from your brilliant example and that your contributions encourage many more researchers to take up your passion. Long may our conversations continue.

Macquarie University funded the research upon which this book is based with two Outside Studies Program grants that relieved me from two semesters of teaching, one in late 2016 and one in late 2020 – I used one semester to travel and research and one to write this book. The Australian government's financial cuts to universities in 2020 and 2021 mean that my colleagues cannot reap the same benefits as I, and that makes me both sad and incredibly angry. I was fortunate to be awarded an Australian Research Council Linkage grant in 2020 which protects my capacity to research as well as to teach over the next few years, but I hope that this book demonstrates what can be done when you get a few months off from teaching to research and write. I also hope that this work reveals the fruitfulness of undertaking international travel and global collaboration with fellow public historians. I miss those days. Our international research collaborations will be sorely impacted by Covid and continued funding cuts.

On that note I want to thank the colleagues who hosted me on my many family history-related travels over the past few years starting in London in 2016. My hosts and collaborators include Nicola Phillips at Royal Holloway, in Leeds Laura King and in Bristol Josie McLellan. In Ottawa, Canada, thanks to David Dean for hosting me at the Centre of Public History at Carleton University. I am also enormously grateful to my International Federation of Public History colleagues Thomas Cauvin, David Dean and others for enriching my work in public history over the last five years.

This book has benefited enormously from my engagement with a number of international research networks including my lovely #HistoriansCollaborate friends including Laura King, Mike Esbester, Nick Barratt, Natalie Pithers,

Mary Stewart and Julia Laite. I have also benefited from many conversations about family history and the history of the family with my colleagues in the #InheritingtheFamily network Katie Barclay, Ashley Barnwell, Laura King and Joanne Begiato.

Thanks are also due to the numerous family history societies who allowed me to talk about my research with members including the Society of Australian Genealogists, Botany Bay Family History Society, the Lake Macquarie Family History Society, Parramatta Family History Society, Orange City Council and Library. Thanks to Heather Garnsey, Ruth Graham and Martyn Killion who have long facilitated my research. Ruth Graham read and provided many helpful comments on a draft of Chapter 4. The city and regional library networks have also been supportive, especially the State Library of NSW who gave me a non-Stipendiary Research Fellowship to work on the project in 2017, thanks to Rachel Franks and Richard Neville for their support. The library remains a haven for Sydney-based researchers.

I am also grateful to readers and audiences of various draft papers and chapters including my Macquarie University colleagues over the years – Paul Ashton, Paula Hamilton, Michelle Arrow, Clare Monagle, Robert Reynolds, Sean Brawley, Chris Dixon, Mark Hearn, Alison Holland, Nic Baker, Keith Rathbone, Penny van Bergen, Malcolm Choat, Rachel Yuen Colleridge, Margaret Sampson, Leigh Boucher and Kate Fullagar. Thanks also to my Canberra-based ANU collaborators on family history, including Melanie Nolan, Stephen Foster, Malcolm Allbrook and Sophie Scott-Brown (who is now back in Britain). For help with Chapter 1 I need to thank Frank Bongiorno for his assistance piecing together the trajectory of social history in Australia as well as James Opp and Del Muise for their help with the same topic in Canada.

I have benefited enormously from my collaborations with Jerome de Groot and his research assistant Matthew Stallard. Jerome and I have worked together on family history since 2016 and he has been such a supportive friend and colleague since then. His scholarship is exemplary, and he is a marvellous academic citizen.

Thanks to the lovely team at Bloomsbury, especially Abigail Lane and the Series Editors, particularly Sasha Handley, for their guidance, words of encouragement and support.

My former PhD student Marian Lorrison read the entire draft of the book closely and helped me with my writing. My wonderful kind, compassionate, conscientious partner Noah Bassil also read the entire draft and has talked about the project with me since it began. I would be lost without your guidance, good counsel and love Noah. Thank you for all you do to support me and my work and thanks for all our many conversations about life, love, family, history and politics. Our blended family Will, Lara and Hugo including our needy but devoted Labrador Charlie did not help me write the book, but they listened to us talk about it over breakfast, lunch and dinner, and they continue to teach us much about the joys, trials and mysteries of family life.

Introduction: The origins and practice of family history in Australia, Britain and Canada

It is through their families that millions of people, all over the world, first engage with the subject of history, listening to family stories over the years and being told about where they sit in their family trees. Psychologists have revealed that these family stories about the past are crucial to an individual's sense of identity and well-being.[1] National surveys across the globe have revealed the overwhelming centrality of family to people's understanding of history.[2] This introduction outlines the origins and practice of family history in Australia, Britain and Canada, while the rest of the book reveals its manifold meanings and significance in millions of people's lives. I want to make clear from the start that this book aims to make a political statement. As part of the broader project of public history, it argues that we should use the practice, meanings and impact of family history to explore the humanistic potential of historical research and learning both inside and outside academe. It is through family history that we can impart the importance of history for its own sake for millions of people all over the world. We can also reveal how much it teaches us about knowledge production on a familial and societal level and why we need a solid understanding of history to become active citizens. As suggested by the editors of this series on New Social and Cultural History, social historians need to make absolutely clear the political motivations of our work and to make more obvious the relationship between the production and consumption of history for all.[3] This is a vital task at a time when the Arts and Humanities, as subjects taught in the secondary and tertiary sector, are under constant attack from governments and commentators across the world.[4] We simply cannot sit and watch while history is demeaned, the Arts and creative industries are destroyed, and STEM subjects and pathways are revered, funded generously and declared the answer to all our neoliberal world's problems. Everyone who loves history as much as we do needs to work a good deal harder at revealing the importance of the subject in all our lives and its significance for the world around us.[5]

Family history is one of the most widely practised forms of public history around the globe, especially in settler migrant nations like Australia and Canada. It empowers millions of researchers, linking the past to the present in powerful ways, transforming individuals' understandings of themselves and the world. This book examines the practice, meanings and impact of undertaking family history research for individuals and society more broadly. It shows that family history fosters intergenerational and cross-cultural, religious and ethnic knowledge, and how it shapes historical empathy and consciousness and combats social exclusion, producing active citizens. Its key argument is that family history can teach everyone the joy and value of history.

This book is not based on my family history, nor does it blend family history with 'traditional' historical research to analyse a particular historical context, as many recent excellent examples, discussed below, have done. Nor does it concentrate on the extraordinary impact DNA has had on family history.[6] The book draws on ten years of research on family history, including survey data, oral history interviews and focus groups undertaken with family historians in Australia, England and Canada collected since 2016. My research reveals that family historians collect and analyse varied historical sources. These include oral testimony, archival documents, pictures and objects of material culture. They undertake critical readings of memories to challenge their families', the state's and other people's versions of the past. This book reveals how people are thinking historically outside academia, what historical skills they are using to produce historical knowledge, what knowledge is being produced and what impact that can have on them, their communities and scholars. Alongside a range of international public historians, who research the production and consumption of history outside of academia, this book continues to trouble people's assumptions about family historians as sentimental, nostalgic, emotional and un-analytical, and to promote their radical potential.

Scholars have shown that the search into local and familiar pasts is a decidedly international practice. The reach of the Internet has opened up archives to anyone with a computer; lines between the production and consumption of history have become increasingly blurred, as local and family historians share methods and data with researchers around the world; and popular historical programmes and resources, such as *Who Do You Think You Are?* and Ancestry. com, continue to spawn franchises globally in response to an apparently insatiable popular historical appetite.[7] We are more likely to see a genealogist or family historian researching in our archives and public libraries than we are to see academic historians in these environments. In historical terms, it seems, the local is indeed global.

When I moved to Australia from Britain in 2008, I discovered that family history was especially popular amongst individuals coming to terms with their convict pasts.[8] Since I first wrote about the practice of family history in Australia in 2011 it has come under increased academic scrutiny by scholars in a variety of disciplines at all stages of their careers in history.[9] Family history has captured people's imaginations at different times, in different countries. It expanded alongside multiculturalism in settler migrant nations such as Australia, Canada, New Zealand, South Africa and elsewhere. We will see how its meanings vary in these different national contexts but also how those meanings are not constrained by national boundaries. Family history helps to reveal the fictive power of so-called 'national histories'. Scholars agree that genealogical work can provide us with unprecedented insight into how history is undertaken, imagined and discussed by 'ordinary people'.[10] As the teaching and research of public history becomes increasingly internationalized, we need to pay careful attention to the practice and meanings of family history around the world for scholars and practitioners – diverse communities both consuming and producing historical knowledge but not often in conversation with each other. This book helps to facilitate that conversation with a focus on three specific national contexts while remaining aware that the focus here is on the English-speaking world. We have much to learn from scholars working in other national contexts and who speak languages other than English about family history elsewhere. This limitation reflects my incapacity to undertake research in languages other than English, but I want to encourage scholars in other countries to tell us more about the practice and meanings of family history elsewhere.[11] One of the other limits of this study is the dearth of survey responses from Indigenous family historians. Aboriginal family history is a subject ripe for future comparative research and it is most appropriate if this is undertaken by Aboriginal historians.

As suggested earlier, family historians were once sidelined by libraries and archives but are now one of their largest client groups. At a workshop on family history held at Macquarie University, Sydney, Australia, in September 2014, Anne-Marie Swirtlich, then Director General of the National Library of Australia (NLA), told the audience that family historians are now a 'significant user group of the National Library, representing 25% of visitors to the reading rooms and 12% of reference queries received'.[12] The Director of Collections, Access and Engagement at State Archives of New South Wales in Kingswood has estimated that the vast majority of users who access their collections are family historians. Academics are a tiny minority of their regular users.[13] The NLA, like libraries and archives around the world, is providing a new suite of services for family historians. The growth of family history from the 1970s has revolutionized access to historical sources within archival institutions and on the internet as many of the family historians with whom I have communicated attest.

Australian historian Noeline Kyle argues that genealogy provides families with a sense of identity in a period when many of them are undergoing transformation and disruption. It 'was once a quest for social status and recognition, but in the 1990s [and beyond], as its base has broadened, it has become a search for identity'.[14] Some family historians suggest that they search for their family trees to find 'something solid in a shifting world'.[15] As a group, family historians are generally situated outside the academy, often marginalized by academics employed in tertiary institutions and their findings and practices deemed irrelevant to the wider historical community.[16] Some people categorize them as conservative, with a big and a small c, for their supposedly nostalgic search for a golden age of the family. They are dismissed by many academics for their naiveté and amateurism and ridiculed for seeking emotional connections with the past lives of their forebears.[17] The histories produced by genealogists were and are often still deemed trivial, of no consequence and little interest to people outside of their own family. However, family history is understood by a range of sociologists and human geographers in Europe and Australia to have an important role in identity formation.[18] As Nash suggests, family history individualizes the past.[19] This book reiterates the significance and value of family history for individuals but also for society more broadly.

I have undertaken collaborative research with numerous family historians since working on my book *Fractured Families: Life on the Margins in Colonial NSW*.[20] The current publication continues that collaboration revealing the fascinating relationship between past and present and exposing how contemporary family historians are challenging the silences that exist particularly in relation to the past lives of women and the poor. *Fractured Families* explored why the life stories of some men and women in the past come to our attention, while others do not. A work of public history, targeted at family historians as readers, it both celebrated the work of genealogists researching their impoverished ancestors and argued the need for academic historians and family historians to consider greater collaboration. That book uncovered the life stories of men and women, boys and girls, who lived on the margins of society, asking how, why and in what ways these individuals are remembered in

Figure 1a Picture of collaborative workshops with family historians in Manchester in September 2017 © Tanya Evans and Jerome de Groot.

Figure 1b Picture of collaborative workshops with family historians in Manchester in September 2017 © Tanya Evans and Jerome de Groot.

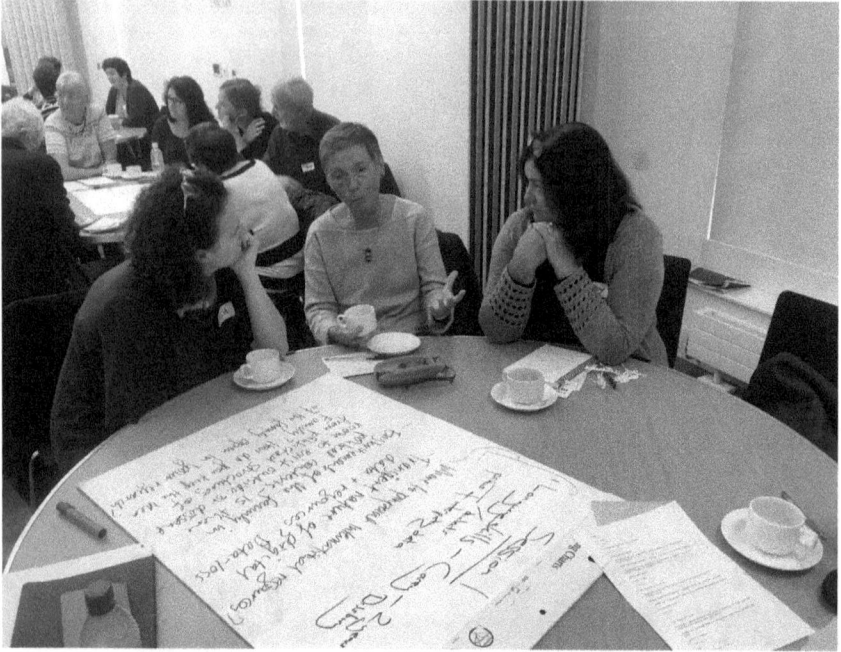

Figure 1c Picture of collaborative workshops with family historians in Manchester in September 2017 © Tanya Evans and Jerome de Groot.

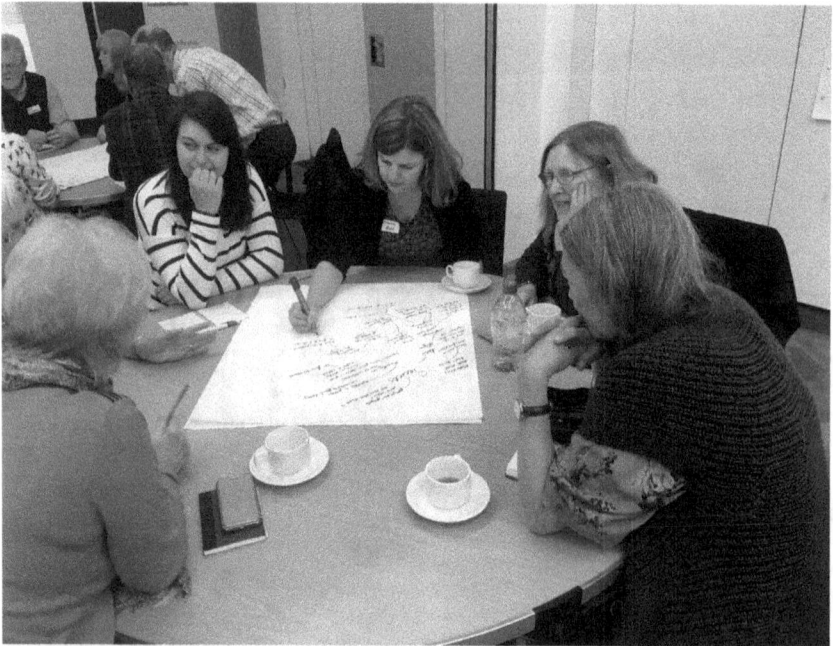

Figure 1d Picture of collaborative workshops with family historians in Manchester in September 2017 © Tanya Evans and Jerome de Groot.

Figure 2 Picture of collaborative workshops with family historians in State Library of New South Wales, Sydney, July 2018 © Tanya Evans and Jerome de Groot.

Australia today. Their lives were refracted through a history of the Benevolent Society and of poverty in nineteenth-century New South Wales, through the institution and its archival record.

I used the book to argue that public history is far more than just a project for academically trained historians, even though people like myself and my colleagues have a significant part to play. Public history is a field in which everyone can take part, but unfortunately different people and groups do not necessarily communicate with one another whilst participating in the process. In that context, I argued that there is a need for all of us to recognize the political significance and consequences of ordinary people producing as well as consuming history in diverse forms. This book and other current collaborative projects continue to work towards that goal.

In my role as Director of the Centre for Applied History at Macquarie University in Sydney since 2016, I have organized several masterclasses and workshops with and for family historians, many in collaboration with the State Library of New South Wales' Education and Scholarship section but also with the public regional library network across Australia, where family history thrives. I am very grateful for the support and collaboration of the Galleries Libraries and Museum (GLAM) sector globally that has helped to facilitate these encounters.[21] Such events have highlighted the benefits of working in collaboration not just with family historians but also with cultural organizations and institutions who cater to large numbers of family historians as clients and who structure our knowledge about the past in terms of the documents and historical sources they collect and allow us to access. In partnership with Ancestry.com.au I helped to co-organize two workshops with British academic Jerome de Groot, one was held at Manchester City Library in September 2017 and one in Sydney at the State Library of New South Wales in July 2018. During these workshops we explored the significant potential to create new knowledge by bringing together scholars with family historians to discuss the extraordinary growth of family history in different nations around the world. We discussed these events in blog posts and

Figure 3a Collaborative workshop with family historians in Orange City Library, Regional New South Wales, August 2019 (credit and copyright Tanya Evans and History Council of NSW).

Figure 3b Collaborative workshop with family historians in Orange City Library, Regional New South Wales, August 2019 (credit and copyright Tanya Evans and History Council of NSW).

Figure 3c Collaborative workshop with family historians in Orange City Library, Regional New South Wales, August 2019 (credit and copyright Tanya Evans and History Council of NSW).

we continued to write about them for a Special Issue of the *International Public History Journal* on Family History which was published in late 2019.[22]

This collaborative networking continues nationally and internationally. In Leeds in July 2018, I spoke at a workshop organized by Associate Professor Laura King, highly regarded British historian of the family, on the benefits of cooperating with family historians. As a result of this and communication that followed (via social media) we planned a successful workshop at Senate House London in January 2019 including family historians, archivists, librarians, representatives of several family history societies, organizations and others to discuss how we might better work with the Galleries Libraries and Museum sector and family historians in the future. All of us believe in the need to challenge the hierarchies and boundaries that exist between family historians and academic historians and prevent their meaningful dialogue.[23] This initiative resulted in the creation of the #HistoriansCollaborate network and the establishment of a new seminar series at the Institute of Historical Research in London titled 'Historians across boundaries: collaborative historical research'.[24]

While academic colleagues often challenge my assertions about family historians being marginalized and held in disdain by academics, it is clear to me from academics, casual conversations as well as from many years of my research with family historians (as Chapter 1 reveals), that genealogists understand themselves as 'less worthy' than academics. Most tellingly they are often snubbed by scholars at conferences and public talks. This book hopes to encourage others to challenge this disdain. Following a University of Sydney colleague's 'sneering reference to "hobbyists"' my Australian public history colleague and friend Peter Hobbins became passionate about undertaking community history on the Spanish flu epidemic in New South Wales.[25] He has joined with me and many other public historians striving to end such dismissive and patronizing responses.

The history of family history

Over the past thirty years, family history has become one of the strongest global cultural industries, capturing people's imaginations at different times, in different nations, and is often explained as a national phenomenon. Before the twentieth century, historians have revealed, it was a practice largely associated with social aspiration. The Genealogical and Historical Society of Britain was established in 1850 and the British Society of Genealogists followed in 1911. Migrants who made their homes throughout the British Empire were amongst the keenest genealogists congregating in formal societies as they settled in foreign lands.[26] In Australia the Society of Australian Genealogists was established in 1938, the same year of the sesquicentenary of white settlement. Elsewhere in this part of the world, the New Zealand Society of Genealogists came into existence in 1967. In other settler nations, the Genealogical Society of South Africa was founded in 1964. While Canada has no overarching national body of genealogists, hundreds of provincial and local organizations have flourished.[27] The Ontario Genealogical Society was founded in 1961, while others followed in the wake of the Centennial of Confederation in 1967, including the British Columbia Genealogical Society, which was founded in 1971. In the United States, the Latter Day Saints' Genealogical Bureau was formed in 1888, and the first US national body, the National Genealogical Society, came together in 1903.[28] Francois Weil has charted how until the late-eighteenth-century genealogy began as a 'private quest for pedigree' amongst status seeking settlers in colonial America, becoming increasingly egalitarian and more widely practised among the middle class and free African Americans from the antebellum era.

From the 1860s to the mid-twentieth century, genealogy in the United States became an exclusionary practice infused by eugenic concerns and anxieties around race. In the mid-twentieth century it was profoundly affected by the civil rights movement and multiculturalism, which broadened its practice among all social groups in many migrant nations.[29] Across the world from the 1970s, the practice of family history underwent enormous growth and democratization and became a global phenomenon after the publication in the United States of Alex Haley's *Roots: the Saga of an American Family*.[30] In both its book and television series format *Roots* reached hundreds of millions of people across the world.[31] The novel's global success led to the establishment of the African American Family History Association in 1977, the organization persisting until 1997 when it morphed into the Afro-American Historical and Genealogy Society which thrives today.[32]

Grassroots, local family history organizations became convinced of the need to join together nationally, and the UK-based Federation of Family History Societies provided an umbrella organization in 1974. There are now 180 societies linked to it around the world.[33] Its Australian parallel followed four years later in 1978.[34] Local historical organizations have been just as active: the Federation of Australian Historical Societies represents about a thousand groups, including nearly 100,000 members, along with around 3000 local and community museums.[35] These organizations, mainly run by volunteers, have all helped to develop an interest in both local and social history, but many members fret about their ageing membership and how best to recruit young people in order to guarantee their survival.

The steady growth in family history at the local, national and international levels preceded the transmission of the enormously popular television series *Who Do You Think You Are?* in the UK in 2004. There is little doubt that the programme, now broadcast globally, has encouraged many more individuals across the globe to research their family's history and to engage with the practice. In recent years, the television programme, a plethora of digital sources and the increasing popularity of family history have had a significant impact on the services of archival offices and libraries across the world. Until recently, production companies based in different nations produced the programmes locally, with different versions being broadcast in Britain, Australia, Canada, the Czech Republic, Denmark, Finland, France, Germany, Ireland, Israel, Norway, the Netherlands, Poland, Portugal, Russia, South Africa, Sweden and the United States. Warner Brothers bought the worldwide rights to the programme in 2017. In 2006 in Toronto Canada, Primitive Entertainment produced the extremely popular television series *Ancestors in the Attic*. Family history thrives in televisual and online forms. Canadian historian John Reid suggests that Facebook hosts over 1000 Canadian genealogy groups and pages. Gail Dever, family historian and blogger, has helpfully collected and listed details on all of them on her website.[36] These numerous sites reveal how family history is practised, produced and consumed in diverse forms.

In recent decades there has been a growing body of work exploring the historical consciousness of national communities, and the everyday historical practices – activities which American historians Roy Rosenzweig and David Thelen term 'popular history-making' – those communities have undertaken.[37] Subsequent national surveys in Australia and Canada reveal the primacy of family history in multicultural settler societies and confirm that for most people the personal and familial remain our 'principal focus for connection with the past'.[38] For example, the Canadians and Their Pasts survey demonstrated that in the twelve months prior, one in five of the 3000 respondents had undertaken family history in some form. It is intriguing to explore how community-based interest in family history is in part a reaction to strictly national narratives, as well as being fundamentally located within them. As Anna Clark's research into community attitudes to Australian history uncovered, while almost all respondents expressed deep connections with their own community or familial histories, many felt alienated and disconnected (in a personal sense) from their nation's 'official' history.[39] Family history research enables them to examine and understand the reasons for such disconnections.

Family history in Australia

A decade ago, I argued that the techniques and findings of family historians disrupt many of our assumptions about the past. The construction of a family tree or the discovery of manifold secrets and lies can throw into question the solidity not only of the history of family, social class and gendered power relations but equally the history of nation and empire. Each newly discovered document encourages the historian to add to or question the narrative so far. The construction of innumerable family trees providing evidence of convict and/ or Aboriginal ancestry forced many to discard the 'pioneer myths' so beloved of a certain class of Australians, usually of European descent.[40] Family historians have also upended our understanding of the heteronormative construct of 'the family' as they have pulled apart and questioned family forms across the ages and revealed the existence of diverse familial forms in different national and community contexts.

Academic and public historians have complicated the picture of the settlement of Australia, providing evidence of the relations between white settlers (whether forced migrants or free) and Indigenous peoples. Australians have become increasingly aware of these discoveries and their implications, and how they can encounter history through genealogy.[41] While the history of early colonial Australia is still considered unfashionable among Australian academic historians and students, genealogists remain fervently and intensely interested in the time. Family historians are hungry for more knowledge about colonial society and its spaces. Many younger family historians now regret not paying more attention to Australian history lessons when at school. I argued then and continue to do so that it is for this reason that when woven carefully with academic history, family history has the potential to change the way in which Australians think and write about the past.[42]

In 2006 Australian historian Victoria Haskins suggested that misogyny informs many criticisms of genealogy.[43] While I believe her observation remains true, historians of women in Australia have long recognized the radical possibilities of family history. Babette Smith, author of the very successful *A Cargo of Women: Susannah Watson and the Convicts of the Princess Royal* (1988), which reconstructed the biographies of 100 convict women transported to

New South Wales in 1830, and of the successful but much more controversial *Australia's Birth Stain: The Startling Legacy of the Convict Era* (2008), began her historical career as a genealogist and remains passionate about family history in Australia today.[44] In her later work, Smith raised the significant role of family historians in revising Australian history. They did so by questioning traditional and largely accepted historical narratives about Australia's early colonial and convict past that strictly demarcated the experiences of convict and free and denigrated or ignored the role that convicts have played in Australian history. The long history of the denial of convict heritage began with convicts themselves, who were already accustomed to telling lies for their own ends. In a new world with the potential to start life afresh, it was easy enough to conceal their true identities. A simple name change was often enough for this, but some convicts grew skilled at creating new identities, moving on and changing nomenclature. The impact of the anti-transportation campaigns of the 1830s lasted well into the mid twentieth century. As late as the 1970s, convict connections were regarded as shameful, and many Australian families worked hard to bury evidence of such ancestry. The rejection of convict connections had important implications for how Australians thought about their nation's past – the first sixty years or so of settlement tended to be ignored.[45] While the silence did not go unnoticed, few were able to challenge it effectively due to political and social pressures. Smith argues that it is only genealogists who have succeeded in exposing Australia's 'real' history, after discovering that their ancestors were rarely victims of a brutal disciplinary regime and were in fact more resourceful and successful in early colonial Australia than we have been led to believe.[46] This means, in the words of colonial Australian historian David Roberts, that 'Convict heritage … which was once a source of anxiety and embarrassment, is now aired and celebrated as something truly distinctive'.[47] Some Australian historians have become increasingly convinced of the unique contributions of family history.

In their quest to reconstruct the early colonial period on the island, historians based in Tasmania have long embraced the methodologies of family historians. Here at least, many historians agree that family historians no longer warrant condescension.[48] Of the 150,000 people transported to Australia between 1788 and 1853, almost half were sent to Van Diemen's Land, which in 1856 changed its name to Tasmania to rid itself of convict identity as quickly as possible. Van Diemen's Land had a far larger proportion of ex-convicts to hide than New South Wales. Like the colonial authorities, ex-convicts worked to bury Tasmania's convict roots. As ex-prisoners went on to establish successful and crime-free lives in the colony the pioneer myth supplanted the island's penal origins. After the end of transportation, many ex-convicts left Tasmania for the goldfields of Victoria while those who stayed simply buried their pasts with silence and subterfuge. Lucy Frost has suggested that, despite Tasmania's small settler population, the secrets and lies of convictism, settler violence towards Indigenous people, theft and murder remained hidden, so that until recently the convict past was successfully expunged from cultural memory. This omission meant that most Tasmanians remained ignorant of their convict heritage even though by the late twentieth century three-quarters of the population sported a convict ancestor.[49] The 'convict cringe' was only successfully challenged with the granting of open access to convict records in 1977 following the 1960s' decline in the stigma of convictism as family historians revealed the extent of convict heritage and Tasmania's archivists squared up successfully to the policymakers.[50]

Frost recognizes her debt to shared scholarship with family historians as they meet in the middle – she working forwards from early convict sources and they working backwards to construct their family trees. Women who had fallen out of historical sight as they left the convict system, moved, married and changed their names were no longer lost, and technology allowed her to find and knot her narrative threads.[51] Convict scholars, blessed with a multiplicity of sources, readily acknowledge the utility of genealogical methods and the value of the voluntary work of genealogists. Hamish Maxwell-Stewart, also based in Tasmania, led a large international team of scholars (members are based in Melbourne, Flinders, University of New England, Oxford and Australian National University) to reconstruct Tasmania's early colonial history. The Founders and Survivors Project enlisted the unpaid and enthusiastic efforts of genealogists, and aimed to 'follow convict founders and their descendants over five generations and build a unique portrait of modern Australian society in the making'.[52] Several of the Australian family historians involved in my study commented on how much they enjoyed participating in the project and expressed appreciation of Australian historian Janet McCalman's support.

Elsewhere in Australia, historians Portia Robinson and Grace Karskens enriched their earlier scholarship on late-eighteenth- and early-nineteenth-century Australian lives by using the techniques of family history.[53] Sophisticated and nuanced work by historians of gender and race in Australia has also recognized the value of genealogy. As Victoria Haskins and Cassandra Pybus argue, the focus on everyday lives, while offering the seductive quality of old-fashioned historical detective work (laborious but ultimately valuable hours spent in the archives, scanning those reels of microfilm), is indispensable when it comes to investigating larger questions such as the complex construction of power relations and their transnational characteristics in the past.[54] The attention to the benefits of family history research has persisted in the Legacies of the British Slave Ownership project and its colonial offshoots around the world.[55]

In recent years, several excellent examples of successful collaborations between academic and other types of historians have proliferated in a range of national contexts.[56] Many of these works have been published in Australia. Using his own family history, historian Graeme Davison has written a history of migration to Australia in *Lost Relations* and is now working on a second volume.[57] Colonial historian Penny Russell continues to research and write about her Congregationalist family who migrated to Sydney from the East End of London.[58] Other examples of a successful blending of academic and family historical research include works by Paul Irish, Betty O'Neil, Marian Lorrison, Alana Piper and Michael Bennett.[59] Since I am most familiar with the work produced in New South Wales and Australia, there may well be many other examples of such collaboration.

Bettina Bradbury's *Caroline's Dilemma* is another excellent recent example of compelling women's history that benefits from an engagement with family history and family historians. It is a carefully crafted piece of detective work, expanding our knowledge of the history of marriage and family life in the nineteenth-century settler colonial world. Bradbury's research and the book's construction have benefited enormously from engagement with descendants of her nineteenth-century protagonists. I would be keen to learn more about the impact of that process on the family historians she liaised with. It is important to ask what can academic and family historians learn from each other as they share their research journeys and how might our knowledge be reshaped considering these collaborations?[60]

In the last few years, I have examined several Australian PhD theses which have used family history as part of their methodological approach. Completed in 2019, Erica Cervini's thesis explores and explains why the life story of the author's great grandmother Rose Pearlman has remained largely invisible until now. Cervini investigates the politics of life-writing, memoir and biography using Virginia Woolf's writings as a springboard. She makes clear the significance of life stories such as Rose's, emphasizing why such lives should be pieced together by researchers and disseminated widely to bring the 'marginalized' to our attention. The thesis begins and ends with a significant discussion about the importance of family history in overturning our assumptions about the past, which is used to construct the larger creative section of the PhD – a memoir/ writing of the life of Rose Pearlman.[61]

Louise Blake's thesis explores and explains the gendered development of different forms of community on the Upper Goulburn goldfields from the mid to the late nineteenth century through the three key themes of geographic locality, gender and belonging. The thesis begins and ends with a significant discussion about the importance of family history, which is used to apply classical theories of community to explain the development of a little-known community in gold rush Australia. Using a wide variety of sources including written archives, maps, material culture (a scrapbook), memoirs, letters and visual sources she shows us how a microhistory of a small, obscure settlement in nineteenth-century Australia can be used to tell us about community making in our contemporary world.[62]

Shauna Bostock Smith's PhD thesis 'From Colonisation to My Generation: An Aboriginal Historian's Family History Research from Past to Present' also blends formal academic independent historical research and analysis with family history research to construct a social history that focusses on the life stories of five generations of her Bostock-Smith family. The thesis also includes a narrative of the candidate's research journey as an Aboriginal family historian seeking to make their mark on 'traditional' Australian historical scholarship while learning more about the construction of their own identity. What marks this thesis out from the others is its very welcome focus on Aboriginal history. I hope it encourages other Aboriginal family historians to undertake similar projects and understand the political significance and potential of that work.[63] As these recent theses attest, there has been a huge growth in family history scholarship in Australia in recent years and the trend is increasing elsewhere.[64] All these scholars are determined to reinforce the value of family history to broader understandings of history in Australia.

Family history in Britain

My research, because it is based in Australia, has uncovered much more about the practice of family history here than elsewhere and the book reveals this imbalance in my knowledge and research. Despite some disciplinary misgivings which I discuss in the following chapter, many academic and professional historians are increasingly drawn to the field of family history outside of as well as within Australia. In Britain, family history was long understood to be an elite practice and associated with social climbing rather than democratization. The practice having begun in the Middle Ages when the College of Arms was established. Given the shift in class focus which occurred after the Second World War, family historians in recent years have been more interested in poor rather than rich relations.[65] Formed in 1911, the Society of Genealogists remained a 'quaint retired gentleman's club' until the later twentieth century when numbers grew rapidly, starting in the 1970s and expanding even more convincingly into the 80s and 90s.[66] This growth has paralleled intensified interest elsewhere and in 1974 the Federation of Family History Societies was also formed to support researchers. It now represents 180 societies throughout the world, but mainly in Britain.[67] The Guild of One Name Studies was formed in 1979 to enable and encourage research about ancestors who share the same name. These multiple and diverse organizations thrive today as active members of the #HistoriansCollaborate network discussed earlier and in the Epilogue.[68]

There are also several examples of British historians writing about their family history. In England, Alison Light's *Common People: The History of an English Family* begins with each of her grandparents' stories and is a living, breathing history of how the Industrial Revolution made its impact on English lives. Light allows us to make some sense of the intimate lives of the English poor over the past 200 years. Using family history, she successfully makes the micro macro – and in her notes, she states that she hopes her book will 'encourage others to write their family history as a public history'.[69] Virago publisher and feminist icon Carmen Callil has recently published her take on the British Industrial Revolution and her family history movements between Britain and Australia.[70] There is plenty of evidence in this book and many others that family historians have responded in droves to Alison Light's request.

We can link the work of these writers on the migratory habits of nineteenth-century English families with that of historians working on their family histories elsewhere across Britain. Alison Baxter wrote her beautifully crafted creative practice PhD, like Erica Cervini, using her Victorian Cornish family history to take us through the Industrial Revolution whilst simultaneously exploring the boundaries between fiction and non-fiction.[71] Laura King's continuing collaborative work with family historians and artists around death and remembrance is particularly innovative and creative, and I eagerly await the publication of her book with Oxford University Press on the topic.[72] Family history is also central to Aoife O'Connor's digital crime history research as part of the Panopticon project at the University of Sheffield. Her experience as an industry insider as a member of the Findmypast team as Head of Project and Programme Management is especially valuable.[73] O'Connor has also compiled a range of resources for genealogists, historians and other researchers to use when researching the history of crime.[74] As we see in a later section of the book, this research in the service of others is a common theme among those who work in family history.

Some people, mainly the well-to-do, have been conducting family history for centuries, but it is time for all of us to recognize the political significance and consequences of others reclaiming their past in such ways. As US historian Joseph Amato states, 'individuals can now give themselves a history' via family history.[75] Technology has been instrumental in the democratization of historical research, as family historians repeatedly articulate in the chapters that follow. These practitioners have moved beyond the archive and online resources to learn about their family history from other sources. DNA is allowing researchers across the world to form new connections, between people and space, being made by researchers across the world. The company 23andMe allows individuals to bring their 'ancestry to life through their DNA' and to 'find relatives across continents or the street'. In exchange for a sample of their saliva and US$99, customers are provided with details about their family history as well as their genetic make-up. Individuals are increasingly turning to science to 'prove' their family history and Ancestry.com is now cashing in on this market along with a host of other companies offering DNA searches. We might suggest that this turn to science has bulldozed over any claims that history might make to this production of knowledge, but Christine Kenneally's and Jerome de Groot's recent research reveals that genetics are 'not as determinative as we feared' and cultural history will continue to shape individuals far more than we may assume.[76]

Family history in Canada

As we saw earlier, American historian Joseph Amato has traced seven generations of his family from Sicily, Prussia, Acadia, England, Ireland, New England and the Mid-West of the United States. The results of his efforts in *Jacob's Well: A Case for Rethinking Family History* reveal a broader history of America's poor as they moved from farm and village to town and city.[77] This trend of academic historians writing about their family history is less developed amongst historians in Canada (as far as I know), but in Canada labour historians have often relied on genealogy to piece together the histories they write. Novelists have also been heavily reliant on the techniques of family history for their own contextual research.[78]

In settler migrant nations such as my own in Australia, and including Canada, New Zealand, South Africa and elsewhere family history expanded alongside multiculturalism. The policy of multiculturalism fuelled the cultural confidence of family history researchers. Historian John Reid, former president of the British Isles Family History Society of Greater Ottawa and author of *Canada's Anglo-Celtic Connections*, put me in touch with several survey respondents and interviewees in Ottawa. He has charted the emergence of genealogy in Acadia, French Canada and of people from Irish, Loyalist and Scottish heritage and organizations.[79]

In Canada, sociologist Ron Lambert's 1990s survey of 1348 members of a Canadian genealogical society has revealed that family historians were motivated to begin research at particular moments in the life cycle, rather than historical moments on the national calendar.[80] Del Muise and Leighann Neilson continued Lambert's extensive national survey on genealogical communities in Canada, which involved large-scale surveys of genealogists. Over 2000 people responded to their 2011 survey. Respondents reported that the importance of family history lay in its potential to help them construct a sense of community belonging.[81] These surveys have revealed that there are many more people practising this vernacular form of history than is often realized. Furthermore, for many groups – such as immigrants and Indigenous peoples (in Australia, Canada and the United States, for example), family histories have existed as counternarratives to dominant national histories from which these groups have frequently been excluded.[82] That these 'stories from below' share important historical methods (such as oral history) as well as political urgency in their various sites confirms both the radical and transnational potential of family history to unsettle national narratives.[83] At the same time, however, many individuals have begun their family history alongside the public celebration of key nation-making dates. In Australia we have seen how genealogy really took off as the country moved towards the bicentenary of white settlement in 1988. In Canada, genealogists were encouraged to begin their research by the Centennial of Confederation in 1967, which was 'a seminal moment that encouraged various initiatives in community history that led seamlessly to an interest in family', and there is a clear link between national celebrations and intimate lives deserving further research.[84] Family history organizations have emerged alongside local history organizations such as the Ontario Historical Society, established in 1949 and the separate Ontario Genealogical Society which emerged in 1961. Genealogical societies sprang up in Saskatchewan (1969), British Colombia (1971), Alberta (1972), Prince Edward Island and Manitoba (1976). After *Roots* made its impact here and the first finding aid for Canadian genealogists was published,[85] other societies followed in Anglophone Quebec (1977), New Brunswick (1978) and Nova Scotia (1982).[86]

In tandem with public historians, Canadian researchers, aiming to examine the development of historical consciousness, have been at the forefront of studies on family history in Canada and shown how popular a pastime it is.[87] The Canadians and their Pasts team in particular have revealed how marginalized groups such as Acadians and Aboriginal Canadians have used family history to challenge dominant narratives about 'the national' past.[88] This challenge may involve a process of inclusion, but it has also resulted in angry responses from Metis communities, who despair at how genealogy is being manipulated by 'race shifters' operating in Canada today.[89]

For these reasons I jumped at the opportunity to undertake comparative research in Canada. In late 2016 I had the pleasure of visiting Carleton University in Ottawa as a research fellow in public history to compare the meanings of family history in Canada with its practice in Australia and England. The surveys and interviews I undertook with family historians largely took place there. Together with Tim Compeau who is based at the University of Western Ontario and other international public history colleagues in July 2021 at an International Federation for Public History conference panel, we will continue to encourage academics to undertake collaborative research projects with diverse local and community historical organizations (https://ifph.hypotheses.org/6th-ifph-international-conference-2020).[90] We desire learning more about the practice elsewhere.

Method

Family history is clearly a global practice, nationally distinctive to be sure, but my research findings confirm how porous boundaries are amongst this global community of researchers. Many family historians have moved between different national contexts and undertake research and extensive family history or heritage tourism globally. Most understand their practice as global, as suggested in Chapter 4 on genealogical communities.[91] I began my project comparing family historians in Britain, Australia and Canada with a call-out on Ancestry.au and.nz and the family history magazine *Inside History* (now folded and reissued as *Traces*).[92] I was quickly inundated with responses from family historians eager to share their motivations, discoveries and the impact of these upon their lives.

Such research reveals the use and strength of social media connections in the family history community and how the Internet is used to produce and consume historical knowledge.

The survey I sent out consists of thirty-seven questions which are listed in the Appendix. These have been collected since mid-2016. The surveys amounted to a total of 136, and included 81 responses from Australian family historians, 27 English and 28 Canadian family historians. Clearly, I have many more responses from Australian rather than British or Canadian researchers. Seven oral history interviews were undertaken alongside the survey collection. Women make up the majority of respondents to the survey and as subjects for the interviews, but men also responded, if not in the same numbers. Among the eighty-one Australian respondents, fifteen (18 per cent) were male; among the British respondents five were men and twenty-two were women; men made up a greater proportion of the Canadian respondents: eight (29 per cent) were men, twenty were women.

It is difficult to gauge the representative nature or otherwise of my survey respondents, given that I collected limited socio-economic data other than asking about their employment. Some respondents chose not to answer all the questions that were posed to them and I did not probe them to share information if they were reluctant to do so. All respondents self-selected to answer the survey. Most, but not all, were non-English-speaking and wrote their answers in English, reflecting my focus on two settler-colonial contexts of Australia and Canada, whereas Britain obviously had a much longer history as a nation. That said, several of my Canadian respondents were bilingual in French. Researchers have much more to learn about the practice and meanings of family history in non-English-speaking nations and the current study makes no claim to reveal this.[93] Most observers assume that more family historians are female than male.[94] A similar gender disparity emerged for the Canadians and the Past survey as well as other similar surveys in different national contexts.[95] Such gendered differences also apply to those people who volunteer for social survey experiments. The University of Sussex's Mass Observation project, for example, has struggled for years to increase male participants in their Directive responses and they have long grappled with questions concerning representation.[96]

Many family historians provided survey responses that were several thousand words long; 3000 words was the average length, but some respondents contributed well over 7000 words while others wrote much less in their replies. Perhaps unsurprisingly if we believe in the strength of gender stereotypes, men were much sparser in their replies than women. It is difficult to find hard data on numbers of family historians. I have consulted with numerous family history umbrella organizations to see if they collect data on the age and gender of their membership. For the most part, unfortunately they do not.[97] Most of these organizations report that their membership consists mainly of older women. It is more of a challenge to learn about family historians who do not belong to formal organizations because they research as individuals using libraries, archives, and the Internet. Some of my respondents were members of societies and thrived sharing their knowledge with like-minded researchers in person, but others were not and preferred to work alone. The Federation of Family History Organizations in Australia estimates that 80–90 per cent of members across Australia are women.[98] This number parallels my survey respondents, but I would not argue that they were 'typical' or 'representative'.

Throughout the book, I use the terms family historian and genealogist interchangeably because many family historians and others who undertake research on family histories do so. In this context, these same researchers debate the conflicting meanings of amateur and professional. As should be obvious by now, my work disrupts the boundaries and hierarchies set up between these distinct categories and labels, and so I use the terms interchangeably. In the same way, I give substantial space to the voices of family historians throughout the book, to privilege their labour and perspectives rather than marginalize them by using mine. This is in line with my feminist practice of providing a platform for diverse and marginalized voices to speak and to share their experiences so that we all might learn from them. It reveals the synergies between their method and mine as social historians as I will explain in the next chapter.

Family historians work or have worked in a range of employment contexts, private and public, and have experienced diverse educational paths. Many are tertiary educated but not necessarily in history or the arts. They are often autodidacts in family history techniques, but also advised by librarians, fellow researchers, related family historians around the world, community organization members, local historical societies and learn from watching global versions of family history television programmes, such as *Who Do You Think You Are?* And *Every Family Has a Secret*. Many of these family historians have themselves become tutors to beginning historians and work as volunteers in libraries and family history societies in various national contexts, as Chapter 4 reveals. They are determined to share their skills with others. The tertiary sector has also recently expanded to accommodate and financially benefit from the global growth in family history. Researchers have benefited from graduate and postgraduate study in history at the University of Tasmania, University of

New England, MOOCS taught out of Monash University in Australia and at the University of Strathclyde, the University of the Third Age and the Open University.

My work will show how many researchers move seamlessly between digital and written archives. These researchers know that without online research, communication, collaboration and presentation of research findings, brick walls would remain insurmountable. Family historian Kay Spence relishes her research on the Internet and feels empowered as 'the Queen of Detectives' when she tracks down information no one else can discover. When she first joined Ancestry.com, Kay was contacted by relatives keen to learn more about her mother's great grandmother, a woman believed to hail from St Petersburg before migrating to Australia. With nobody succeeding in finding out when her great, great-grandmother's precise arrival had occurred, Kay had

> Within a year ... tracked down an advertisement in a newspaper on TROVE which resulted in a breakthrough and [learned] the year she arrived, what ship she was on and who she travelled with to Australia. I received thank you emails from people all across the world ... I now feel like I am indomitable when it comes to discovering details no-one else can find in the digitised newspapers.[99]

This important sense of prestige and empowerment is key to understanding the affective aspect of family history research. It is emotional insofar as it considers family links, but it also contributes to feelings of self-esteem and self-worth, particularly amongst retired or older people. Surprisingly, such an effect is also true for younger family historians. Kay hosts her family tree online and has made it publicly available for nine years (in 2016) and she corresponds with family historians on Ancestry.com, Genes Reunited and My Heritage. She has shared her DNA test online as well. She is 'very happy for anyone to use anything they find on my tree'. She loves research so much that she monitors Ancestry's Facebook page and answers people's questions when they post them, even helping some of these people to undertake their research after making contact.[100] Family history is the reason these practitioners love history as a subject, and they work hard to share their love with others. Therefore, this book argues that their work requires thoughtful analysis, some celebration and to be offered as an example to others.

'Giving Little People a Voice': Family historians, the 'new social history' and public history

This is a book that sets out to challenge the nation-focused/state-driven patriarchal history that populates the popular histories and older academic scholarship many family historians and the people situated outside the tertiary sector understand as History. The introduction reveals how this research brings family historians into conversation with contemporary social and cultural historians, public historians as well as historians of the emotions. It is crucial that this conversation includes as many people as possible so that people far and wide can recognize and reiterate the importance of history in daily life for each and every one of us. This chapter asserts that family histories are often constructed by those who as a collective can unwittingly challenge our early twenty-first-century neoliberal focus on the individual and the market, sometimes consciously, if often not.

As it is practised in Australia, Britain and Canada today, family history privileges the history of intimate, everyday lives. It draws on broader themes to reveal the power relations that valorize some forms of knowledge and labour over others. As discussed in the Introduction, family historians were once believed to be in search of illustrious and aristocratic relations, but my research, as well as that of others, reveals how family historians are particularly fascinated by the lives of their working-class and migrant forbears and especially women – the lives of ordinary people in all times. As a feminist historian, I am interested especially in how family historians, many millions of whom are women, can trouble the gendered order of history making, as well as our wider knowledge of the history of the family and social history. As discussed in the following chapter, the micro and macro historical knowledge that is produced through their research and collaboration with others can have a profound impact on their identities. This encourages them to challenge family storytelling and the structures of power within which they, their families and communities are situated. It reveals how important the subject of history is to understand the self as well as society.

As we saw in the Introduction, there have been several excellent recent examples of successful collaborations between academic and other types of historians which have proliferated in a range of national contexts.[1] My book *Fractured Families: Life on the Margins in Colonial New South Wales* was a history of the marginalized and impoverished in colonial New South Wales and examined the methodologies and motivations of public history and family history. Here I am building on the potential of those efforts to think about creative ways to co-create historical knowledge, I suggest that academic and family historians need to work collaboratively on family history, sharing a commitment to a feminist social constructionist method and continually reflect on the relationship between their subjects and objects of research.

This research on family history builds on the genealogy of women's engagement with alternative modes of making history and how they use it in their everyday lives. In their research on women historians Bonnie Smith and Mary Spongberg have shown how women's diverse contributions to history have been marginalized by male (and later, female) academics since the early nineteenth century.[2] Joan Thirsk has also revealed how women have always made significant contributions to family and local history, often outside of the academy but are typically denigrated for their efforts. Academic disdain for genealogists remains hard to document because it is usually articulated orally and rarely in writing.[3] Academics, sometimes even feminist historians, have been quick to distance themselves from genealogists in the desire to set themselves apart from, and better than, those 'amateur' family historians, from those who supposedly 'wallow in self-indulgent nostalgia'.[4]

Family history has been imbricated in the peaks and troughs of social history since the 1960s. My continued research with family historians is committed to the belief that the historiographical projects of social and cultural history, with the history of emotions, are mutually constitutive; that learning and teaching should be collaborative; and that history researchers should aim for pedagogical and political impact. We should be engaging with family historians because they are our history students beyond the classroom. In producing empirical knowledge that transforms their own and others' understanding of the present they have developed significant historical skills and critical understanding. It is for this reason, I argue, that contemporary public historians, inside and outside academe, would benefit from revisiting the efforts of their social history forebears in the 1970s, especially the work of the History Workshop movement.

Such revisiting would 'enable popular participation in historical research' in new ways for the twenty-first century. This means we can reap the benefits of the popularity of historical research among family historians around the world.[5] This book suggests some ways that family historians might work with academic historians in the future to fulfil an emancipatory educative agenda with productive political effects.[6]

Family historian Julie Poulter, who lives in Albury, New South Wales, Australia, has been a family historian for over thirty years.[7] She was actively involved in the writing of *Fractured Families*. She wrote to me after reading the book post-publication to tell me how much she appreciated the focus on the 'failures' of colonial Australian society. She had always enjoyed the stories her grandmother told her about her family's lives. When she was still a teenager Julie took detailed notes as she and other female relatives spoke. This process laid the groundwork for her love of history. Many family historians in varied national contexts have told me how their passion for history was fostered in such a manner – through conversations with older, often female, relatives. Like other family historians I have worked with, Julie acknowledges her family history research, as a feminist project:

> Perhaps why I have become so attached to Jane's (her ancestor's) story is informed by my own mother's family history. ... On my maternal side I come from a long line of strong independent women ... I am the beneficiary of those who have come before me and fought for equal rights ... researching history and genealogy gives me a more rounded view of how marriage/motherhood/fatherhood has changed over time and allows me to advocate for a fairer system all round for fathers, mothers and most importantly, the children.[8]

Julie works full-time in administration but hopes to become a professional historian one day. She began her formal research using the support of her local historical society in Dubbo, New South Wales. She wrote up her family history after many years of research and travel, both national and international. She claims that 'Family history research is almost my favourite thing in the world to do! I have decided to not have children, and as a result have much more time to devote to the family history cause! This will be my legacy.' It is due to the diligence and detective work of an army of family historians like Julie working globally and often collaboratively that we can learn about her maternal ancestors. Julie is giving voice to these long-marginalized women in the present.

Family historians are often motivated to undertake research by their affective ties to female ancestors. Feminism informs their work, and they are using family history to learn about women's history, producing new knowledge about mothering and women's diverse historical roles, urging them to challenge the gendered expectations of women's labour in the present, as well as other gender norms. Male family historians are doing the same and are passionate about reclaiming these lives and asking their contemporaries to learn from them. I argue that the emotional as well as intellectual engagement of family historians with the past has the potential to not just reveal the power relations that have worked to marginalize the activities of women in the past and present – to do the work of 'women's history'. But they can also subvert them – doing the work of 'feminist' and 'gender history'. Many family historians begin to produce their family histories because they 'owe' their female ancestors the benefit of their research skills, historical knowledge and the time it takes to reveal their life stories. My argument is that research and communication about the past have enormous pedagogic and political potential. They provide family historians with social, emotional and cultural capital to transform their understandings of themselves and the world in which they live. It is for this reason that the synergies of family history with the broader project of social history demand emphasis.

Social history

I trained as a social and cultural historian in Britain during the 1990s and 2000s, studying my first degree in history and politics at the University of Edinburgh, which had large, distinct departments awarding separate degrees in economic and social history as well as history. I undertook my MA in Women's History and PhD at the University of London under the supervision first of Anna Davin and then Sally Alexander, key constituents of the History Workshop Movement since the 1970s. When I moved to Australia in 2008, I was struck by the different ways in which social history seemed to be understood, structured and practised in Australia. This difference undoubtedly has had an impact on academic and community perception of family and public history in both national contexts.

As an academic discipline, social history had diverse beginnings and laid roots in assorted institutional contexts across Britain. This is a well-known story amongst British academic historian readers but is perhaps less well known in other national contexts and among many family historians, which is why I repeat it briefly here. I also want to draw out the different trajectories of social history in Britain, Australia and Canada because I think they help explain some of the derision displayed towards family history and public history revealed in these different contexts.

The widespread efforts of the Communist Party Historians Group beginning in the 1930s and beyond the post–Second World War period endured for generations and were crystallized in the establishment of the journal *Past and Present* in 1952, by Christopher Hill, Edward and Dorothy Thompson and Eric Hobsbawn. The journal was committed to using scholarship to understand how societies functioned, and to this day remains committed to internationalism and the collaboration between history and other disciplines, especially sociology and anthropology.[9] Fabian socialists including the Webbs and Hammonds had left their significant social historical mark in the London School of Economics in the late nineteenth century, hoping to 'reconstruct society in such a manner as to secure the general welfare and happiness'.[10]

It is important to remember that social history had non-Marxist as well as Marxist roots. The non-Marxist Harold Perkin became a lecturer in social history at the University of Manchester in 1951, and the first Professor of this freshly minted sub-discipline in 1967.[11] Elsewhere and simultaneously the charismatic Marxist historian EP Thompson set up the Centre for the Study of Social History at Warwick in 1968.[12] And from 1964, the Cambridge Group for the Study of Population and Social Structure collaborated with family historians working in the community, transforming academic and popular understanding of the history of the family whilst using quantitative analysis.[13]

As social history found institutional homes, journals followed. The US-based *Journal of Social History* was set up in 1967 by Peter Stearns. The History Workshop movement, formed largely from the Communist Party History Group, set up the *History Workshop Journal* in 1976. Their form of Marxist-influenced social history was reshaped by the formation of the Women's Liberation Movement and from 1981 the journal was re-titled '*History workshop*: A journal of socialist and feminist historians'.[14]

Non-Marxist urban and labour historian Asa Briggs was the first president of the Social History Society established in 1976 and remained its president for the next forty years until Pat Thane took over. Briggs was a powerhouse in the Labor history movement in Britain, the first Chair of the Society for the Study of Labour History formed in London in 1960. He also had significant influence in Australia when he became a Visiting Professor at the Australian National University in 1960.[15] The Australian Labor History Society was established much along the same lines as the Society for the Study of Labour History while he was based in Australia. These societies in both countries worked hard to include professional and 'amateur' historians in their remit, if not necessarily successfully. Always interested in the perspectives of ordinary people, Briggs was responsible for bringing the Mass Observation archive to Sussex when he took up a post there on his return from Australia to England in 1961. In 1967 he became an enthusiastic supporter and powerful advocate of Open University (founded in 1971) and remained passionate about 'wide access, technology and new approaches to life-long learning' but was criticized by many commentators for 'debasing' higher education in the process. His enthusiasm continued unstinted, and he became responsible for adult education initiatives at Sussex where 'he organized day release courses for shop stewards, weekend schools for GPs and seminars for magistrates' clerks'.[16]

Marxist scholar Keith Neild and socialist Janet Blackman established the Hull-based journal *Social History* in 1976. For most practitioners, the power of social history at this time lay in the ways in which it blended political engagement and pedagogical purpose with academic study. Advocates were passionate about diverse forms of community engagement. Blackman, for example, helped to establish the Hull Arts Centre.[17]

Despite maintaining a powerful community presence from the 1960s, especially within family and local history societies, social history as an academic sub-discipline fell by the wayside following the emergence of cultural history in the 1980s and 1990s. There had always been divisions between Marxist and non-Marxist historians within social history, but theoretical tensions became inflamed when established notions of class lost their explanatory power. Attention shifted from people and their everyday lives to language and discourse.[18] Cultural historians sometimes dismissed social historians for their naïve empiricism.[19] The Social History Society created the *Cultural and Social History* journal in 2004 hoping to bridge social and cultural history when the 'epistemological challenges' of the linguistic turn threatened to split them asunder. The editors hoped to emphasize 'the ways the "social" and "culture" are mutually constitutive and that study of one enables a deeper understanding of the other'.[20]

In Australia, as Frank Bongiorno has discussed, social history had far less of an impact in the 1970s and 1980s than it had in Britain and is rarely mentioned explicitly in academic historiographical discussion. Nonetheless, as we have seen, British historian Asa Brigg's influence was significant in the creation of labour history as a sub-discipline. Briggs also had an enormous impact on a range of scholars who were to become prominent practitioners of social history in Australia including Ken Inglis, John Merritt, Bob Gollan and Graeme

Davison.[21] In the 1960s labour history was 'associated with partisanship and antiquarianism'[22] but by the 1970s and 80s *Labour History* was publishing the type of innovative scholarship with political purpose that might appear in *Past and Present, History Workshop Journal,* and *Social History* in Britain. From 1984 *Push from the Bush* called itself a journal of social history and became key to the expansive bicentennial *Australians* project of social history proposed by Ken Inglis in 1977.[23] In May 1981 the journal *Labour History* was briefly re-titled '*History workshop*: A journal of labour and social history'.[24] When the Australian Historical Association was formed in 1973, there was some talk of setting up a Social History Society, but the plans came to nothing.[25] In Green and Troup's *Houses of History* 'social history' gets no dedicated mention and in the index, it is stated that 'most of the major schools of history in this volume fall under the head of social history'.[26] This statement makes little sense to me. Social history continues to exist with no institutional roots, Australian-produced journals or academic appointments. It seems that the sub-discipline's strength and popularity outside the academy remains unrecognized and few practising historians in Australia with tenure would describe themselves as social historians.[27] The same was and is not the case in Britain where institutional identity and respectability remains far stronger for social historians and there are proud professors of social history plying their trade. Social history struggled to lay strong roots as it grew alongside cultural history. This means that social history has less sway as a sub-discipline within the Australian tertiary context. Nonetheless family history has made an impact on the academy in recent years. The University of New England has taught local, family and applied history since the 1980s.[28] The University of Tasmania continues to teach thousands of family historians with a Diploma in Family History developed in 2016 (mainly online) while the University of Western Australia has introduced a new unit convened by Jane Lydon using family history techniques.[29]

In Canada social history followed different paths in French and English-speaking regions.[30] In Quebec, social history was focussed on demography and quantitative analysis, and this was a context within which genealogy and family history flourished.[31] However, English-speaking Canada followed a similar trajectory to Britain where the growth of social history, as we have seen, was linked to social movements and their impact on universities around the world.[32] Social history seems to have been more highly valued in Canada than in Australia and linked, as in Britain, to labour history and political activism. As the tertiary sector expanded in the 1970s and 80s it became increasingly popular as student numbers grew, so did the number of teachers and professors from whom they learned. After 1967 social history was especially fashionable among the burgeoning intellectuals and the diverse student body of the post Centennial of Confederation period. This following included more women and students from diverse immigrant groups, who became passionate about tracing the histories of politically marginalized peoples, often their forebears. The development facilitated an institutionalization of diverse historical perspectives of Canada's national past that flourished in the tertiary sector, on television and in other public forms.[33]

Historians became a large cohort of the Toronto Labour Studies Group established in 1981.[34] Social history was also crucial to the growth of museums and historical sites established across Canada after 1967. Journals and social history publications also expanded including *Social History/Histoire Sociale, Acadiensis,* the *Urban History Review, Labour/Letravail,* etc., which emerged in the late 1960s and early 1970s.[35] Since the 1970s, the successful University of Toronto Press has supported a thriving social history series that has now published almost fifty monographs, many under the leadership of prominent labour historians Greg Kealey and Mike Cross.[36] Politically activist work and collaborations between labour and social historians remained strong throughout the following decades as the field flourished and continue today with institutional recognition of its strength.[37] Social history as a sub-discipline thrives in Canada and Britain, more so in Britain than Canada and a lot less so in Australia.

Public history

We have seen that family historians are at the heart of the production and consumption of history in public. Therefore, family history falls under the expansive umbrella of public history. The term was first used in 1970s' America and came into common use in Australia in the 1980s but did not take off in Britain until the 2000s. That said, as Graeme Davison reminds us public history 'is a new name for the oldest history of all'.[38] For centuries public history was practised as local, family and community history and flourished outside academic contexts following the formalization, professionalization and masculinization of the discipline within universities in the late nineteenth century.[39] During the 1970s following the growth of social history, public history allowed the kinds of political and community engagement that had been key to many international social history projects, academic and otherwise. This was especially the case in Britain where people's history thrived. Applied history dominated the US scene, while Canada and Australia practised and produced a mixture of both. One of the reasons why I have come to understand my scholarly work as public history in recent years is due to its political purpose. I, like others, use my work to critique the elitist, professionalized, hierarchical and exclusionary discipline that some historians work hard to protect, and I want to encourage others to collaborate with audiences and researchers outside of academia, working with history in everyday life.[40]

Public history expanded, alongside social history, across the world from the 1970s.[41] This was partly as a result of economic change and as the labour force restructured. The expansion of tertiary education from the 1970s and the production of increasing numbers of highly skilled, qualified history graduates led to an expansion of public history in America, Europe, Australia and elsewhere as employment opportunities diminished in academia. The journal *The Public Historian* was launched out of the University of California in 1978 and The National Council of Public History was established in 1979. University graduate programmes in public history expanded in Australia and Canada in the late 1980s and took off in Britain in the later 1990s with the establishment of an MA in Ruskin College in Oxford in 1996.[42] In 2010 there were only two public history Masters programmes in the UK, but ten years on there are twelve postgraduate programmes. Now British public history programmes are offered at numerous universities including Royal Holloway College London, Bristol, Bath Spa, Swansea, Derby, York, London South Bank, St Mary's Twickenham, Birkbeck, Plymouth, Goldsmiths College, Leeds, Manchester Metropolitan, Hertfordshire, University of the Highlands and Islands, Greenwich, Queens University Belfast, while Sussex teaches public history as part of a heritage studies MA. A Public History Seminar series was established at the Institute of Historical Research in 2013.[43]

Public history took different forms in these different national contexts.[44] In Australia, public history was taught at Masters level for many years at the University of Technology Sydney and Monash from 1988. It has been discontinued at both these universities.[45] It survives for the time being at the University of New England, University of New South Wales and Deakin. Public history is also taught within courses on Heritage, Museums and Digital History for example at the University of Western Australia, University of Sydney, Flinders, University of Queensland and the Australian National University. The University of Technology Sydney established its Centre for Public History in 1998.[46] In Canada public history is taught formally at Carleton University in Ottawa (begun in 2002), the University of Western Ontario, at Universite Du Quebec at Montreal and York University. The University of Victoria offers a new joint undergraduate programme between Brandon University, Assiniboine Community College and Concordia University. The University of Waterloo ran a public history MA between 1983 and 2005, when it ended.[47] Public history is thriving in different forms across Canada as the popularity of the active blog site attests (http://activehistory.ca/) and it also has a Franco-phone site Histoire Engagée (http://histoireengagee.ca/).[48]

In Australia, Britain and Canada, many public historians remain inspired by the early work of the British History Workshop Movement and are committed to engaging everyone in their passion for history.[49] Therefore, a public historian like me is struck by how many family historians consume history in diverse numerous forms because of their great passion for the past. Family historians are avid museum goers, historical television and film viewers and history and heritage tourists. In their path-breaking study, 'Australians and the Past', Paul Ashton and Paula Hamilton argue that most Australians gain a knowledge of the past not through the formal teaching of history, in the classroom or at university, but rather, through an understanding of their family's past, which they acquire from a range of evidence (oral, material and visual). This knowledge is developed and augmented during visits to museums and by television programmes and films about history: 'The past that inspires genealogists, local historians, and collectors', Ashton and Hamilton argue, 'is not random but connected to their personal identity, most often their genetic heritage ... the family is the principal site for exploration and teaching about the past across all cultures'.[50] Participants in the survey conducted by Ashton and Hamilton for their research saw the familial and the local as central to understandings of an individual's personal history. Many of the individuals Ashton and Hamilton surveyed felt strongly about the importance of 'researching and remembering' the histories of their families using objects as key triggers for family memory making. Pictures and objects give the histories of families a sense of time and place and a legitimacy that remains absent when using the written record alone.[51] Canadians became increasingly interested in their history as a nation and as individuals in the 1970s mirroring much of what was occurring in other settler colonial nations like Australia.[52] Practitioners of public history celebrate history as 'a social form of knowledge'[53] as suggested by Raphael Samuel and often aim to share their authority, as argued by Michael Frisch,[54] with diverse members of communities.[55] This was why, like many other public historians intent on making our discipline more democratic and inclusive, I became set on a path of collaborative endeavour as I planned my history research projects from the late 2000s. This is also why I wanted to learn more about the passion for the past that family historians so obviously feel.[56]

History of the emotions

My interest in family history and the history of the family has been framed by an increased scholarly interest in histories of the emotions. This is because family history researchers, working outside the academy, have been dismissed for their naiveté and amateurism and ridiculed for seeking emotional connections with the past lives of their forebears.[57] These criticisms are linked. The research practice and interests of genealogists are often defined as unscientific, uncritical, emotional and of little value to the academy or anyone else bar their own family – we need to overturn these assumptions and to show how family history is enabling people to think historically and to produce historical knowledge.

Most scholars now reject the family as a transhistorical, essential unit. Since the turn of the twenty-first century, historians (and sociologists) have also become more entwined in the scholarly analysis of emotions. The affective turn of the mid-1990s urged scholars to grapple with the theoretical and epistemological legacies of feminism, post-structuralism and queer theory. Scholars working with affect theory pushed at the limits of textual representation to reintegrate the body and mind back into our subjects of study.[58] They have suggested that we need to understand emotions as social and cultural practices and urge us to question the division between reason and emotion, just as feminists of the eighteenth and nineteenth century did before them.[59] As Frevert reminds us, '(H)istorians are above all interested in the social and cultural complexity of emotions as well as their historicity'.[60] We now accept that emotions and the family are rooted in our past and present bodies and their meanings change over time.[61]

In recent years historians have questioned the facade of academic objectivity, proposing that we examine how emotions structure academic research and scholarship.[62] As Emily Robinson has suggested in *Rethinking History*, getting in touch with one's emotions as a researcher does not have to mean being labelled a 'regressive, nostalgic, empiricist'. Reflecting on one's feelings holds enormous intellectual potential for scholars. Robinson argues that the discipline of history has been 'able to withstand the challenges of poststructuralism and postmodernism' because of the intensity of historians' affective engagement with the past. It is for this reason that all researchers' emotional connections with the past deserve greater scholarly attention.[63]

Emotions have long been associated with being female and femininity; as Sara Ahmed reminds us, 'emotions are associated with women, who are represented as "closer" to nature, ruled by appetite, and less able to transcend the body through thought, will and judgement'.[64] I argue here that we need to embrace the positive political consequences of an emotional engagement with the historical subjects of family historians, and the broader social impact that such engagement can produce. I want to reveal the complex ways in which family historians are using their increasing knowledge of stories, social structures, bodies and minds to piece together their family's history, changing the way they think about history and the world more broadly. There is a close relationship between family history, social history, women's history and public history. Family historians are passionate about the lives of 'ordinary' people in the past. They feel like family history 'speaks to them' in a way that other forms of history have failed to do. A focus on family history and the history of the emotions allows us to trace the symbiotic relationship between social and cultural history. Minds, bodies and feelings are at the heart of this book.[65]

Peter Stearns, one of the key protagonists of the field of emotions history as well as social history in the United States, maintains that the history of emotions was entwined with social history. He suggests that it was the history of the family in the 1970s and 80s which helped give birth to the field.[66] Unlike emotions scholars who preceded him, Stearns focused on 'common folk' rather than the elite by researching 'emotionology' in advice manuals.[67] However, other history of emotions scholars like William Reddy who mooted the notion of an 'emotional regime' have argued that it needs to be understood as a distinct field, separate from social and cultural history.[68] Medievalist Barbara Rosenwein rejected Reddy's modernist focus on the nation and to bridge the medieval and modern divide put forward her notion of 'emotional communities'.[69] Rosenwein claimed that groups such as families, schools, churches and locales worked within proscribed understandings of emotions and constituted distinct communities. She suggested that many communities could be in operation at one time, potentially overlap or create offshoot subcommunities, but they nonetheless over time shared distinct emotional understandings and vocabularies. These communities were structured by shared 'systems of feeling'.[70] I will return to this label 'emotional communities' in Chapter 4 when I focus on family historians as emotional communities.

The benefits of collaboration

Public historians have been increasingly keen, as Jorma Kalela has suggested, to 'encourage and support non-professional people to engage with history – and to be available when needed'.[71] In the wake of Michael Frisch's scholarly contributions, oral and public historians have been sharing their historical authority and expertise with 'ordinary' people for decades.[72] However, we saw in the previous chapter that family historians around the world have been subject to derision and certainly not understood as equal to academic historians or researchers understood as 'professionals'. Historians such as Michael Kammen and John Tosh have been notable in their insistence on acknowledging the distinctions between scholarly and family history – between professionals and amateurs. '[F]amily and pastness are clearly not the same as history and should not be conflated with it,' argues Kammen.[73] But to some extent, times have changed for many family history researchers.

Many of my survey respondents have practised family history for decades and enjoyed the increasing acceptance of their work over this time. Robin Dryen, an active member of the Australian Jewish Genealogical Society, says that 'there has been a gradual acceptance, helped by programs like *Who Do You Think You Are?*, that there is value in family history. When I started many people thought it was an indulgent or nostalgic looking backwards.'[74] Like Robin as we will see, these researchers are often very well read, communicating with a wide global community of researchers in person and online, in the process they have become deservedly more self-confident and articulate about their practice.

According to my research, family historians read widely in academic scholarship but express the desire that more scholars could communicate their work in a more accessible way. This complaint is something that academic historians and writers might find confronting to hear or read but need to consider when presenting their research in written and oral forms. Caryn Patterson thinks 'a lot of academic historians are boring'.[75] Janine McMinn finds 'that they are often difficult to read, you wade through pages of prose and then they gloss over the point that interests you!'[76] Patsy Trench also wishes, 'some of them could be a tad more readable'.[77] TB thinks 'they operate in their own narrow worlds' and she does not feel like they respect her, 'And I don't give a shit. Fuck 'em. I appreciate them if they take interest, though.'[78] Others also feel disrespected and dismissed by academics: 'I feel that generally the academy does not respect family historians … it is often judged as "less"'.[79]

Many family historians hope to reap the benefits of collaboration with academics and others. They want their work to be taken seriously by family historians, family members and 'professional' researchers. John Dean believes that 'family history is very important in understanding the social history of communities and its worth should be given more credence by academia and publishers'.[80] Brenda Lee also wants academics to take their work seriously.[81]

Several have enjoyed their collaborations with academic researchers as part of the Founders and Survivors network based in Tasmania and Melbourne and other projects in Ontario, Canada. Stephanie Hume lives in regional Victoria and has helped with three projects for the Founders and Survivors project. She respects Professor Janet McCalman enormously and thinks family historians and academics have a lot to learn from each other – 'in general they probably realise they [family historians] could be highly trained in a completely different area … and yet can turn our minds to historical research'.[82]

However, while most family historians have had little to do with academics, many are committed to the possibilities of collaboration in the future, for themselves and others. John Shrimski thinks that benefits include 'a disciplined approach to research, rigorous examination of facts without jumping to conclusions, different ideas for presenting family history results with proper annotations'.[83] That said, Peter Keeda worries that 'taking it [family history] into academia has the danger of making it exclusive, elitist and inaccessible'.[84] He hopes the practice can be as democratic and inclusive as possible. Barbara Barclay thinks academics and family historians should collaborate, contending that 'Academic historians bring such knowledge and context to historical events, as well as professional practice. Family historians have intimate knowledge of "history from below," and often a huge passion for their stories. What a great mix that can be'.[85] Donald Davis believes that 'academic historians acknowledge that the preservation of records and access to them has been enhanced because of amateur genealogists … academic historians have opened doors to better practice on the part of amateurs'.[86] It is clear to me from this data that family historians want to be part of conversations and collaborations with university-based historians and to be treated as equals, to co-produce and to co-research. Contributing to the project of social history together is where we can meet in the middle and produce beneficial outcomes for the field.

Family historians' passion for social history

Most family historians are extremely passionate about social history. They could spend hours talking about the subject. They believe that it is key to their broader knowledge and understanding about themselves, their families and the world. CA found history 'dry as dust' at school but as she researched her own family 'the social history of their times suddenly became meaningful'.[87] Similarly, for Liam Roberts, 'Family history research has taught me so much more than all of my schooling in my formative years'.[88] Julie Jones agrees, 'I love anything to do with the social history of ancestors, as it gives more substance to their lives'.[89]

Family historians admit to thriving on the minute details of peoples' lives in the past and how they fit within a broader picture. For Ken Mckinlay 'history is no longer just about names, dates and places but also how it has affected migration and employment patterns, and how the "little" players in history are impacted by the big events'. His research has 'humanized' history. It has also shown how important it is to put lives and events in context.[90] Brenda Lee seeks out the company of family historians who are as passionate about social history as she is: 'to me the social history is the most important part of the research. It tells the story. I can spend months researching one decade'.[91] Hannah Frost now much prefers to read social history compared with other forms of history. 'I think history was seen to me as a national/global concern, not how it affected the average person.'[92] Frost studied history at university, but it was 'only when I looked at my own family did I really understand the human element in history … I think what has changed is I prefer to read about social history – who people were, how they lived – and how this impacted history as a whole.'[93] She likes the 'lack of snobbery in family history. It doesn't matter where family come from geographically or socially – it's an accepted part of the research'.[94] JH's family history research has shown her that 'History is made by people, not just leaders or characters but by bog-standard working-class people'.[95] Kate Hurst has also found that learning personal details about her ancestors has made history come alive for her. She's been made 'more aware of how "ordinary" people lived and what their experiences were'.[96] Family history has made history come alive for Barbara Barclay as well as many others, so that 'social history is definitely my main interest'.[97]

A focus on social history reminds these researchers of the politics of their research. PC, a professional researcher and self-employed genealogist, born in Ireland but now based in Scotland, believes that

> Family history has democratized access to the history I felt I should have been taught. What the state omitted through the teaching of 'official' history, I was able to explore through the lives of each of my individual forebears – they became my conduits to the past, but also to a past that was actually relevant to me in a direct sense.[98]

This book argues that social historians, public historians, feminist and gender historians in partnership with historians of the family should work with and practice a more inclusive form of history that embraces academics and non-academics alike. We should collaborate with others to feed the passion for history shared by so many people all over the world and recognize the politics that structures our knowledge about the past. 'Giving little people a voice' enables us all to better challenge exclusionary and discriminatory politics and practices in the past and present.

'She told me I had destroyed her memories': How family historians work with memory

Canadian Brenda Lee, who now combines work as a professional genealogist alongside administration, used to hate history but 'that changed when grandmother started telling me stories'. She became a family historian in 1989 after taking her elderly grandmother for long drives to Toronto to get her out of her nursing home for a few hours of respite and a breath of fresh air.[1] This chapter explores how family historians like Brenda use diverse sources during the research process to construct their family trees and memories. It shows how they utilize oral history, archival documents, material culture and explorations of space to construct and reconstruct family stories and to make meaning of the past, inserting their familial microhistories into global macrohistories. In asking whether family historians undertake critical readings of these sources when piecing together family stories, the chapter reveals the impact of that work on individual subjectivities and the construction of historical consciousness. It explores how family historians might join with social historians of the family to reshape our scholarly and 'everyday' knowledge of the history of the family in the twenty-first century.

While some family historians have loved the subject of history all through their lives, many tell me of first falling in love with the stories told by aged relatives and how family history has led many to their passion for the subject. Oral historians have long identified women as the major 'keepers' and disseminators of family stories, the custodians of family memories.[2] My research has shown that family history shares many parallels with oral history in this regard. The construction and sharing of family stories are also gendered practices.[3] Gloyn and her co-authors suggest, 'contemporary gendered practices of family archiving and memory processes have long historical roots'. They suggest 'that this strong gendered nature of different archival practices is part of the reason why informal and family archives tend to remain undervalued within the historical discipline'.[4] The same is true of family history which typically begins with these private archives and feminine realms. Family historians expose the value of combining private and public sources, joining micro and macro histories that influence their own subjectivities but also contribute to our wider knowledge of the family. This blending enables them to challenge what is understood, by themselves and others, as 'normal' family life and social structures. As oral historians have revealed, oral histories are crucial for memory work – the process of remembering and reconstructing stories about the past.[5] Family history research depends upon, deepens and consolidates a research process that often begins with oral accounts and storytelling.

Individuals sometimes share reconstituted histories among some family members to expose intergenerational secret keeping, with the explicit aim of improving lives in the present and future. These researchers learn how to and are then compelled to engage in a critical reading of all sources – written, oral and material. The research process thereby transforms how individuals remember their families and understand national and global history. All use family history to better understand how their families have contributed to the nations in which they settled and travelled. These accounts challenge much of what researchers learned at school. The memory-making undertaken by family historians allows these researchers to use their personal histories to insert themselves and their families into wider historical narratives from which they felt themselves excluded. This chapter affirms how family historical research and communication about the past provides practitioners of family history with social, emotional and cultural capital – transforming them, their lives and the lives of those around them. It will reveal the complex ways in which families construct, reconstruct and disseminate family memories as they use the diverse historical sources and methods found in public and private archives. In the process, family historians share some of the same intellectual and political endeavours in which social historians of the family engage.

Family history has been understood by a range of sociologists and human geographers in Europe and Australia to have an important role in identity formation.[6] As Nash has suggested and many of my family historians articulate, family history individualizes the past.[7] Scholars have established how important family history research is for memory work and the construction of identity. What is distinctive about my work here is the focus on how family history develops historical knowledge, linking the individual to the social, producing alternative accounts of the past that transform people's lives both personally and politically in the present. The process of individualizing history and using it to understand one's self is a deeply affective practice and one that allows family history researchers to claim crucial agency over their lives.

Throughout this book, I show how their stories, the memories that family historians produce, have ample potential to be used for broader historical and political purposes. Academic and family historians need to work collaboratively on this form of family memory work because it will produce more productive outcomes.[8] In the spirit of Haug's model of memory work, I suggest here (and elsewhere) that barriers between academic historians of the family and family historians must be eliminated if we truly envision a shared history in which we create and enhance knowledge on the family for everyone.[9]

My research on the meanings and impact of family history was not originally designed to examine how family historians move between different forms of historical sources or use them to construct family memories. For the purposes of this chapter, I have re-read my evidence with these questions in mind and asked some of these family historians further questions about the material culture they have collected. I also asked them what meanings they make of this evidence in the process of undertaking their research and piecing together their family stories. I return to some of these questions around material culture in the final chapter of the book.

'Humanizing the past' – memory work in families and research communities

As indicated above, in researching the lives of their ancestors, family historians humanize history. For them, this humanizing process is what gives history its emotive and intellectual power. An affective connection to ancestors is key to the development of family historians' passion for history and the foundation of their historical knowledge.[10] While some family historians have loved the subject of history all through their lives, first falling in love with the stories told by aged relatives, many family historians discovered their passion through family history.[11]

As argued in the previous chapter, family history practice is targeted at 'giving little people a voice' and rescuing past relatives from anonymity. Family historians find this process of historical resurrection empowering both for their ancestors and themselves.[12] Like Barbara Barclay, most are passionate about social history because 'making national history personal, gives a greater insight into the lives of Australians through different periods of its history'.[13] The passion for family history leads to a focus on the historical lives of 'ordinary people' and everyday life that has a significant impact on an understanding of the present for its practitioners.

We have also seen how the construction and sharing of family stories is a gendered practice. This can be a double-edged sword, because while family history may give women authority within their own families and communities, it can also be used to disparage them as individuals within families who do not support their research and those who ridicule the broader practice outside the familial unit. This form of historical research and memory-making is often feminized, derided, trivialized and marginalized, and typically contrasted with 'professional' knowledge production on the family that takes place in academic journals and publications.[14]

As we have seen, women make up most respondents to my survey and as subjects for my interviews. Many of these predominantly female family historians state in their surveys that by sharing familial stories, female relatives encouraged and fostered their practice of family history. One of my respondents, Australian-based Shane O' Neil, was drawn to become a family historian because 'as a child, family artefacts in our home fascinated me as well as the stories my mother told me of her childhood and family life, and the special significance she attached to these things'. While Shane suspects she 'was being groomed for the role [of family historian] by my mother', she admits to being 'a willing acolyte'.[15]

Many of these researchers (male and female) feel an obligation to continue their research as a way to honour the efforts of the women in their family trees and to reveal the details of their lives in the present. Men have also been inspired by the women who first motivated the research they continue to build upon enthusiastically. England-based KD explained that he became a family historian in 2005 because his 'mother had been researching our family history and when she died I took over her papers and felt obliged to carry on her work'.[16] Although mature women predominate among these participants, men are also clearly passionate about the practice and so are much younger women. While older family historians are retired and now more leisured than they used to be, younger researchers are juggling the demands of busy lives and multiple caring responsibilities with the labours of family history. Kate Hurst is thirty-two and works as a freelance family history researcher in the North-East of England. She became a family historian, around the age of eleven, gathering details from her grandmother, but became more active once the 1901 England/Wales census was released online in 2002. The Internet, as Kate suggests, has clearly motivated many younger researchers like herself: 'I think people may feel more connected to family history and records related to themselves because of the huge changes in data available via the Internet now'. For Kate, online searches revealed census images and once she was able to drive, she visited record offices to fill in missing gaps using parish registers.[17]

BL was born in 2000, reared in a ghost/gold mining town (which is where her love of history was fostered) and now lives in rural Victoria (Australia).

> From a young age, I was intrigued by the stories my parents would tell me about those who had once lived and worked on our land ... There were many stories that I was told that ended abruptly, with missing information, and this was what captivated me when I was old enough, to fill in the blanks of our history. Over the past 5 years, I have helped my father, who also has a keen interest in genealogy, to uncover the stories of our family, and whilst doing so, learning how to do it myself.

She combines her oral history research with archival research and writing, affirming in her survey that her research had made her grow as an individual. It

> makes me want to make something of myself, to leave an impact on the world. There are many people in my family that have dozens even hundreds of records etc on them. There is [sic] others where their life followed them to the grave, and they leave nothing. I don't want my life to mean nothing, and to be forgotten, I want to make change.[18]

She is using her research to better understand herself and her contribution to society. It is important to use responses like hers to question stereotypes of family historians regarding gender and age and the significance of that work for them and others. It is not just the elderly who are keen on this form of memory work – teenagers and young people in their twenties are also eager to participate in such labour, to construct memories about their ancestors and to show others its social utility. Therefore, family history research has significance, value and meaning for society's younger citizens as well, helping them to better understand their lives and their contribution to the world.

This personal connection to the past, a past that is begun with oral testimonies and then fed by family history research, has had a significant impact on the social and self-confidence of family historians. As they make memories and their historical knowledge increases, they develop pride in their skills as historians. Practitioners use empirical evidence to challenge normative accounts of the history of the family and the nation produced by previous generations. This makes them feel better about themselves and their futures.

From microhistory to macro history – using family history to understand national and global histories

As we have seen above, while Shane O'Neil was drawn to family history through her mother, an affective connection to the past has led her to better understand the links between the historical, the personal and political. Her passion for family history,

> Came from a mixture of curiosity, empathy, desire for truth, a conviction that the ordinary was in itself extraordinary, a belief that in a life you could demonstrate social and economic change on a large scale (the microcosm and macrocosm), as well as a strong sense of wanting to give little people a voice.[19]

These family historians are explicitly using their family history research to connect their lives to broader historical narratives. When Barbara Barclay thinks about "'big" history – of the nation/the globe – I now think about how all of those big stories are made up of everyday, normal people'.[20] Researchers like Barbara want consumers of history to recognize the contributions of 'ordinary people' to our nations in the past as well as the present.

Family history researchers are reconstructing the lives of many of their working-class forebears to challenge the knowledge of history that they and indeed most people possess which has been constructed by mostly elite, white and patriarchal sources. In the process they aim to transform the construction of history and encourage others to think about how we build our knowledge about the past. Helen Jenkins works as a personal assistant and lives in England. She became a family historian in 2003 and since then has learned that

> history is made by people, not just leaders or characters but by bog-standard working class people … Ordinary people fuelled the industrial revolution and went overseas to build an empire (whether you consider this to be good or bad).[21]

This focus on the ordinary is a common refrain in these responses, along with a frustration at the lack of historical documentation of 'ordinary' lives and how little we know about them now. Barbara Hearn was born in North West Kent in 1953. She trained as a social worker in the 1970s before settling in North London. She found that family history had made her

> aware now that the Royals and Military history is a very narrow view and that the way ordinary people lived adds up to a richer and truer story of our past. For example it has become clear that women and black and ethnic minorities have had a much greater part to play in UK history than I had been taught.

I see that it is the majority of the population who make history but are too easily forgotten. I also realize that everything we all do is making history.

She is using family history to reframe her understanding of the past, but this is also making her aware of how power relations structure our lives and lead us to value some forms of labour, certain races, classes and genders, more highly than others. As historians, family history practitioners are self-consciously using microhistory to better understand macro-histories and they delight in the significance of this newfound knowledge and the connections between their families and the wider world. They are using their ancestors to seek out new knowledge of diverse historical contexts and to develop their historical knowledge. Some are also undertaking family history research within academic contexts and undertaking postgraduate degrees to further their knowledge and establish their expertise. Sydney-based academic and writer Betty O'Neill used her family history to write a creative practice PhD at the University of Technology in Sydney, but she is not alone among family historians in understanding that her 'family history is a microhistory, an individual and family experience of a particular time in history and geography that reflects many of the larger national, transnational and global themes'.[22]

Not only are these family historians becoming new social historians, using their family histories to understand social, cultural, economic and political change over time, they deepen their knowledge of the discipline of history in the process. In doing so, they are accessing and using the same language as scholars of history utilize. Canadian RG told me that 'we're doing micro-history' while academics are doing macro-history'.[23] The evidence shows, however, that some clearly understand themselves as doing both.

Research makes Canadian Barry Cobb feel like 'we are all just small cogs in a very large wheel'.[24] In Donald Davis' words, 'Family history is like a bristle in a brush. The small national brush is, in turn, an integral tuft in the broad global brush'.[25] Now that Peggy Beckett is 'more able to link my family contextually to world events, [she is] therefore more interested in both'.[26] All now better understand their families' contribution to the nations in which they settled and travelled through and these accounts challenge much of what they learned at school.[27] Brenda Lee states that 'the history of a nation impacts a family history … A family history impacts a nation as well … Our national history is interesting. At times it is glorified and the wrong people are made into heroes'.[28] Through their family histories many Canadian and Australian family historians have become aware of how their countries are 'largely a nation of immigrants'.[29] Several are 'proud' of the achievements of pioneer ancestors who settled far from home in difficult circumstances.[30] While these migrants are often English-speaking settlers, others are not, and largely as a result of family history these histories are becoming part of the rich multicultural history of these nations. The memory-making undertaken by family historians allows these researchers to use their personal histories to insert themselves and their families into wider historical narratives from which they have been excluded up to now.

For family historians researching the lives of non-Anglo Australians, Canadians and Brits and other underrepresented groups in our history books this process of growing awareness can have a profound political effect. Their research makes them realize how they have been excluded from national storytelling about the past. One fifth of Canada's population and over a quarter of Australians are foreign born. Canada introduced its multicultural policy in 1971 and Australia was declared a multicultural nation in 1975. Family history grew exponentially alongside multiculturalism which has fuelled the popularity of family history among younger researchers in all these contexts under examination. Justina Lui is a fourth-generation Australian/Chinese woman whose great-grandfather arrived in Melbourne, via San Francisco, in the 1890s. In an email discussion and interview she told me that her

> family history has given me a personal insight into Australian history – I have personal connections to many key events in Australian history … Although at times it feels like a parallel narrative – we do not fit the typically depicted Anglo-Saxon profile of early 20th century Australia. It made me realize there are millions of stories like my family's hidden behind every sentence in the history we were taught at school.[31]

A young woman in her twenties, she has become committed to sharing her family history with relatives in China and Australia, young and old. Through her developing knowledge, she has become conscious of how her family history has both familial and broader political purpose.

Other migrant groups in Australia and Canada are using their family histories to challenge predominant and misleading narratives about the foundations and growth of their nations. The Australian Jewish Genealogical society (AJGS) members I spoke with were using their research to flesh out the stories of ancestors destroyed by the Spanish expulsion and the Holocaust and to show that Australian Jewish family history is not just a footnote in the Anglo-Australian national story.[32] By understanding his family's journey to and settlement in Australia, Peter Keeda feels like he can 'better understand issues such as prejudice, immigration, refugees and social integration … Having been so central to Western thought and philosophy I believe that, as Jews, we DO have a mission. Understanding our history helps to clarify what we should be doing, or what we would like to do.' Research on the impact of anti-Semitism 'is a major theme in my thinking, which in turn has shaped my political beliefs and has significantly influenced my life in general'.[33] For John Shrimski, 'Sometimes parents, grandparents gave the impression that their ancestors were almost aristocracy, and are quite demeaning about the "lower classes." A minor scratching of the surface can often reveal that they are actually from these "lower classes." This knowledge gives you better insight into your background i.e., knowledge is empowerment.' John's love of family history and its broader impact upon his life led him to enrol as a continuing student at Macquarie University. Studying ancient and modern history as an external student and 'reading, visiting actual locations, visiting galleries, museums and cemeteries has given me a fuller perspective on Australian history'.[34]

Another young Jewish family historian, Dani Haski is deeply involved with the AJGS in Sydney. She tells me that

> community groups coalesce around a geographically or culturally specific cohort – whether that be Jewish, Greek, Italian etc. Then we self-select into amorphous larger groups based on the areas our ancestors come from. When I'm asked where my family is from, or what my background is, I reel a list of half a dozen countries – Egypt, Poland, Ukraine (Galicia), Lithuania/Latvia via the UK – plus my religious ancestry (as being Jewish has both religious and cultural connotations).[35]

The AJGS is a member of the International Association of Jewish Genealogical Societies which runs an international conference annually and supports the work of societies around the world. Diverse cultural family historians are dependent upon sites other than Ancestry to undertake their research and develop thriving communities of practice to encourage others in their research journeys.

My work with diverse groups of researchers has revealed the ways in which Ancestry.com does not adequately meet the demands of non-Anglo researchers. Members of the Jewish family history community use alternatives methods and modes to undertake its research. Many genealogical societies in Australia, England and Canada are overwhelmingly British, Irish and English language focussed. So perhaps it is little wonder that people from other ethnic and cultural backgrounds have turned towards other sources of knowledge and forms of collaboration, constructing subgroups of family history communities.

Italians are among the oldest and most established migrant groups in Sydney and one of the largest non-Anglo ethnic groups in Australia. Co.As.It. was established in Sydney in 1968 to fulfil two distinct aims: 'to promote the Italian language and culture in NSW and to assist the growing number of migrants arriving from Italy'. Co.As.It. launched its Italian Family History Group in 1998. I contacted them through their highly active Facebook group.[36]

A past Chair of this group, Maria Linders nee Ravesi was born in Darlinghurst just after the Second World War. Her parents migrated to Australia as children following the First World War. They came from Salina (an island in the Aeolian Islands north of Sicily). Maria is now semi-retired and became a family historian less than ten years before we met in 2016 – she is tall, blond and blue-eyed, and was keen to discover why she looked and felt so different to her southern Italian parents – who were short and dark-haired. The story she told, of growing up in post-war white, assimilationist Australia was similar to those I have heard from the handful of non-Anglo Australian family historians I have spoken with. In response to the racism that surrounded her every day, Maria fiercely rejected her Italian heritage in her youth. Her parents spoke Italian within their home but did not encourage their children to speak the language in the hope that they would assimilate into white Australia as soon as possible. Maria knew she could pass as an Anglo Australian

Figure 4 Maria Linders and I in the Friends Room of the State Library of New South Wales (credit Joy Lai).

with her colouring and looks, and she told no one she was Italian. She attended a Catholic girl's school in Bondi where there was only one other Italian girl. She learned quickly how to suppress her cultural background. Her brothers did not reject their Italian identity in the same way but according to Maria they looked Italian and were subject to less personal restrictions because they were male.

Maria describes herself as a rebel, rejecting her parents' authority and insistence on certain behaviours within and outside the home and escaped the parental home, marrying a Dutch man soon afterwards. It was only in the previous decade that her family history research has enabled her to feel 'more Italian than Australian'. Family history has fostered 'a greater love for my parents and Italian heritage'. She has also become reunited with many members of her family around the world. Family reunions that she has organized in Australia and Italy have played important functions in facilitating these connections. Her work and these reunions have also encouraged other family members to begin this work themselves and to learn more about their Italian heritage and connections. Each time she travels to Salina Maria feels like she is returning 'home', although she never travelled there as a child. In her autumn years Maria embraces her Italian heritage, but her language skills have been largely lost and only partly reclaimed in that process.[37] This is not an uncommon story among post-war second-generation migrants, and by analysing similar data, we have much to learn from others about the impact of migration and multiculturalism over time. The existence of migrant community groups like these reveals the ways in which people strive to create continuity with the past, which is significant to the maintenance of local identity. My research reveals the ways in which family history has the potential to generate significant political consequences and encourage cultural confidence and cohesion among diverse community groups.

Family historians are using their research to challenge national narratives about the past produced not just by their families but by governments, the media and the education system. Their research has important personal as well as public and political effects. They are using this historical knowledge to understand how 'I became the person I am today' and to question the history they learned as children and have since imbibed. When Brenda Lee reads history now, she questions how accurate it is because she knows that 'the truth is creatively told. If the true story was told we could move forward better as a nation'.[38] It is for this reason that family history can have a powerful effect on researchers' subjectivities as well as their broader communities. Family history research enables these individuals to recognize and utilize their agency as individuals in the present.

Using history to challenge 'the truth'

We have seen how family history is being used by researchers to challenge 'the truth' about broader national narratives. I now turn to how they are using their research to challenge familial truths and to piece together individual microhistories that allow them to better understand themselves and the changing world. These reconstituted histories are shared among some family members to expose intergenerational secret-keeping with the intention to improve lives in the present and future. Family researchers demonstrate that they read critically all sources – oral, written and material. Some family historians have vast private archival evidence to work through, discovered in attics, cellars and gathered following the deaths of family members, but there are others who have very little material or memories to sift through. Family history research allows those individuals to construct memories when no oral or material evidence exists. With no, little or conflicting information some individuals use family history to create replacement memories. This is certainly the case for those seeking to find out the details of familial adoptions, for the Stolen Generations, Forgotten children and children in care, in the Australian context as well as elsewhere.[39]

Other researchers use family histories to uncover secrets and lies and to seek out the 'truth' of family stories. In many historical and sociological accounts of family secrets it is assumed that most family members are deeply invested in the process of keeping secrets in the family. Ashley Barnwell's work on the ways in which family secrets impact upon Australian people's sense of national history is important here.[40]

Keeping secrets allows these families to sustain kinship relations and fictive national identities that occlude the brutality of a settler colonial past.[41] However, as Jerome de Groot has suggested, family historians can work as both 'truth seeker' and 'secret keeper'.[42] This capacity is the double-edged sword and the power central to family memory-making. The family historians I have heard from are all 'truth seekers' but some also recognize the need to continue to keep some family secrets to protect the sensitivities of older generations.

Dianne Johnstone heard me speak at a meeting of the Australian Jewish Genealogical Society and delighted in telling me her family story and the many years she spent uncovering its secrets, describing the enormous effect these discoveries had upon her. When she was fifty-five years old, Dianne found out that she was adopted. Her identity was a source of concern all through her childhood. Her birth mother was Jewish, her family migrating to Australia in the

1930s and hiding their Jewish religion to avoid being persecuted. Dianne was adopted in 1944, when she was six weeks old, into a large Christian family that worked hard throughout their lives to keep her adoption secret from her. Her adoptive family told her many stories about her roots lying deep in Australian convict history and the Trade Unions. As she aged, she remained convinced that they were hiding 'the truth' about her origins. After she survived breast cancer, she became determined to seek out some answers. When Dianne discovered the story of her adoption, she recalled it was 'a shock to me but not a surprise'. She eventually found her birth mother, half-sister and cousin and 'it was a happy reunion'. She has travelled the world piecing her birth and adoptive families' histories together, through England, America and Lithuania, and she has been welcomed into familial homes in all these places. When I last communicated with her, she was looking forward to travelling to Texas to visit her birth father's family. She had recently discovered that her father Jack had been raised on a ranch. She relished learning about his cowboy ways. Dianne used her research to write two books and to produce a DVD of her family's story titled *Secrets My Mothers Kept* and *The Kalvarija Story*.[43] She has become committed to sharing her story with others to encourage them not to keep secrets like these. She believes they wreak untold damage on families who spend their lives hiding them and contends that her adoptive mother's lifelong ill health and stress were caused by the perceived need to keep the secret. According to Dianne's account, there is no doubt of the 'slow violence' that Ashley Barnwell has recently written about, wreaked on this family due to the secret guarded for so long and by so many family members. The social stigma associated with illegitimacy and adoption is 'an often unseen and accretive form of social violence' that has affected families like Dianne's for hundreds of years.[44] Family historians are calling out this violence – reworking and publicizing these memories to bring an end to intergenerational trauma.[45]

The family historians I have engaged with are mostly keen on seeking out truths, but many are also aware of the ethical requirements of secret keeping. They hope their research will allow secrets into the open, making them public so that they can help to reconfigure kinship relations and remake their families into the future with hopefully positive outcomes. The practitioners I have corresponded with want to use their research to question what is meant by 'the truth' and to trouble people's attachment to fictive 'happy families' but they are also well aware of the tensions involved, especially the consequences of these secrets and truths on older relatives. Deb McAuslan has realized through her research that 'history is taught rather black and white' while it is the grey that strikes her and others now.[46]

Northumberland-based Irene Blackburn became a family historian in 1981 and has enjoyed reconfiguring her family's stories through her research even when her efforts were resisted.

> My sister told me to stop tracing the family tree when I came across a branch with names like Isaac, Sarah, Ishmael, Ezekiel as she thought they were Jewish. I ignored her (they were Primitive Methodists but I wouldn't have cared anyway) …
> My father was disappointed to find that his Huguenot ancestress Barbara Murdelle was from Sussex and called Muddle (as were her ancestors back to 1598). My other grandmother asked me not to trace her family so I didn't until after she died aged 89 in 1988, I discovered that her eldest sister was illegitimate and so was her mother.[47]

In almost all family histories, such stories of secrecy and stigma are ten a penny. Many family historians have become adept at using their research and retelling family stories to seek out such truths.

Scholar Gillian Rose in her book *Doing Family Photography* suggests that it is women who usually order family photos with the explicit intent of constructing familial memories. She tells us that feminist critics can be hostile to the veneration of family photography arguing that many images of family life are oppressive to women. They paint misleading pictures of how families work, concealing the fragility of relationships and women's domestic labour and emotional work. While images of family life can clearly be deceptive, Rose wants us to interpret the use and presentation of these images as more complex than this.[48] I propose suggesting something similar for family history memory-making in its various forms. Family history reconstructs memories about family lives in the past and in that process reveals the 'invisible' labour of secret keeping, emotional familial management and its effect on people in the past and present.

Many of us recognize the proliferation of those images that represent key life-cycle moments – birth, death and marriages – and fill the walls, mantelpieces and bookshelves in the houses within which we live and visit. The representation and celebration of these moments might help create the familial 'myths we live by' as suggested by John Gillis who argued that family homes are mini museums representing the imagined 'nurturing and protective' family of myth and legend, the idealized family that we 'live by', rather than the fragmented and challenging reality of the families that we live 'with'.[49] While it is often argued that family historians love seeking out Golden Ages and familiar motifs in the telling and retelling of family stories and memories[50] the family historians I have worked with, as we have seen, are primarily keen to overturn assumptions and oft-told stories they remain suspicious of. For many 'memories are reworked over time in light of subsequent experiences and the meanings attached to these'. They relish the ambiguity revealed by the historical record. Erll using Halbwachs' theory of collective memory suggests that 'family memory is not a monolithic, stable entity, but an ongoing process shaped by the multidimensional *cadres sociaux* of family members. The shared construction of memories produces a variety of "viewpoints" on mnemonic contents and meanings which, depending on the particular family structure, can lead to a continual renegotiation of the past.'[51] 'To Halbwachs, family memory is a type of collective memory characterized by the strength of its group allegiances and its powerful emotional dimension ....an exchange of "living memory" takes place between eyewitnesses and descendants.'[52] Examining how family historians work with memory reveals how memory work is reshaped by different generations in varied historical contexts and why younger family historians typically work so hard to continue to obscure family secrets of illegitimacy and bigamy to protect the sensitivities of their older relatives. Paradoxically, these younger family historians want their work to reveal those secrets to future and younger generations and to reshape people's understandings of 'the family'. They are using their historical research to undermine and overturn ideal and fictive representations of family life, to reshape present and future lives.

Constructing memories critically and collaboratively

Family memories are constructed by family historians collectively and collaboratively. This socialized construction of knowledge is what gives it its strength, power and long-term potential. Through the channels of a vast global community, family historians learn how to question the data they collect and use to construct stories about the past, and they communicate and share their stories in diverse ways. They know how to maximize the Internet for their research and how to read the data they mine critically. They aim to share and reveal their skills and capacities with others.[53]

Many enjoy working in teams as I will show in Chapter 4. As I have indicated above, most of the family historians I surveyed took real pride in their research skills, challenging, constructing and reconstructing mnemonic communities and the global network in which they undertook their work. They experience visceral joy in knowledge acquisition and the sharing of skills, knowledge and expertise. They also take real pleasure in using different sources and discuss their knowledge in a range of forums – within local and community societies, at huge family history conferences, on cruises, in family history magazines, on blogs and online forums (which are especially popular in Canada) – they take pride in the acquisition of historical skills and describe the critical readings they undertake. Through the development of their knowledge, they claim authority and expertise on their subjects amongst their community of learners. While such authority is performed within families, it is also enacted at a community level as positions of authority are claimed and long held in local and family historical societies.

As we have seen from many of the previous responses like that of Maria Linders, family historians are fuelling a rise in family history-related tourism and global travel undertaken to connect and reconnect different branches of newfound family trees.[54] Their discovery of family, familial spaces and historical places makes a significant impact on their understanding of past lives and contexts. Canadian-based Carole Whelan adores travelling with her husband 'to ancestral villages, churches and cemeteries' but the rest of her immediate family show little interest in her passion: 'long-lost cousins are the most excited when we make contact and share'.[55] Barbara Hearn lives in London but was reunited with her Australian family through her research. After losing all contact with these relatives when she was fourteen, Barbara's Australian uncle visited when she turned fifty.[56] Travel and face-to-face meetings with long lost family members have an enormous impact on these researchers, who savour new social interactions and engagements. These social engagements with familial spaces give them the capacity to use written, oral, material and embodied evidence to better piece together fragmented family stories, to contest particular forms of storytelling and to reconstruct the meaning of families and nations so that they can live with equanimity in the present.

This chapter suggests that academic historians of the family need to think more creatively about bringing family historians' work with memory into the centre of our scholarly and political endeavours because of its individual and social benefits. This research reveals how critical family history research is to understand the complexity of family life in the past. It also reveals how lives change over time and in different historical contexts and can result in many researchers achieving peace in the present. Social historians should work collaboratively with family historians not only because we share many of the same methods, research questions and motivations for undertaking our research but also this is how we might best reveal the potential of this form of memory work for identity formation, social inclusion and citizenship to scholars and the wider public.

The evidence above reveals how the memory-making undertaken by family historians occurs in complex ways and on multiple levels. Many people link 'private' knowledge on the family, with 'public' and popular knowledge of national histories; in the process they reshape their understanding of both. Their affective engagement with the past enables family historians to develop deep personal and cultural insight that has significant benefits for them and for others.

As shown through several examples of family history memory work above, this research reveals the significance of historical knowledge for understanding the self and the social, and how these might change over time. The process enfranchises family historians and emboldens them to challenge family lore, the historical authority of others, and to assert their own expertise, giving them agency over many aspects of their lives. Some family historians have been prompted to use their research for political purposes, challenging normative understandings of the family as well as national mythological storytelling. These 'private' histories are working to challenge the 'public', popular histories they were previously led to believe were hegemonic.[57] Newfound knowledge is then disseminated in diverse ways in written, oral and material form among family members across the world and shared with the broader family history community to challenge dominant narratives and to contribute to collective knowledge. However, for the most part, their labour sits apart from academic knowledge production on the family even though some family history researchers consume such work and aim to reach and engage with broader audiences. Moreover, as this chapter suggests, there are many links between the research undertaken by family historians and social historians. Academic historians need to engage with, inform and facilitate this process of memory work, and to share the work of formal and informal 'memory-making' with family historians. Such a transformation is vital if we are truly committed to increasing knowledge of the history of the family for all. If historians can understand and explain people's affective engagements with the past, we will be better placed to impart the social value of historical knowledge.

It 'makes me come alive': The emotional impact of family history

Harriet Jones, a heritage librarian who works in Queensland Australia, told me in her survey response that she enjoys enormous satisfaction, in her terms 'a hint of serenity' when she undertakes family history. But she is also

> inspired … I regularly come back to these when I think my life is challenging to help me get some perspective and inspiration.

She uses her learning to galvanize her in the present and her knowledge about the women in her family tree also helps her to mother today:

> The research process … makes me 'come alive'; it's so stimulating and engaging. As a sole parent, when my daughter was young and I was only working part-time family history was a great way to pass the naptime hours or evenings after she was in bed; now that I'm working more than full-time … it's easy to not find time, but sometimes, for a 'treat', I'll say to myself 'All the things I should be doing can wait; I'm going to do some family history tonight' and pull out a file and choose a dangling thread to pursue … It's also been a great distraction or focus point during traumatic or emotional periods in my life.[1]

Harriet's lengthy survey response reveals many fascinating insights like these into how her family history research makes her feel at different moments in her life. This chapter explores how researchers in Australia, Canada and Britain report how family history makes them feel. It demonstrates how the process of individualizing history and using it to understand oneself, as we saw in the previous chapter, is a deeply affective practice, allowing family history researchers to claim crucial control over their lives. This chapter explores what it is that motivates family historians to undertake family history work. It also considers how research discoveries can emotionally affect individuals, families and communities and the effects of that emotional response on others. It suggests that we can recognize the broader social impact these engagements can produce by embracing the positive political consequences of an emotional engagement with family historians' historical subjects.

This chapter builds on the powerful relationship between feminism and family history I gestured towards in Chapter 1. It asks how feminism informs the work of these family history researchers. Much of the discussion and analysis is focused in this chapter on information provided in questions seven to fifteen and question twenty-eight in the survey (see the Appendix for the survey questions). As I discussed in the Introduction, the survey responses were highly gendered. As is to be anticipated, this is especially the case with regards to questions concerning emotional responses and motivations. One male participant gave mostly one-word answers in his replies. In answer to my question on whether he had experienced emotional responses to his work, he stated that his research made him feel 'rewarded'.[2] Australian respondent John Stanhope was balder in his assertion that he felt no emotional response to his research.[3] John Bennett also replied that: 'No really emotive words like the above apply … I am not really a very emotional, heart on sleeve person, more analytical (bit like Spock)'.[4] Perhaps some men are not comfortable admitting to emotional responses or find it difficult to articulate them?

It is hard to know whether these men were being flippant and/or performing stereotypes about the gendering of emotions.[5] However, most of the male respondents took pride in their so-called 'objectivity'. Matthew Benson finds: 'I am objective and somewhat detached when I write the story of my ancestors'.[6] English respondent Neil Spurgeon was a retired Royal Navy Chief Petty Officer and College Lecturer/Manager, living in Hampshire, who became a family historian in the late 1950s because he was curious about the characters his mother and grandmother discussed in his presence. His emotional responses captured those of many others: 'I am very proud of my ancestors who made something of themselves, won medals or awards … I am sorry for those in workhouses or who found themselves in trouble through no fault of their own.' However, he made clear that because he was 'a Royal Navy CPO, emotion doesn't really exist in me!'[7] Some of his initial answers detailing his emotional responses above suggested otherwise, however.

One or two respondents contended that my questions about emotions were 'leading' but did not articulate what they meant by this. My question probing whether their research had made them feel 'proud, sad, happy', etc., did encourage respondents to detail these specific emotional responses in their answers, but others listed several other emotional triggers and responses. Some people queried whether the questions about emotions were appropriate even though their participation and consent form made clear that this project was focused on eliciting data about their emotional motivations and responses to their research. My experience as an oral history researcher has made me aware that some people loath talking about and sharing details of their emotions with strangers. It is possible that this is a concern for more mature participants, or personality types not comfortable talking about their feelings with strangers.[8] However, as will be clear from the following discussion, many of my respondents were content to describe their feelings at length.

Like many of my respondents Harriet Jones, who opened this chapter, detailed her manifold emotional responses across several pages and long paragraph answers. These listed how she felt inspired, entertained, joyous, competent, sad, responsible, excited, blessed/privileged, satisfied, exasperated and wistful as a result of her research.[9] A few like MP emphasized that they had experienced 'a lot of emotional responses, Sadness, happiness, anger, shock, intrigue – it is like watching a movie of your life unfold'.[10] Catherine Ong had experienced 'a multitude of emotions ranging from intense sadness to pride/joy'.[11] The emotions most frequently listed and experienced as a result of family history research by my respondents was pride, excitement, joy, happiness and sadness. Most rejected feeling any shame or anger towards their ancestors or as a result of their research. However, as we will see, they sometimes found themselves carefully walking on eggshells with older members of their family, hoping to hide skeletons in their closets. Exploring the broad emotional impact of family history in this chapter enables me to reiterate the value of all historical researchers reflecting on the relationship between their emotions and research and to consider how emotional responses to family history research have changed over time.

Emotions and affect

As suggested in Chapter 1, there is an important relationship between family history and the history of the emotions. Using the sociologist Bourdieu's work, I suggested that family historians need to be understood as 'feeling bodies' located within complex relations of power to history and the world.[12] My study shows that family historians are using their research, both the knowledge they create and the communication of that knowledge, which might be driven by the desire to connect emotionally to the past, to challenge the 'repetition of norms'. This is important because such projects produce different forms of knowing to those that queer theorist and philosopher Judith Butler suggests rests at the heart of the discursive power of family, heterosexuality and the nation.[13] Family historians are using their research to challenge their own and broader assumptions about and definitions of the so-called 'normal family', gender relations and 'the normative' more broadly. This questioning disrupts people's assumptions about the history of the family and how greater knowledge of family lives in the past can have a significant impact on people's present lives and make a difference to future generations.

Family historians understand their place in the world as relational and as situated within complex structures of power. They are, to take Bourdieu's phrase 'socialized subjects' situated within their own, their family's and broader social histories.[14] The knowledge that is produced through their research and collaboration with others encourages them to question the structures of power within which they are situated. They are transformed by their research and reflections on the past lives of their forebears and often use their knowledge and expertise to help others. Family historians who learn how to become social historians reap the benefits of cultural capital. What my research demonstrates is that historians, and especially feminist historians, should embrace the 'amateurish', the 'emotional' pursuits of often (though not always) female family historians and recognize its educative potential and political significance.

The practice of family history has become well integrated into the burgeoning practice of lifelong learning across the globe since the 1970s.[15] It is one of the world's most popular leisure pursuits, understood by sociologists to be a form of 'serious leisure', a means of both enjoyment and education.[16] This educative function among lifelong learners, at all stages of the life cycle, is often unappreciated.[17] Despite its conservative practice – archival, patrilineal and often heteronormative (but not always – there is more I will say about the disruptive potential of queer and adoptive family history for example) – family history is radical in the way it has shifted modes of historical practice and exponentially expanded its production and meaning.[18]

In the eyes of many family historians, 'national history' tends to be 'male and political' and does not engage them in the ways that social history – with its focus on women, the ordinary and the everyday – does. They want national history to become 'personal' so that they can connect to it. This means they will learn more and engage with the past more passionately.[19] Jeannette Tsoulos, a mature part-time piano teacher, is a passionate and active member of the Australian Jewish historical community in Sydney and past president of the Australian

Jewish Genealogical Society. She told me: '[T]he written history of the nation or globe takes no account of family history unless it's that of kings and queens. It's invisible, like women's lives.' When women's lives are marginalized in these ways people more easily ignore them and devalue mothers in the present.[20]

Feminism informed the research of a significant proportion of respondents, including two British, five Canadian and nineteen Australian respondents. This amounts to almost a quarter of the Australian sample. It was through their family history research that many became aware of the gendered bias of historical records. As Australian CA reports it is 'hard ... to find the ancestral women in my family ... I suppose feminism is one aspect that I have become aware of as I research the women in my family.'[21] Canadian Deb McAuslan labels herself a feminist, as she says, 'I do consider myself a feminist and find it discouraging that the history of women is much more difficult to trace.'[22] These women and others find that they have more respect for their female rather than male ancestors 'because history is just that HIS story.'[23] Through the stories of their female ancestors and the pride they elicit, as women today they are inspired to live better lives as women.[24] Harriet Jones, who we met earlier, was inspired 'by the bravery and hardships, particularly of the women in my family tree who intrepidly left their homelands and travelled across the seas to an unknown land ... They went on to marry and raise families, often in the harshest and most rudimentary of circumstances.'[25]

Family history is understood as bringing women's lives to the fore when other forms of history marginalize them. It was framed by several researchers as a feminist practice.[26] In response to my question: 'Has your research challenged the way that you think about the history of the family or national history more broadly?' NM, one of the few family historians who asked to remain anonymous, stated:

> For sure. I have become more aware of the role of women, especially in relation to their work. I think national history emphasizes women's roles in history as mothers and wives, whereas my family history research has shown me that they were also great workers. My family history research has challenged my previous views of women in national history.[27]

In the previous chapter, we were introduced to Kay Spence who was born in Townsville, growing up in Brisbane, Queensland, Australia. Kay has spent decades devoted to learning more about the women in her fascinating family tree. She was inspired to do so by her great-grandmother who accompanied her husband around the world, helped him settle in foreign lands and gave birth to thirteen of his children. Kay was shocked to discover that his memoirs contained barely a mention of her in over twenty-nine pages,

> Once was where he got 'married to Mrs. Spence' (no maiden name), and the next was in a paragraph on the final page where it seems she had died. Her lifetime was summed up with these words: 'A very great sorrow came to Mr. Spence a short time back, when his faithful helpmeet of nearly sixty years, passed away quietly in her sleep ....Sixty years of marriage and she warrants <u>no more than a few lines</u> ...

Kay now knows that family history has transformed her understanding of Australian history.

> This was a very interesting survey to complete. It made me think about the possible connections between local/national/global history and my own family history. I had never thought of family history in this way before.[28]

Respondents to my survey in Britain are also using family history to better understand the lives of their working-class forebears as well as the lives of women. Many have thought carefully about how their knowledge of history has been constructed by particular sources and alternative accounts pieced together over time. We saw in the previous chapter that Barbara Hearn is using family history to complicate her understanding of the past. This has compelled her to undertake feminist historical activity. She told me that

> the slow progression of women has been informed by my family research. Inevitably it has influenced my choice of working on a campaign with some of my free time www.maryonthegreen.org.uk about the Founder of Feminism.[29]

This project is now complete. The memorial by Maggi Hambling to the founder of feminism was instated in 2020.[30] Barbara helped set up The Wollstonecraft Society but has now stepped aside to work on a different initiative addressing racism through conversation.[31]

Learning and teaching scholarship in the discipline of history has been mainly focused on the primary, secondary and tertiary sector or broadly on historical consciousness among 'ordinary people'.[32] We have much to learn about how lifelong learners use history to understand their place in the world. Education scholar Emma Shaw has used her research on Australian family historians (1406 survey responses and eleven oral history interviews) to suggest that many are using substantive history (first-order historical concepts) and procedural history (second-order historical concepts) following Peter Lee's use of these terms.[33] Like her, I believe that family historians think historically because my research has shown that they understand how historical knowledge has been constructed and because they work hard to contextualize this knowledge using the techniques of social history to do so. They are using stories about their ancestors' past lives to argue for better lives in the present for themselves, their families and others less fortunate than themselves. They are using their research to learn more and reveal to others about the impact of structural disadvantage and social inequality. This focus on the ordinary is a common refrain in these responses, along with frustration regarding the inadequate documenting of their lives. Some male respondents are also firmly committed to a feminist project. HSN, a retired teacher born in Hartlepool England in 1955 and now living in Laibin City, Guangxi Province, China, believes

> that women's contributions to society are just as valuable as those of men. Unfortunately, in the past people didn't always see it that way. I consciously do what I can to redress the balance but there are far fewer records available for my female ancestors.[34]

Researchers like HSN relish discovering details about mothers in the past over many decades of research. Others talk about experiencing great joy in piecing together significant details about how childbirth has changed over time, maternal and infant mortality, child labour, women's work, domestic violence and migration in different national contexts.[35] They also delight in sharing this knowledge with others.

These researchers have developed a strong understanding of social history and the politics of history making. Many take enormous pleasure in producing microhistories of motherhood as part of their efforts to recover women's lives in the past. These stories have become significant for the present lives of these researchers and the lives of women more broadly. This process of synthesizing and making sense of empirical detail is not a simplistic and naïve enterprise.

When family historians undertake their research, as the previous chapter revealed, most are thinking critically about the ways in which our knowledge is constructed, how we think historically and how that new knowledge can be shared for political purpose. As academic historians worry about declining university enrolment numbers, I take enormous pleasure reading, hearing and watching the passion that family historians have for their subject.[36] It transforms them because family history involves student-centred, active learning, which is deeply dependent upon technology and communication.[37] The Internet, social media, local and family history societies serve as the classrooms for family historians.

In these learning spaces they actively share their love of history, affectively and cognitively with others, to share satisfying learning outcomes that sustain them for many years as a community. Many articulate that the physical and emotional connection they have to their subjects is key to their learning process.[38]

Harriet Jones is an excellent example of this. She wrote in her survey that her family responds to her passion in different ways. Her mother

> is always interested and keen to come on family history adventures with me and help where she can ... it's one thing I've done that Mum things I am very clever at (I'm actually very good at lots of things, but this is one of the few she has acknowledged and acknowledges publicly, which is even more amazing).

Her fifteen-year-old daughter

> does lots of eye-rolling (as she feels she must) but is generally interested and has actually absorbed a large amount of information over the years and knows many names and stories .... She has also been extremely tolerant throughout her childhood of the random places we have travelled to in the pursuit of family history and very patient entertaining herself for long periods of time in family history societies.

It has also taught her to be reflective about the information she shares with other family members:

> Something that I simply find really interesting (or perhaps a bit funny) could be upsetting for others. For example, finding out my granny had two abortions which caused her to suffer great emotional distress later in life (and there's nothing at all funny about that; I just feel sad for her and her circumstances and wonder at what point in her life this was – was it before she married and was she therefore a bit of a free spirit as a young woman? Or was it during her marriage and she just couldn't face having any more children?) While I find this really interesting, I haven't shared it with Mum as instinctively I feel she would be quite upset by this knowledge.

This survey response reveals how Harriet's historical thinking and emotional engagement with the past and her present works in a multiplicity of ways. Her research is allowing her to produce counter narratives to challenge familial knowledge passed down the maternal line as well as dominant national histories from which members of her family (especially the women) have frequently been excluded. Women like Harriet are challenging our understandings of 'history', of motherhood and 'the nation' in this process.

My family history respondents demonstrate that they are thinking historically by aiming to contextualize information about family lives in the past. They demonstrate rigour in the collection of historical evidence, triangulating their sources and hoping to understand how and why historical change has occurred, acquiring many of the skills academics associate with advanced historical research. Many of these family historians possess a sophisticated understanding of a variety of primary and secondary sources, have developed the capacity to read and think critically and learned about the complex ways in which our knowledge is constructed.[39] However, emotions and affective engagements with the past are front and centre of this process.

Pride

Pride is the emotion most articulated as a response to family history research. Most family historians – fifty-two out of eighty-one Australian (64 per cent), fourteen out of twenty-seven British (52 per cent) and eighteen out of twenty-eight Canadian (64 per cent) respondents – said that they had experienced pride as a result of their research. We might expect that family historians were most interested in seeking out connections with and being proud of aristocratic and illustrious ancestors, as they were prior to the 1970s,[40] but only one respondent Ron Sinclair wrote that he was 'Proud that [he has] been able by DNA to connect to the Peerage of Scotland'.[41]

Most family historians expressed the greatest pride in those in their family trees who were poor, resilient, marginalized, opportunistic survivors. Irene Morgan is 'proud of all my ancestors the ones who did it tough, as well as the pioneers, and the ones who had an easy ride'.[42] Dee Leamey, like others, is 'intensely **proud** [emphasis is hers] of my forebears and what they overcame to live their lives. Intensely **proud** of those who started off with so little and made a success of their lives providing a livelihood for their children and subsequent generations'.[43] This pride seemed strongest amongst migrant descendants to Australia and Canada, who appreciate the sacrifices made by their intrepid ancestors as they travelled the world seeking opportunities and becoming nation-builders.[44] Glenna Morrison feels 'proud to know that my ancestors were brave souls who left all that was familiar to come to two Canadian outposts (Newfoundland and Quebec) and help build a new nation'.[45] Pennie Griffiths feels 'very proud of all my Ancestors in the making of the Australian nation, the brilliant, the good, the bad and even the naughty'.[46]

Learning about the resilience of ancestors makes others feel proud of their forebears. Brenda Lee feels 'empowered. I look at what my ancestors endured … They inspire me … My family had humble beginnings but they were survivors.' She is proud of her ancestors because 'I thought I came from "bad stock", from lower class … Now I see how rigged the system was, and how strong my "lower class" ancestors were to fight against it. They were survivors.'[47] Brenda is using her historical knowledge to critique and challenge contemporary class and gender social structures and government responses to refugees and global migration.

This pride is often directed at female ancestors by men as well as women. Donald Davis felt 'proudest in discovering foremothers who survived frequent childbirths and skilfully raised large families to adulthood in times and places where infant mortality was high and where epidemics are known to have been devastating to many'.[48]

Others articulate pride in their own research achievements rather than their ancestors, revealing the identity-affirming qualities of research, personal historical knowledge and reflection.[49] LB encapsulates both senses of pride, his research made him feel, '**Proud of my ancestors** [emphasis is his] for "holding it together" in the tough times and seizing the opportunity to venture elsewhere to seek a better life when times and circumstances made it tough. **Proud in myself** [sic] for sticking to the task of research about research, and achieving goals with same.'[50] Tracey Treloar feels the same way, 'I am proud of my ancestors and their associated histories, and also a little proud of myself for keeping their memories alive and acknowledging their existence.'[51]

Anger

A handful of these family historians admitted feeling anger as a result of their discoveries. This group included three English, four Canadian and fifteen Australian family historian respondents. Dee Leamey feels '**Anger** by the futility of the loss of some of their lives in warfare and poor social conditions. **Sad** about the children left motherless or orphaned.'[52] Jenny Wilson has experienced being 'angry, when a great uncle is found to have been executed by the Japanese on the Burma – Thai railway, for the offence of stealing food to feed starving prisoners.'[53] Others also express anger at historical racial and ethnic persecution: 'I get angry thinking about the things I have learned about how the Protestants in Northern Ireland torment the Catholics. My family may have been involved. It sickens me.'[54] This shows that anger can be coupled with guilt on occasion. Others are angry at the omission of women in historical sources: RG, for instance, is 'often angry at the lack of recognition for my female ancestors' struggles and contributions'.[55] Others are angry at social inequality and prejudiced legal systems. Tracey Treloar has been 'angry … at injustices that may have caused suffering and loss'.[56] HG has felt anger 'when the mores of the time were particularly judgmental about human foibles eg public shaming (outing) of individuals seeking a divorce in the 1920s individuals written about in the local paper or in the 1960s when government policy required those who were divorcing to give cause'.[57]

Sadness

Most of this anger is a response to the sadness researchers feel on learning about poor people's suffering in the past. Eleven Canadian, thirteen British and forty-one Australian researchers expressed feeling sadness upon their research discoveries. Ian Devenish has been 'saddened at the tragic lives some of my ancestors experienced, quite unnecessarily in some cases'.[58] Jenny Wilson feels 'sadness about their circumstances, when discovering that an ancestor is described as "died as a pauper" or "died in childbirth."'[59] CA sometimes feels 'very sad for the tough life some of my ancestors led, but then I remember that they survived, or I wouldn't be here'.[60] Marilyn Myers feels 'sympathy for their plight and the difficult times they had to negotiate. It has given me a deeper understanding of and sympathy for the difficulties experienced by people in poverty today and their need to do the best they can for themselves and their families'.[61]

The sadness that other researchers feel is gendered and directed, for the most part, at poor women and children. Jan Brown feels 'very sad about the babies/ children who died, the times my family ended up in the workhouse, the large numbers of family who died prematurely of TB, the women who died in/soon after childbirth'.[62] AM experiences 'sometimes intense sorrow at the hardships and losses endured, and the inequities of the times – and frustration that "it should never have happened" – (in case of loss of so many babies …) and also intense pride at the determination, skills and sheer courage of these people who despite many setbacks survived and thrived and contributed to their new communities'.[63] Maureen Cooney is 'never shameful, certainly proud and happy, and occasionally sad about the hardships endured, especially by mothers. It makes me grateful for the time in which I live'.[64] Irene Blackburn wrote how 'I feel sad when I see how many children died before the age of 5, it must have been heartbreaking. I feel sorry for women who died in childbirth. I feel sorry for those who went into workhouses.'[65] Others have experienced sadness when they have realized 'a husband has deserted his children after the wife's death. A sadness, when I discover an elderly relative living her last years in the poor house.'[66] Grief at child mortality was mentioned by many respondents. They were frequently 'sad because of the deaths of young children'.[67] CA feels 'sad for all the mothers that died in childbirth or the lost babies'.[68] JA was 'sad about the deprivations and sorrows they endured, that put any we suffer into perspective'.[69] Brenda was 'sad – for what they had to endure'.[70]

Sadness could be personal as well as political. For Betty O'Neill,

> I have felt sad that my family, and my father's other secret family and my father suffered so much loss and trauma. The violence and fear endured during WWII and the concentration camps engender great sadness in me that we as human beings can treat each other in this way. I am also saddened that this is still happening today and that we really do not learn from history.[71]

Dawn Spriggett has been 'shocked by some of the social circumstances I have uncovered. There are errant fathers, severely judged single mothers, mental health issues, selfishness, people who clouded the truth and premature deaths due to illnesses that are no longer a death sentence ... I mostly feel very sad. So many opportunities lost'.[72] These responses trigger empathetic reaction at a time in history when we are discouraged from caring for others, as I discuss in Chapter 5.

Shame

Most survey respondents rejected shame as an emotional response to their research. This group included eight Canadian, six British and nineteen Australian researchers. If they talked about shame it was usually in relation to the responses of older relatives to their discoveries around illegitimacy, adoption, homosexuality, mixed-race and sectarian relationships. Deb McAuslan's 'mother was worried about what family secrets I might unearth and who I'd tell'.[73] RG conceded that she was 'more likely to encounter shock in older family members'.[74] As Carolyn Jones suggested 'living relatives who are in their 80s and 90s still hold on to the old ways of keeping stuff really private'.[75] Most of these family historians were careful not to offend older relatives but they also wanted to share secrets openly to discourage shame as a response to these topics. This generational sensitivity was important for many, as Barbara Barclay suggests when writing about her emotional responses: 'Angry or shameful – never. I think we are a different generation in how we view/talk about family.'[76]

Michelle Goldsmith, a reference librarian living in NSW, suggested the same when she wrote that responses really depended

on the age and education of the researcher. Younger researchers don't care as they are more accepting. People were people and things happened. However, as part of my job I assist people in their research and many older customers still view those things negatively. If they have an image of a beloved grandfather being an upstanding citizen, to find out that they had contracted an STD in WW1 whilst married to grandma is very confronting.[77]

In his book *Shame: A Brief History* Peter Stearns challenges the perceived decline of shame in the United States from the nineteenth century, revealing its uneven and inconsistent continuance and shows how new paths for shame were forged across the Western world.[78] Most of the family historian responders were aware that the different emotional regimes structuring generations across time have had a huge impact on understanding these episodes in family histories.[79] Throughout much of the nineteenth century and well into the twentieth century public shaming was used by communities to discourage pre- and extramarital and non-heterosexual sex. However, despite this shift, shame did not vanish.[80] With regards to social mores these survey responses support a story of significant change over time. As family historian Gail Wright suggests, 'there doesn't seem to be many secrets anymore.'[81]

Even though more communities became increasingly critical of the public use of shaming rituals in the nineteenth century, Stearns suggests, 'middle class Americans retained a huge stake in sexual regulation because of birth control needs ... more attention began to go into guilt as the key emotion in sexual self-regulation ... Women worried about their reputations should they lose their virginity before marriage: shame anticipation strongly influenced behaviour and also encouraged concealment, well into the twentieth century.'[82] While almost all the family historians pointed to this shift in attitudes over time, others are aware that the results are mixed, and we have not moved our way towards a more progressive present. As Ian Devenish thoughtfully suggests:

As a white Anglo-Saxon person, and living in a Western culture I would be inclined to say we are much more tolerant of the issues you have mentioned. Thinking a little more deeply about it, however, I'm not so sure how that is. We're pretty tolerant of children born out of wedlock, also mixed-race unions and homosexuality, but some sections of our community are still struggling with the issues of asylum seekers and people of the Islamic faith. The original Australians, the Aborigines, are still living as outcasts in some parts of the country, therefore we appear to have contradictory issues occurring in our midst.[83]

Through their research and reflection many family historians have become aware of such contradictions and disjuncture. There is no doubt for many researchers that new categories of shame emerged in the late twentieth century, especially in the hands of the Conservative right, with a focus on poverty and immigration.[84]

Many family historians admit having to hide stories of illegitimacy among their ancestors from older relatives, but also suggest that they would rather name and confront this source of shame head on for the sake of future generations.[85] As J Brian Hardaker suggested, he felt 'all those things, except shameful' but he was well aware of the shame that others might feel about the lots of babies born before marriage or too soon after, and several born to single women.[86] 'Carolyn Jones said she did not' think I have felt angry or shameful. I try to learn all I can about people without judging what I find. I can't understand all the circumstances surrounding their decisions to act a certain way so best not to judge.[87]

In the same way Canadian Alison Madden stated that she experienced 'absolutely all of the above [emotions] except for the shameful part'.[88] Respondents who articulated shame and guilt for the actions of their ancestors focused mainly on the wealthy exploiters in their family trees. As we will see below, this group included those who committed domestic violence as well as criminals and slave owners.[89] Patsy Trench is 'slightly ashamed, knowing what the colonists did to the Indigenous population of Australia'.[90] Descendants of settler colonists have been confronted by the legacies of colonialism and its dire impact on Indigenous populations in Canada and Australia through their family history research. Deb McAuslan was horrified learning how 'Indigenous peoples had suffered at our hands'.[91] Australian respondents referenced the well-known change over time with regards to how the nineteenth- and early-twentieth-century response of shame towards convict ancestors is now a source of pride, with 'everyone desperately wanting a convict ancestor'.[92]

Domestic violence and shame

Shame as a response to research revelations was particularly strong with respect to examples of domestic violence. As we have seen, for the most part,

Australian family historians are no longer ashamed about discovering convict ancestry, illegitimacy and mixed raced relationships in their families' past, but they are embarrassed about discovering domestic violence. In early 2016 a domestic violence survivor described family violence as a 'silent tsunami' engulfing Australia,[93] its effects rippling out to overwhelm not just its immediate victims, but their wider networks of family and friends.[94] In 2020 the problem has worsened rather than improved.[95] Many victims have difficulty admitting experiences of violence to their loved ones, let alone to the police or courts.[96] Meanwhile, those who observe violence from outside the family unit still often struggle to describe it to others.[97] We live in a time when the language of domestic violence is changing rapidly and in different national contexts. Having worked on the history of the family for over two decades, I remain shocked by the many terrifying tales of domestic violence I unearth in my research on families in Britain and Australia from the eighteenth century to the present.

Family historians are challenging these sorts of silences around women's lives in the past. I wonder how much the high-profile media and political campaign led by Rosie Batty in Australia since 2015 has heightened people's interest in the broader history of domestic violence? Batty, whose eleven-year-old son Luke was murdered by his father in 2014, became Australian of the Year the following year. A prominent campaigner, she has played a crucial role in bringing domestic violence into the public eye. Many family historians I have communicated with note Batty's role in their understanding of domestic violence in contemporary Australia. The attention attracted by her campaign has fed their thirst for knowledge and reframed their understanding of partner violence, past and present. We need to recognize the opportunities for knowledge acquisition available to us in this historical moment, and then use it to acknowledge and document the long history of domestic violence in Australia – the structural circumstances that result in the ongoing perpetration of violence – to figure out how it can end. Might confronting family histories of violence in the past help us become more willing to begin conversations about violence in the present?

The accounts of domestic violence unearthed by family historians are often horrifically shocking. Revealing stories like these can teach us valuable lessons about history and humanity, but not all family historians agree that this is the case. Some normalize the incidence of domestic violence towards women in past societies, because 'men were men', even though media reports at the time were deeply critical of perpetrators' actions. As a feminist historian it is important for me to challenge this assumption about 'the olden days' and attitudes towards women. Therefore, I continue to collaborate with family historians and to ask them about the emotional impact of discovering domestic violence in their family histories.

Gay Horsburgh was born in 1958 and became a family historian in the early 2000s. She works as a health planner within a local health district in NSW. In her family history research, she has 'mainly been interested in … the female side of the family as usually existing trees focussed on men'. When the wife of one of her ancestors left him, this precipitated acts of domestic violence:

> He pursued her through the local press, denigrated her and then burnt down his father-in-law's house. He then spent years justifying these acts by saying that his wife deserved it. This form of domestic violence and justification continues to resonate with the current world. This behaviour is inconsistent with the values I hold.[98]

Through their family history research, practitioners like Gay have come much closer to understanding the impact of legislative reform on individual lives in the past and present, through their family history research. Gay's parents divorced before Prime Minister Gough Whitlam introduced the Family Law Act in 1975 and she relished the opportunity to read her parent's divorce papers as part of her research:

> I realised how unfair those laws were for the individuals concerned – in revealing their lives and in having to do 'illegal acts' to get a divorce; and the value of more progressive legislation.

As I have suggested already, family historians are often criticized for seeking out the past lives of their forebears for nostalgic reasons. However, many researchers love discovering the secrets and lies their research reveals and the lessons they learn about past and present lives, as well as the impact of legislative change on individual lives, on their journeys. It makes them much more aware of how the law structures our lives in the present and what impact it has on ordinary lives.

I am struck by how many contemporary family historians in Australia have described the shock and shame of discovering ancestors who have been violent towards their spouses. I think responses to domestic violence have changed dramatically in recent years. Yet if people have difficulties confronting the realities of domestic violence in the past, how much more difficult must it be to acknowledge its presence in the present?[99]

Caryn Patterson was born in Moree but she has spent most of her life living in Sydney where she became a family historian in 1985. She has had powerful emotional reactions to her research. It's 'made me cry to learn just how hard the lives of some of my ancestors were (for example, my 3 times great grandmother was subjected to abuse from a very violent alcoholic husband … and he was jailed numerous times for it)'. This has shocked her, because some of her ancestors 'were subjected to some awful treatment'; she reflects, 'I think I've learned to be much more aware of the way people live and their right to live the way they chose'.[100] My research has revealed that many family historians like Caryn have become increasingly sensitive and empathetic to cases of domestic violence since discovering its existence in their own family trees.

Another passionate family historian who works in education, Margaret Nelly,[101] was born in Darlinghurst, Sydney, in 1963, and began working on her family history in the 1990s. Through a growing interest in social history and the history of 'ordinary'/commoners like her ancestors, she felt herself becoming more 'connected' to her ancestors. She feels that this personal connection enables her to understand the past, and especially domestic violence in the past, better:

> I have found so many heart-wrenching, sad stories that have increased my empathy for my ancestors. Sometimes I also get annoyed and feel shameful when I find out an ancestor beat up his wife so badly that she was expected to die.[102]

Karin Davis grew up in Victoria and she became a family historian in 1970 at the age of fourteen. She knew there was a story her family was trying to hide. She was desperate to learn more details about her father's side of the family but all her relatives were 'so close mouthed'. She

> wanted to make them understand that ANYTHING and EVERYTHING is ok by my standards and not to feel shame or fear – I failed.

In response to my question – 'Do you think emotional responses to family history have changed over time?' – she replied:

> Yes, whilst we no longer stigmatise illegitimacy, we do as a society however have a far less tolerant attitude to family violence. This may have been more accepted in the past (a husband's right and all that) but now I am sure a woman may well feel the object of ridicule in some ways for not leaving an abusive partner. After all, it is 'easy to leave' people think ….[103]

Karin claims that her work as a family historian has enabled her to become more empathetic, 'it has made me much more understanding of what is sometimes termed people's "shortcomings"'. She is not alone among my cohort of family historians to believe passionately that their research has made them generally more empathetic, an issue I discuss in Chapter 5.

Les De Belin likes discovering the skeletons in his family's closet, but he doesn't understand why people get so emotional about these sorts of discoveries. He's unearthed Aboriginal ancestry and:

> Love affairs resulting in divorces, illegitimate children, criminal offences, and even my 2 × great grandfather attempting to murder my × great grandmother by cutting her throat. That was something nobody in the family knew of until I found it in an old newspaper.

While Les disputed other people's emotional responses to family history discoveries, he cannot understand why more do not undertake their family history in order to learn further details about the world.[104] He agrees that it remains a significant conduit to historical knowledge and understanding about the world in the present.

'Ordinary' family historians and 'professional' feminist academic scholars are working in tandem to reveal many of these troubling stories of historical domestic violence. This effort is one of the many legacies of the women's liberation movement, when campaigners finally listened to the 'quiet screaming' occurring behind closed doors during the 1970s. More and more research has revealed how these quiet screams have a long history and can be discovered among families of all classes, nations and races.

Historian Zora Simic's chapter in *Gender Violence in Australia* reveals the political and methodological purpose of her current (now Australian Research Council-funded) research project on the history of domestic violence, a task shared with fellow historians Ann Curthoys and Catherine Kevin. Simic shows how the knowledge production spurred on by feminist academic historians in the 1980s was a vital phase in helping to label and generate campaigns for the rights of domestic violence victims. Let us use the knowledge production among celebrities, 'ordinary', everyday people and millions of family historians across the globe, created partly by the high-profile campaign against domestic violence led by Batty, to demand change for women and their children now and in the future.[105]

Excitement and joy

These emotional responses outlined above are always accompanied by visceral pleasure in the process of research and discovery. It is important that we acknowledge the joy, elation and excitement that many family historians express for their work, both its process and outcomes. As suggested earlier, Sally Newman has lamented the fact that academic researchers often forget to articulate their passion for research.[106] By contrast family historians love to emote about their work and its impact upon their lives. Barbara Barclay told me that her research has made her feel 'huge excitement at times when I just want to tell every person that I meet what I've found'.[107] For Harriet Jones – 'there's nothing like the thrill of the chase and then finding the answer to a stubborn question; even better if the answer to that question leads to greater discoveries … The research process brings me great satisfaction and makes me "come alive"; it's so stimulating and engaging.'[108] Susan Hinds is 'thrilled, wanting to know and do more. My husband reckons "I'm like a dog with a bone."'[109] Carol Turner finds that her research gets her 'so excited and bursting to share what I've learned'.[110]

This chapter has demonstrated how emotionally driven empirical research by family historians around the world is helping to challenge myths and assumptions about family life in the past and to redefine familial and other relationships in the present, giving researchers enormous pleasure in the process. Family history facilitates the rediscovery of women's and men's lives in the past, allowing researchers to reimagine families, familial relationships and individual legacy. Developing a long-lasting passion for family history is changing how men and women think about their roles in society today and encouraging them to advocate for change. The following chapters will show how family historians are using their affective engagements with the past to work through the gendered and classed expectations of society and to challenge them.

Around the world millions of family historians busy producing women's, feminist and gender history through family history research have the potential to have a far greater impact on our knowledge of women and men's lives in the past than most academics do. It is for this reason that academic historians need to revalue the labour of family history so that we can continue to subvert the gendered structure of the discipline of history, as well as the gendered social order. Let us recognize and facilitate the ways in which 'ordinary' people are using history to rethink women's paid and unpaid work, their contribution to the family as well as to the nation, in the past as well as the present, and to reject the reproduction of mothering (and fathering) that has sustained unequal relationships between men and women for centuries.[111] Most importantly of all, let us celebrate the life-affirming impact of family history research.

'Random acts of genealogical kindness': How family historians share their knowledge and break down national boundaries

Carol Turner's enthusiasm for family history leapt from the pages of the survey response she sent to me in 2016. Carol is the mother of three young children and lives in Victoria, Australia; she adores the way the Internet makes it possible to collaborate with a global community of researchers. 'Learning from others and sharing what I've learned are what keeps the passion alive,' she writes. 'Otherwise, it's just me, a box of dusty documents and a bunch of dead people.' Carol is convinced that her practice of family history has transformed her – it has been her 'life's work'. Social media and the Internet have facilitated this labour and they enable her to share it around the world with family members and strangers. This gives her, and millions of others, enormous pleasure.[1]

Of those family historians who responded to my surveys, participated in oral history interviews, and focus groups, most understand themselves as part of a global community of researchers who are working together to increase their knowledge and understanding of family history. As Simon Michael Titley-Bayes suggests in his 2006 thesis on family history in England, in the late 1970s and 80s, family historians became 'both a self-defined and self-conscious group' within family history societies, helping to feed the global family history boom. As the century turned, the expanding use of the Internet by this emotional community of researchers caused the boom to rise exponentially.[2]

Drawing on the work of historian of emotion Barbara Rosenwein, sociologists who work on the concept of community and educational scholar Barbara Rogoff, I want to suggest in this chapter that the family historians with whom I have communicated are dedicated, loyal and committed members of emotional communities of learners. Piecing together family histories, both their own and those of others, the people working within such communities aim to share their knowledge and expertise far and wide.[3] Family historians learn to develop crucial historical skills when participating in the endeavour with others. It is being part of these communities that teaches them the rules of the discipline and the ethics of their practice. As we have seen in our brief discussion of the history of emotions in Chapter 1:

> [Emotional communities] are precisely the same as social communities – families, neighbourhoods, parliaments, guilds, monasteries, parish church memberships – but the researcher looking at them seeks above all to uncover systems of feeling: what these communities (and the individuals within them) define and assess as valuable or harmful to them; the evaluations that they make about others' emotions; the nature of the affective bonds between people that they recognize; and the modes of emotional expression that they expect, encourage, tolerate, and deplore.[4]

This chapter outlines some of those systems of feelings that family historians possess, and which I introduced in the previous chapter. It investigates how the process of engaging with emotional communities gives family historians the language, knowledge and confidence to become empathetic agents of change. A development I discuss in the following chapter. As Pamela Fane in Canada suggests, 'Any hobby that engages people, brings them together for a common purpose, makes them think, causes them to look outside themselves and help each other is a wonderful thing'.[5] This chapter will show how engagement with communities of family history learners creates a set of shared values and knowledge that provide the seeds of the social and cultural capital reaped by these researchers.[6]

Communities of learners

UK-based Jan Brown became a family historian in 1985. She believes wholeheartedly in 'random acts of genealogical kindness'.[7] Several family historians used this precise phrase to describe a broad range of activities and experiences in their surveys. Random Acts of Genealogical Kindness (RAOGK) is a formal global organization set up in the United States in 1999 by the late long-time family historian Bridgett Sneider.[8] The organization was established to help family historians with their research, via a network of global voluntary labour whereby volunteers help others seek out evidence, copy details on gravestones and locate archival documents. This is precisely the sort of voluntary activity that allows this community of global family historians to flourish and certainly such acts are evidenced in many of the survey responses shared with me. In her American PhD thesis Amy Smith traced out the sense of community (abbreviated to SOC in her thesis) that family historians develop. Smith argued that this community shares 'recognition, identification, support, relationships, emotional attachment, and obligation'.[9] I am extending her argument here to suggest that the community is sustained as an emotional community.

One of Jan Brown's favourite family history moments was when a family historian in New Zealand 'offered to take a photo of the grave of her 2 × great-grandfather (on her way home from work!) and email it to me. I now treasure that photo'.[10] Like most of the family historians discussed in the book, she treasures collaboration and the impact it has on her knowledge and research because it allows her to grow her historical knowledge and understanding. Irene Blackburn in Northumberland England was born in 1956 and became a family historian in 1981. She collaborates 'most often with a friend in Australia' and exchanges 'information with people all over the world' but she is also part of a local community of researchers who she meets at 'Record Offices etc and we bounce ideas off each other and help where we can'.[11] These people show us how family historians are active and collaborative learners and teachers, and many enjoy the voluntary labour that helps to cohere their community.[12]

Through such acts of global, collaborative, public pedagogy these contemporary family historians are reconstructing and learning from family lives in the past. As we have seen, it is only recently that historical thinking among lifelong learners outside of the school system has become a focus of scholarly research. The PhD thesis of Australian-based education scholar Emma Shaw explores the ways in which family historians practice 'public pedagogy'.[13] Danish digital historian (and passionate family historian herself) Henriette Roued Cunliffe has revealed the widespread practice of 'helpful information behaviour' among family historians. She shows how 'ordinary people' are engaged in participatory heritage projects and the diverse ways in which this has significant community impacts building valuable partnerships between archives, libraries and different communities of researchers.[14] In the previous chapter on the emotions of family history I argued that family historians understand themselves as 'socialised subjects', their place in the world as relational and as situated within complex structures of power.[15] Other earlier chapters have shown that they are transformed by their research, its sociability and their reflections on the past lives of their forbears. Scholars who research the benefits of lifelong learning suggest that people assert its positive impact anecdotally rather than via empirical evidence. This research presents empirical evidence of the positive benefits of lifelong learning and the forging of learning communities among family historians engaged in this survey.[16] Researchers who learn how to become social historians, with and through others, reap the benefits of increased knowledge and cultural capital. Bourdieu's classic formulation of cultural capital describes how the elite used cultural capital to increase their power, using it to maintain rather than destroy privilege. There was no space in his analysis for the possibility that the marginalized could use social and cultural capital to challenge the power of the elite. I want to suggest in this book that family historians gain social and cultural capital and through their research they use such capital for political purposes, challenging the power of the privileged in the past and present.[17]

This chapter explores the diverse sociability of family history researchers and random acts of genealogical kindness, considering why family historians are motivated to help others with their research and what effects that has on them, their families and communities. It also explores some of the ways in which they police one another. Collaboration and sociability are crucial to their research and the dissemination of that knowledge. This process has the potential to foster community inclusion and belonging among diverse migrant communities in different national contexts. We want to encourage more migrant groups to undertake the practice and to grow their communities and others' awareness of their existence and contributions to 'nation building'. As academic historians and their employers around the world respond to declining enrolment numbers in university history departments by cutting units and staff, I take enormous pleasure reading, hearing and watching the passion that family historians have for their subject in the community. We need to use their passion and collaborative endeavour to show others how important an attention to history can be in people's everyday lives. Their passion transforms them because family history research involves student-centred, active learning, a process deeply dependent upon technology and communication.[18] The Internet, social media, local and family history societies provide people with virtual as well as face-to-face classrooms. In these spaces family historians actively share their love of history, affectively and cognitively with others. Here they create satisfying learning outcomes that sustain them, as a community, for many years. Many articulate how the physical and emotional connection they have to their subjects and the process of sharing them with others is key to their learning process.[19] With these collectives crossing national boundaries, we can see that family historians participate in a range of different communities, online and in person on a level that ranges from community to local, to national and international.[20]

Reciprocity

The communities that I describe are nurtured and sustained by extraordinary acts of reciprocity. English family historian Dee Leamy loves 'to make contact and connections and above all share and help and solve. We really are a community of like-minded people and enjoy the companionship of being a part of it.'[21] Fellow Brit Peggy Beckett is also 'very pleased to give and receive help from other people. Over the years I have been fortunate to have had contacts that have helped me in so many ways, and I hope that I have been of use to others.'[22] Others have limits to their sociability, as is the case for Brenda Turner, who does not like engaging too much with groups of family historians. Brenda tends to find them self-interested; she still loves sharing her knowledge with others on her own terms, 'It's especially fun to share something I have learned.'[23]

Canadian Donald Davis describes many of the different relationships he and others enjoy with other family historians all over the world. These relationships 'entail that of learner, collaborator and mentor. It is multifaceted. I enjoy sharing my findings by writing and publishing. I equally enjoy studying the work of others whose experience and expertise lies in areas I have not previously explored. Archivists are my best allies in my research.'[24] Donald greatly enjoys these multiple collaborations, with diverse others, and has travelled to four countries as a guest speaker on family history and shared his expertise because 'family historians are a collegial and highly curious lot in my experience. Archive lunchrooms are always a locus for lively discussion among researchers keen to share what they are working in and always willing to answer questions.'[25] Similarly, fellow Canadian Ken McKinlay values 'the sharing of information due to the simple fact that one cannot be an expert in all areas and regions of family history. Through sharing I can leverage the knowledge of others and I benefit by also learning more about a different region.'[26] Over half the respondents in Moore et al.'s study on the psychology of family history also declared that they enjoyed sharing their knowledge with others.[27]

Many of the researchers who wrote to me fervently believe that information is useless unless it is shared. 'What is the point of finding all of this great information about ancestors if you don't tell anyone else about it? Family history gives you a sense of being part of something larger, and in sharing, you are connecting more strongly to the family group.'[28] This 'being part of something larger' motivates many of these community members.

There is no doubt that collaboration is crucial for these communities to function so successfully. Many are profoundly committed to the concept and practice of sharing across different levels. Brenda Lee loves 'to learn and it is so valuable to get information from others who share an interest. I love sharing what I have learned as well as it helps people move forward with their research. Collaboration is crucial for a broad education'.[29] Peggy Homans Chapman values 'collaboration tremendously and I see it as essential in family history research. I cannot be knowledgeable about every local level area and there are "gems" of knowledge who live in every small town and rural community. Family historians for the most part are extremely generous with their time and knowledge. I know I get great satisfaction from helping someone and I suspect most people feel the same'.[30]

These family historians are passionate about extending their knowledge of social, local and cultural history and sharing it with their community. They are always searching for more information to contextualize their family trees. Barbara Barclay really enjoys learning from some people

> whose family history research ends up making them excellent local historians, whose research and interests spread much beyond their own family history. These are the people that I enjoy engaging with the most. I also think that in the pre internet days, people were much more guarded with their research and information. Probably understandably, given the amount of hours and personal visits to repositories to gather that information.[31]

Caryn Patterson thinks 'the whole idea of doing family history is the sharing of information'.[32] As Shane O'Neil sums up this section perfectly, 'sharing is what makes a community. It's how you learn and grow'.[33]

Generosity

Many survey responses and interviews reveal a powerful generosity of spirit amongst fellow travellers in the family history world. This extends to family (near and far, close as well as distant relatives), local community members and complete strangers. Many advertise the voluntary work they are willing to do for others, on a local and global scale, often via the Internet's various groups of family historians. Debra McAuslan told me that 'I put on Ancestry.com that I am willing to help others. For fundraisers (Silent Auctions) I put in that I will do 5 hours of genealogy for people ... I enjoy helping others discover their roots and the money goes to a good cause. I have helped cousins' spouses, my daughter's boyfriend's parents and friends working on their family histories'.[34]

Caryn Patterson benefits from the kindness of strangers like Debra and finds 'the family history community an absolutely wonderful source of assistance when I am really stuck. There are some fantastic people out there who are willing to give their time to help, and in turn I help out whenever I am able to.'[35] Jeannette Tsoulos agrees and has found 'nothing but helpfulness and generosity from those involved with family history, officially or as amateurs. I am always happy to share research.'[36] As Harriet Jones suggests, 'There is much enjoyment in helping someone else find a piece of information that was eluding them.'[37] Barbara Hearn really wants 'to help as many people as I can get the best out of their own research.'[38] This process of giving to the family history community and taking back in return when required enables the community to function effectively and to grow exponentially.

Sociability

These family historians relish the social aspects of their research and being part of an active, diverse and engaged community of learners, of all ages, shapes, sizes, backgrounds and levels. Anne Sherman finds that 'being a self-employed researcher can also be very lonely at times, so I value the time I can discuss things with my peers.'[39] Bob H has 'been most impressed by the friendliness and willingness to help worldwide'. His collaborations 'are friendly and mutually productive.'[40] Julie Jones loves 'talking about our research to each other. Shared knowledge is a wonderful thing ... We share information via blogs, forums and emails.'[41] This sociability takes different forms and is shared in a variety of ways.

Before the emergence of Ancestry.com in 1994 and other online family history research platforms, much of this socializing and community-building was undertaken face to face. Many family history societies with members in their thousands before the launch of Ancestry.com experienced a sharp decline in membership as a result. Now much of family history communication occurs online but my evidence suggests that has not diminished or prevented the formation of communities of researchers. Sociologists are divided on whether the online world has destroyed some forms of social capital generally, but it is clear from most of these researchers that it has created new and more inclusive forms of sociability and cultural capacity. Field suggests that quantitative evidence concerning online social capital shows that it 'complements face to face engagement'.[42] Sociability among family historians frequently takes place both online and in person. Jenny Wilson enjoyed 'the sense of camaraderie' she felt in belonging to a member of a local history group.[43] Members of local history groups have articulated concern in many different national contexts about declining membership, the increasing age of their members and the reliance of researchers upon digital resources rather than paper-based archives.[44] It is perhaps useful to know that many of our family historians depend upon local, family and community history organizations and the resources they create. They adore interacting on a local, national and global level and multiple physical and digital levels. PC, a self-employed genealogist who was born in Northern Ireland but now lives in Scotland, describes his family history community as multilayered. It is 'local in the sense of community based family history societies, national to an extent through national bodies, and international in terms of online collaboration .... I greatly value what I learn from other speakers and writers about the research process itself, as I am constantly learning'.[45] Like many others, LB has 'found many friendships both domestically and internationally as well as willing participants in the exchange of information and see them as a valuable asset and ally in conducting research'.[46] In Canada, a self-employed stained-glass artisan, Alison Madden, belongs to her local genealogy guild and the provincial Ontario Genealogical Society. She attends their yearly conferences and 'loves all the workshops and comradery'.[47] AM always enjoys interacting with family historians and believes that 'anything that encourages positive human interaction and a common goal results in a win-win. We can share in small successes and support each other in many ways'.[48]

Despite the anxiety many family historians express about the reliance of millions of family historians on digital sources in the early twenty-first century, many of these researchers enjoy extensive face-to-face interaction despite the increasing online context. For Canadian researcher RG, 'One of the chief reasons I joined a family history society is to get the "face time" ... my fellow researchers are my tribe and it's in my best interest to be as courteous as possible because, after all, who else could possibly understand the overwhelming pull of this hobby'.[49] Brenda Turner likes 'being with people who love what I love'.[50] Carole Whelan also loves 'to tap into the excitement of sharing a passion with someone else'.[51] That said, several suggested that being a member of local, voluntary organizations can be testing at times. As Debra McAuslan proposes, 'Like any volunteer organization – it is a bunch of people doing their best to help others and leave a legacy of encouraging others to value family history and history. They have their issues, but they do good work'.[52] Most acknowledge some difficult moments of tensions and rivalry, but as Donald Davis suggests 'there is no greater fun than joining forces with cousins following the same lines and building a story together'.[53]

Retired Nova Scotian Peggy Homans Chapman finds herself on good terms with many family historians because she provides training and information sessions

> I enjoy many of the people and find these are people I would not have met otherwise and we keep contact through social media and occasional meetups. I also enjoy communicating with people across the country and across the world. It adds a dimension to my life that might not be there otherwise ... The universality of the genealogical language is one that provides instant connection.[54]

In countries as large as Canada and Australia where many people are physically isolated, interacting with family historians online provides important social interaction. Even in small countries, with dense populations, isolation, whether physical or mental, is common, and the online environment remains a vital space for much needed socialization.

As we know, even though many of these researchers relish in-person interaction, much of their communication is undertaken online as well as face to face. Amy Smith estimates that there were sixty-six million websites dedicated to family history when she undertook her PhD in 2008.[55] Since 2004, Facebook has been a goldmine for family history researchers, both for finding individuals in their family trees and facilitating research support groups. Lilian Magill is 'on several Facebook pages, for genealogy and also about half of my Facebook friends are from the genealogy world'.[56] As members of family and local history societies and undertaking online family history courses, others are also very active on social media, attending conferences, writing blogs, making podcasts and travelling on genealogy cruises.[57] TR enjoys sharing his research and suggests that 'the social interaction is also very beneficial'.[58] Barbara Barclay thinks that 'whether we have a family member in common, just a passing connection, or just a general interest in family history research, it is usually wonderful to engage with someone else who has the same passion'.[59] In late 2020, I asked one of my undergraduate students undertaking a public history internship with me to research the number of Facebook sites dedicated to family history in Australia, Britain and Canada. She found 19 in Australia, 85 in Britain and 142 in Canada. There may be more she missed, and many are established daily.[60] Several family historians in these different contexts have also established podcast sites to share their knowledge, expertise and resources.[61]

Not so keen on sharing

Not all family historians feel comfortable within these emotional communities of researchers, and indeed some actively shun them. Others are more reluctant about sharing their knowledge and information and prefer to keep their research cards and discoveries closer to their chests. As a volunteer for her local and provincial genealogical groups, Debra McAuslan says that most of her collaborations with family historians work well but she's 'had a couple of people who were competitive ... "hoarding" their data. I don't get that. Most people are happy to share and gracious in their help.'[62] Some will only share their information if others have shared with them 'on a quid pro quo basis.'[63] Others do not like sharing at all, even if the process is reciprocal. Helen Jenkins admits that 'being quite private I find it difficult to share my research ... There is a definite limit to how much contact I want.'[64]

Others are, in their own words, 'very selective' about who they work with.[65] Janelle Collins likes to 'swim in my own little pond ... Unless I'm researching something in particular I tend not to visit local family history societies because I think those places tend to be a breeding ground for people who like to feel like kings/queens of their domain.'[66] Several researchers identified problems with people guarding their territory and power within particular research domains. Kath Robinson finds interacting with family historians almost always enjoyable but 'very occasionally I have come across someone who wants lots of information from me but is not willing to reciprocate and share their knowledge.'[67] Some are cautious about what they share because they have had their data 'stolen' in the past. Alison Madden in Ontario has been 'stung on occasion when I have shared information and/or photos or documents. In particular those who post things online without asking for permission and/or using them and then going on to make false assumptions or errors in their work. I am now very careful about what I share and with whom.'[68] RG contends that

> a growing problem online, and you will find this discussed at length on genealogy web sites, blogs and forums, is the practice of copying other's research without acknowledgement, and worse, without checking for accuracy. I had a public tree online for a decade, and after much soul-searching, have recently moved it to private mode as I kept finding my data, photographs and even phrasing copied sloppily on to other trees that, because of poor research, had no relation to mine.[69]

Barbara Barclay has also been 'burned' in this way,

I've only had one unpleasant experience, and that was a connection via a distant relative made on Ancestry. We shared information, and I later found that he had uploaded some of my documents (which I had annotated) and shared them freely online. I was annoyed that he had not acknowledged that the documents had come from me … His responses to me on email were quite rude, and he broke off correspondence.[70]

Harriet Jones also revealed that the politics of family history can be a bit of a minefield, 'The family history community is a very sharing one, but like any community there are scurrilous elements that make everyone that bit more cautious and I feel like there are more and more family historians taking a "once bitten, twice shy" approach.'[71]

Those researchers who take pride in their research skills and the accuracy of their results are also wary of 'family trees which have endless mistakes in them' and trees with 'glaringly obvious errors' and many blame the ease and access of Ancestry for these errors.[72] Kay Spence communicates with family historians through Ancestry.com, Genes Reunited and My Heritage and has let people know about their errors but this 'has resulted in a few fallings out with my Ancestry. com "found" cousins. It seems that not everyone appreciates being told they have errors in their tree – not even newly found 4th cousins.' This hasn't stopped her making her trees public on Ancestry because she finds it a compliment when people copy hers. She thinks that there are cultural differences between varied communities of researchers and finds that American researchers are most likely to be rude and ignore messages 'I haven't heard back from any of them.'[73]

Others find the internal politics of family history societies difficult to negotiate. As Peggy Homans Chapman suggests from her experience, there is a

hierarchy that runs along lines of educational and social background. In my experience, institutions such as libraries and archives may treat less knowledgeable people differently … Recently, some colleagues and I have commented on the expansion of family history/genealogy as a business for some and this is very competitive among English speaking countries. Competition for gaining lecture spots at conferences can be somewhat fierce.[74]

This leads a couple of researchers to be cynical about whether 'communities' of family historians actually exist. Robyn Dryen is sceptical about the concept of a family history community and does not 'subscribe to the notion that there is a family history community. There may be a community of practice – it is global, and at its best is sharing and caring. At its worst it is insular and feeds nationalism and racism.'[75] As we have seen, for the most part, others hold firm to the existence of their community and remain committed and loyal members for decades. For them, the wins far outweigh the losses.

Dead ends/brick walls

Many family historians find that their community of learners and researchers has helped them overcome 'brick walls' – these are well-known blocks in the family history research process and are frequently bemoaned by family historians.[76] As MP suggests, 'Sharing my information and taking advice has helped me get over blockers'.[77] Stephanie Hume uses Internet forums to get over her brick walls and enjoys sharing 'the joy of freely exchanging information'.[78] Donald Davies, a retired epidemiologist, 'could not progress in my understanding of historical records without inviting other researchers with expertise in fields I have not explored to share their knowledge with me'.[79] Working in groups means that you can put different pieces of the puzzle together: 'There is always a chance with family history research that you can look in one place (or at one type of record) for so long that you can't think of any other logical way to find an answer to the problem, and another perspective can be very useful'.[80] This is true too, of all researchers, committed to disseminating their work as widely as possible. Robin Dryen has discovered that 'most of my breakthrough moments have been due to tips from others. My most rewarding moments are when I can break down someone else's brick wall'.[81] Learning within a community is vital to breaking down one's own brick walls and helping others overcome theirs, allowing researchers to progress with their research. The process involves moving between archival and DNA evidence, gathering as much diverse data as possible and using the Internet widely in all forms of research.[82] Dissemination of research is also vital to the process.

Generational conflict

As we have seen, the community is not always as united as might appear to certain eyes. Some researchers describe the unique needs revealed and practices undertaken by different generations of researchers. In the same way, some of the individuals involved with family history societies identify a stark division between younger and older members. Harriet Jones feels like she has been excluded because she is younger than most she meets with.[83] Janet Few mentioned 'a divide between old-school (where I probably fit) and the get-a-tree-quick-using-only-the-internet generation ... As I have been a researcher for many years I am now far more likely to be giving information about individuals and research techniques but that's fine.'[84] Kate Hurst is a committee member of her local family history society in the North of England but at the age of thirty-two is 'by far the youngest person to be present at such meetings (most others tend to be of retirement age) ... I like being part of my society because I feel involved and able to use and share my ideas in a way that will benefit more people.'[85]

For younger family historians, social and virtual networks are key to the acquisition of their knowledge and the communities within which they feel most comfortable. That is not to say that they are not interested in the work and resources of local history organizations, but they do not always feel at home or welcomed within them. Kate Hurst feels 'that websites like Facebook will be very useful for sharing information both with other societies and other family historians in years to come because news can be found and spread quickly, in many cases between societies who might be based thousands of miles apart, and at virtually no cost, other than time spent by volunteers'.[86] Mary Holland observes that 'the younger ones are all online and have trees with Ancestry which I don't really want to have any involvement with'.[87] There is certainly work still to be done to bridge the divisions between younger and older family historians at a local and global level, as many organizational leaders and members attest to.

New non-familial communities and friends

Many family historian survey respondents have really enjoyed discovering and meeting with new family members as well as strangers face to face, around the world as well as locally. Australian Dawn Springett has

> met the most interesting people and we have helped each other to unravel the past. I belong to the Society of Genealogists in Sydney and my local family history group. I have attended conferences, workshops, lectures, coach trips and lunches. Most of my guests for luncheons are family historians because we have so much in common. Guests are writing down information in between courses.[88]

Many of these respondents write and talk of the friends they have made in this community and these friendships tend to last for years, decades even. They are active, engaged learners who thrive in each other's company. Tracey Treloar told me that 'great finds and breakthroughs have been shared. New friends have been made'.[89] Kay Spence described how

> on the local level, I've met up with 2nd cousins I played with in the 1950s but hadn't seen since. We regained contact when I put my family tree on Ancestry in 2007 ... Nationally it is mostly by Ancestry messaging, email or on the phone. I'm happy to get out and about in Brisbane to take a photograph of a headstone and this is sometimes a request from a national community member. Globally is probably the most exciting ... Who else knows their 8th cousins other than family history researchers.[90]

These bonds amongst distant relations are often firmer than those amongst nuclear families.

Indeed, many would argue that these friendships and reunions with distant kin often bring more pleasure and comfort than closer and more immediate familial ties and relationships. Harriet Jones described how her

> research has, for me, resulted in some unlikely or unexpected friendships, most notably with a retired Canadian mathematician who provided voluntary family history help to the public in the library where I work ... We co-hosted many family history workshops together over a period of years and reached a point where we didn't really need to prepare – we just turned up and did what we call our 'song and dance' routine ... We also used to bounce off brick walls with each other. When he became suddenly ill last year, I was one of very few people he asked to visit him in palliative care and, at his request, delivered one of the eulogies at his funeral.[91]

Here the connection that bound Harriet and her friend was not familial but focussed, nonetheless, on family history. MP delights in the '"friends" [made] through this research, although I've not met them face to face, I have continual contact with people where our paths have crossed'.[92] Continued and /or frequent face-to-face engagement is not necessary to sustain and strengthen these bonds. Similarly, RG has 'made wonderful contacts online, some of whom I even dare to call friends, even if I haven't met them in the flesh'.[93] Gail Wright also loves her connections with family historians – all via the internet.[94] Walter Crites has enjoyed 'a communal journey of interacting with total strangers who are more than willing to lend you the experience of their own research journeys. I have received emails right out of the blue offering to help me in my own journey. That gives me great faith in the humanity of what I am doing'.[95] Gail Wright has also been amazed at the connections she has made: 'people are always anxious to help out and never ask for anything in return. What they do get in return is a very genuine friendship.'[96]

Others have forged ties that mimic and replace their familial bonds. Hannah Frost told me that she has

> mainly collaborated with distant cousins who I've met during the process ... One person I've met used to go to school with my Dad but they didn't know about their link. He's been the one constant contact and we regularly pose each other questions to see what the other thinks. I actually feel quite close to him, although we've never met, and it was good to have him around when Dad died 2 years ago.[97]

These ties that bind reveal significant bonds of friendship, reciprocity, generosity, commitment and are familial as well as non-familial. Family history researchers reveal powerful community commitment and cohesion on multiple levels, both real and virtual. Amongst most researchers, such commitment and affective bonds help to structure an awareness of ethical practice and the careful regulation of their community.

The ethical practice of family historians

As we have seen, some family historians have been 'burned' by others when they have shared information online and are keen to complain about it publicly and warn others against the practice.[98] This is one way in which family historians police their emotional community of researchers.[99] Family historians who communicate online provide numerous resources guiding researchers in the ethical practice and use of their research.[100] Most of these discussions involve the sharing of data and what sort of data should be shared. So – how do our family historian respondents understand the ethics and emotional boundaries involved with their research? Christine Clifford believes that the politics of family history research requires 'being sensitive about what you tell and to whom, and being non-judgemental ... Not putting information, especially trees, online without permission, and respecting privacy.' These family historians expect certain standards to be kept. Christine finds sharing information 'enjoyable when I am collaborating with those whose standards of research and aims I can respect.'[101] Jill Gregory is careful about the information she shares and is presented with, admitting that 'I always check information I receive with at least three reliable sources, I have taken great care to make sure my family research is correct, as far as I can make out, unfortunately this is not always the case with other family historians'.[102] LB always undertakes his research 'with the thought always in my mind that family research other than your own family can be viewed by some to be invasive, intrusive and upsetting, I will always consult with the person or persons I represent regarding the prospect of an expose that might offend and acquire their permission to proceed'.[103] WS insists, as do many others, that 'it is necessary to be sensitive of other people's feelings and their experiences'.[104]

The impact of unearthing secrets

Family historians use collaborative archival research, the sharing of photographs, oral histories, material culture and DNA to unearth secrets and break down brick walls in their research – some of those secrets are shared while others are kept well under wraps so as not to hurt or harm family members. Perth-based Barry Cobb was born in 1945 and became a family historian in the 2000s. He told me that he became a family historian:

> To try and sort out truth from fiction in oral family history some of which seemed (to a child when I first heard the stories) rather unbelievable. Some remain unresolved while others have been explained ....

Barry has had to negotiate conflicting stories about families in the past, often with problematic responses:

> I was surprised to find my maternal g-grandparents had not married until all their children were adult. This seems to have been the result of a Catholic-Protestant rift with neither party prepared to accommodate the other's views. ... revealing to my elderly Aunt that her grandparents did not marry till late in life, after the children were adult, seemed to shock her and she has refused to believe the historic documents. Her brother was not happy when the belief that a branch of the family had a peerage was shown to be incorrect; oral family history he had long accepted .... I had discussed it with her children before telling her to gauge the possible reaction but we were nevertheless surprised at the response.[105]

Like many family historians familiar with asking others how to handle this information, Barry has become adept at using his research to trouble other people's 'stories' and memories about their family but does so with great care and respect. Brenda Lee has also had to negotiate negative responses to the fruits of her research and polices her activities carefully:

As the family historian, I am cautious on what I say. Most people are open minded but some have an agenda. There are many skeletons that I will not make public to protect the living, but it is documented in my private research so that future genealogists in my family will know the truth ... I know now that so many family stories are not accurate. The passing years have a way of changing the story to something different from its original.[106]

These secrets have seemingly had little impact on the lives of many of these family historians but there are others who wish they had learned these 'truths' earlier, like adoptee Dianne Johnston who we met in Chapter 2. Gail Lewis waited until after her mother died to begin to research her family history: 'She was always very secretive about her family and always changed the subject when it came up, making it very obvious it wasn't something to be discussed'. She thinks her life would have been very different 'if some of my family history had not been kept secret for so many years. I missed out on knowing relatives I never knew I had, which I greatly regret.'[107]

Carol Smart suggests using her research on Mass Observation Directive responses discussing family secrets: 'Counter memories do not just tell another story but they construct the family, and the characters in it, in completely different ways which can lead to surprising re-evaluation'.[108] This has a significant impact on individuals, families and societies as well as our collective knowledge about the history of the family. Like many other family historians, CA has learned through her research that, 'despite the mores of past times, ordinary women did leave their husbands and have affairs'.[109] Research has troubled their assumptions about what is 'normal' and socially acceptable in different historical contexts.

A common theme in my surveys and interviews is the transience of families across the generations. JM was born in Brisbane in 1952 and lived a transient life in her youth. Her father was in the army and they moved to Victoria Barracks in Melbourne when she was one. She became a family historian in the late 1970s.

I knew nothing whatsoever about my mother, who died when I was six months old, in 1953. My father had never spoken a single word to me about her, and once I had children of my own, I decided to go looking for her family ... I missed meeting my maternal grandparents, I was eventually able to make contact with cousins who have welcomed my contact and given me wonderful family information, photos, etc ... I grew up virtually as an only child (with a half brother living in another state), knowing bits of the story, but never the whole story, from my stepmother ... Even when my father was made aware that I was beginning my research, he still remained silent. I did not even have a photograph.

Over the years, as I unravelled my mother's story, for the most part since my father's death, I have felt progressively more distant from him, and whilst hate is certainly not the right word, anger certainly is. ... I will never forgive him, simple as that. I have also realized what a lot I missed out on, growing up with no connection to my mother's family, which makes me feel sad and angry. ... I feel that perhaps I now have an explanation of sorts for why I felt as I did as I was growing up. I realize that there are countless hidden stories in most families, but it is definitely a bit of a shock when you make these sorts of discoveries about your own. [Family history] has taught me to verify, verify, verify, and to take nothing at face value.

JM's research has enabled her to fill the gaps in her knowledge about her family and to reconnect with her maternal family but her relationship with her father suffered drastically as a result.[110]

Social scientist Sian Lindley has undertaken a field survey of eight people aged over fifty years and concludes that they used inherited archives and new archival documents to construct two different sets of memory work – one for themselves and one for posterity in order to create a joint past with other family members 'reinforcing a wider family narrative'. Memory worked on two levels for these individuals and each level was quite distinct: 'Memories are not retrieved but formed; narratives are actively reconstructed (and co-constructed) with others'.[111] As we have seen among these survey respondents, for some their discoveries are a source of liberation, for others, they expose and exacerbate familial conflict, but they can exist with both of these stories of their families in play. It is this knowledge that gives them the power to live their lives differently as individuals.

PS lives in Humpty Doo, a small town in the Northern Territory of Australia. She became a family historian when she retired and embarked on a mission to solve a mystery about her mother. This did not result in a positive outcome.

Maternal family [was] always a mystery, mother claimed she didn't know her name, where she was born ... Claimed her life started when she married my father. When young I just believed she was probably illegitimate so did not make any attempt to find out anything from her ... So with my own found family, I can share my actual family. (my son actually went to Sydney to meet a cousin once removed, and we've all stayed in touch).[112]

PS's mother kept her life in England a secret from her children and Sandra later discovered family letters and photos allowing her to piece together the story with additional archival research. Her discoveries made her very angry.

At my mother who knew the family existed, she had in fact been writing to her sisters until I was about 15. I have a copy of one of these letters. The family in England knew about me, but I knew nothing about them, although my mother did have her wedding photos, a war time wedding 3 bridesmaids, 2 flower girls, all of whom she said she couldn't remember although I later got photos of both my mum & Dad attending the weddings of her bridesmaids and flower girls (her nieces) and her brothers and sisters in many of the photos matched the few photos she had. For some reason she stopped writing to them although there was no known reason and certainly her English family were perplexed about it.

… I had lived in England for 2 years in the mid 70s before I was interested in genealogy. Most of my aunts, uncles and cousins were still alive and in fact I often went to the very districts they were living in, in my travels, but didn't have a clue. So I really resented the fact that my mother knew all this and kept it from me, because she decided around 1958 to change her lifestyle … I spent her final years really resenting the fact that she had kept me, and my children, from their extended family for no known or understandable reason.

When I gave my mother a copy of her birth certificate and explained that both she and her mother were born in London, her parents were married and that her father had been at Gallipoli and had been killed in an accident when she was little. **She told me I had destroyed her memories** [*author emphasis*]. She didn't know anything about it. When I later showed her photo of she and my Dad at her bridesmaids' weddings, she … refused to talk about it. Yet she had seen her brothers and sisters regularly for 30 years and had lived close by most of them until she married in 1941 and came to Australia some 8 years later …

I have probably valued my husband, 2 children, 3 grandchildren much more, because I have been determined that they will have memories of family life, birthdays, activities, outings, time spent with them etc.[113]

In this particular family unit, intergenerational memory work created profound familial conflict over whose memories counted for more. This form of memory work clearly remains challenging for PS today. Perhaps further continued research and self-reflection continues to provide her with agency over her family story and her life.

When LG, who lives in Gatineau, Quebec,

uncovered my great grandfather's stay in the lunatic asylum, and the circumstances leading to it, my brother was upset, and wanted to move the portrait he has of him on his wall away from public consumption … When I told one of our cousins about her great grandfather in the asylum, she was actually thankful, and said for her it explained so much the relationship and behaviour of her great-aunts and grandmother.

She thinks now 'there is a lot more openness about the existence of hidden information, and its uncovering ... They want to be a part of more, and seek to find things that their ancestors did their very best to hide'.[114]

So, while some family members will reject and refuse one family historian's version of their family's past – others welcome the revelations with open arms. They use their newfound knowledge to reconfigure contemporary family relationships and overturn existing assumptions and dynamics. Robyn Tassicker was born in Western Australia 1953, where she lived until she was sixteen,

> I feel proud that I was able to discover and reconnect broken links in our family tree. I feel sad that there was such pain and hardship experienced by so many along the way ... I now appreciate the opportunities to make new ties with people who I should have met when I was young, had my family of origin been different.[115]

Similar discoveries have had a transformative impact on families with a history of foster care or adoption. SM's father was adopted. He died when Michelle was three, and she moved to live with her maternal grandparents, learning little about her paternal side of the family until beginning family history research in the 2000s. This allowed her to re-establish relationships with her half-siblings that were severed following her father's death. They now 'happily exchange photos, stories and memories. On my father's side of the family, only his adoptive mother remained by the time I was in my early twenties. Any relationships I've established with this line since then are distant rellies. I would say that each time I've (re)opened communication with a family member, no matter how distant, it has been a very excited and happy occasion.'[116] The discovery of SM's newly extended family has given her enormous pleasure.

Alan Campbell from Ontario is one of the few male respondents who detailed deep emotional responses to family history research. As we have seen, most men dismissed any emotional reactions at all to their work, taking pride in their emotional detachment and 'objectivity'.

> My most emotional response came not as a result of my research but because of the research of a half-sister. I had a 61 year old half-sister, given up for adoption prior to my mother's marriage to my father, who reached out to me. I was totally unaware of her existence. I met her once in person in November and attended her funeral the following March – an emotional roller coaster. I stay in touch with her children via Facebook and annual get-togethers.[117]

These reunions result in the reconfiguration of contemporary families. Susan Hinds became a family historian inspired by her stepmother who was writing up her father's family tree

> I never knew much; my (birth) Mother rarely spoke of her family ties. Today as I have learnt so much more, I can understand why my Mother never raised the connections. I did meet my eldest two aunts on my first trip to Adelaide during a Spring school holiday as a young teenager. It was great, meeting cousins ... Aunt Betty filled a void in me, she was so gentle, loving, quietly spoken, something I never received from my Mother.[118]

So, while family history research has allowed families to be reconstituted and expanded, it has also changed people's definition of family and enjoyment of diverse, non-nuclear kinship ties. As the previous section of this chapter argued, many family historians do not feel like their work is enjoyed or respected by members of their close families, but they find enormous comfort in the shared purpose of a global community of often unrelated researchers, together with distant kin. Carole Turner says that 'none of my immediate family members have an interest in family history, so my enthusiasm leaves them bemused ... Extending the experience out to more distant relatives than my immediate family, it is overwhelmingly positive.'[119] Social media and the Internet are allowing the creation of broader intimate and affective ties, expanding people's concept of family and blood relations. Barbara Hearn thinks that 'having 8th cousins contact me about information and then wanting to stay in touch feels a bit mad. Finding that I am related to people I went to school with and when we had no idea, was amazing.'[120] There is a disjuncture between the ways in which family historians often chart the so-called decline of the extended family and harp back to a golden age of extended family support as the result of their research. At the same time, they clearly relish the process of creating and extending family ties in the present through the use of technology and travel. In the process, they are forging diverse friendship and familial bonds that sustain them in the present and galvanize them for future change.

Conclusion

Family historians are committed to teamwork and voluntary work in family and local historical societies but also in other areas of life and the world. Many of our respondents, but by no means all, work or have retired from work in the public sector, as teachers, librarians, archivists, researchers, academics, etc. These are people who are well aware that a focus on the self alone makes no one happy. They tell us that their work on family history is encouraging them to become more active in their communities and to think about their impact on the world around them. Research in multiple national contexts, undertaken by Western and non-Western, Indigenous and colonial-settler researchers, broadens understanding of global history and politics. This form of lifelong learning has the potential to have an enormous impact on the discipline of history and teach others about its value.

Researchers believe that family history research and writing has given them valuable written and oral communication skills. Others feel that collaboration with others and tutoring new researchers in family history techniques has provided them with important listening skills and enabled them to pass their knowledge on more effectively. JA finds that 'helping out at a Family History Centre means you have to listen carefully, and also accept the confidences people entrust you with about their family'.[121] Harriet Jones, as we have seen, works as a heritage professional and has undertaken postgraduate studies in history. Although she is extremely well qualified as a professional working in history, Jane admits that 'family history has really pushed me to focus on listening skills, particularly when interviewing older family members and asking questions'.[122] Family history research has helped these individuals to bind together as emotional communities in formal and informal networks that create relations of trust and reciprocity. These relations produce social and cultural capital that encourages the political engagement of citizens. This political engagement fosters civic and community engagement and a spirit of cooperation, compassion and tolerance that can lead to increased social inclusion.

'I'm much more empathetic now': Family history, historical thinking and the construction of empathy

In 2006 Barack Obama bemoaned the 'empathy deficit' that he believed was destroying contemporary societies.[1] Many commentators concurred that our capacity to care about the lives of others was waning in the twenty-first century. The prediction of declining empathy was one of the reasons I became so excited in 2016 when England-based Kate Hurst told me in her survey response that 'research has improved my ability to put myself in another person's situation and to try to see things from a new perspective'.[2] Family historians like Kate give me hope for our shared future when they tell me how much their research has increased their empathy for those less fortunate than themselves and compelled them to become more active citizens within their communities. Such optimism comes at a vital time given the terrible year that has just past, wrought by the destruction of COVID-19, when many of us are searching for hope in the future amid worldwide environmental disaster and political turmoil.

Chapter 5 reveals the pedagogical and social value of family history for learners at all stages of the life cycle and shows that family historians use their historical learning and thinking to produce empathy and rational compassion. Learning and teaching scholarship in the discipline of history has been mainly focussed on the primary, secondary and tertiary sector while public historians seem much more interested in the construction of historical consciousness among 'ordinary people'.[3] So far, this book has argued that there is a strong link between family history research, community engagement and myriad forms of voluntary activity that has benefits for individuals and society more broadly. For Carol Turner in Australia, 'small acts of kindness are my oeuvre. I try to give through acts of transcriptions, sharing resources, teaching what I've learned'.[4] In this chapter I argue that these small acts of kindness can help change the world. We learn in this chapter about how lifelong learners use history to understand their own and other people's place in the world and how that process encourages them to act differently within it. When family historians undertake their research, these findings reveal that many of them are thinking critically about how their and our knowledge is constructed, about the value of historical thinking and how that new knowledge can be shared for political purpose and social benefit. This chapter argues that family history research has a transformative impact upon researchers and those around them.

History of the term 'empathy'

There is some debate among scholars and contemporary commentators about the cognitive and affective processes involved with the construction of empathy.[5] Over the past 100 years, understandings of empathy have changed dramatically, with many authors becoming increasingly suspicious of the concept.[6] Although the term 'empathy' was invented in the early twentieth century, by the 1960s most people had barely heard of it.[7] Prior to this, sympathy took the place of what we now define as empathy.[8] Its popularity as an affective response has waxed and waned over time. After the Second World War, understandings changed in response to an increasing critique of the concept growing in force from the 1970s.[9] Up until then, psychologists and educators argued that it was beneficial if we all 'put one's self in another's shoes' and tried to understand what life and circumstances might be like for people unlike ourselves. From the 1970s, policymakers increasingly suggested that such an emotive response could lead to social inclusion, meaning that the concept had activist potential to change the present.[10] In recent years psychologists Paul Bloom, Fritz Breithaupt and others have argued that empathy is not necessarily a force for unqualified good with progressive potential, as previously assumed. Broadly speaking these scholars suggest that people mostly only feel selective empathy for those like themselves, meaning that empathy could be used for evil ends, and so deepen not lessen social division. It is for this reason that they insist we dismiss empathy as a tool for social change and democracy. Breithaupt argues that we need to acknowledge the dark sides of empathy and to become more self-aware about our complex affective responses to events and circumstances. We need to learn when empathy is not an appropriate response to particular situations. Instead, we should strive to become selfish empathists. This means that we should aim to 'put one's self in another's shoes' not to learn about the lives of others but rather in order to learn more about ourselves and to enrich our own lives.[11] These criticisms of the concept bear some thought and reflection but, in this book, so far, where my focus on the meanings and impact of family history is concerned, I have made quite clear that I am more interested in 'the importance of empathy as a feeling connection that could also transmit knowledge'. [12] I want to better understand the disruptive potential of family history learning and research. How do family historians' affective responses to their research help them learn and behave differently in the world as citizens?

History education and historical consciousness

Stemming from the concept's heyday of the 1970s, a large body of literature exists on the fostering of empathy and its educative uses among primary and secondary school students.[13] However, there is little scholarship on how empathy is constructed among lifelong learners of history or its educative potential for older learners outside the school system. My research with family historians allows us to gather data on its impact.[14] Since the 1970s, and with increased focus from the 1990s, history teachers have argued that empathy is key to the process of historical thinking and understanding.[15] In 1983 Peter Lee argued influentially that 'empathy is central to history'. It became a key concept used in the teaching of school history, emphasizing how school students might mirror the practices of trained historians in the academy.[16] In the wake of the success of the English School's Council History Project from the 1980s, pedagogues argued passionately, that empathy was an essential prerequisite to understanding different historical contexts.

Endacott and Brooks suggest that empathy involves a three-pronged process: historical contextualization, perspective taking and affective connection.[17] While the term was dropped from the English school curriculum in the 1980s and replaced by the concept of 'perspective-taking,' empathy remained central to history education curricula in Canada and Australia. It was situated at the heart of classroom history learning and teaching and went on to form the basis of those 'second-order concepts' that Peter Seixas argued were essential for the development of historical thinking and consciousness among school students. Seixas's model remains extremely influential in education systems around the world.[18] These educational concepts were heavily influenced by cognitive science and psychology and understood as crucial to the study of the past as a historical discipline and the construction of the content of historical knowledge.[19]

In an educational history of the concept of empathy and an intellectual history of the history discipline, Tyson Retz draws on the foundational work of British educationalists like Peter Lee to suggest that Canadian scholarship on historical thinking has emphasized the 'benefits of historical learning for social democracy'. In this model, which I suggested above is influential in all the nations discussed in this book, history education is vital for teaching ethics and the importance to democratic process of historical thinking.[20] Through the means of history education, historical consciousness is understood as crucial to the formation of moral citizens.[21] It was argued that knowledge of social, cultural, economic and political systems and structures in the past were important for active citizenship. Knowledge in these areas had the potential to encourage students to become more actively engaged with democratic societies.[22] Peter Seixas suggested that history helped to augment democratic citizenship by encouraging the study of political institutions, through comparative analysis, comparing the past with the present and helping to foster 'democratic habits of mind'.[23] As a result of this scholarship and its impact on educational systems around the world, empathy and perspective-taking remain core business for history teachers across the globe. While Retz suggests that the understandings and uses of empathy in educational contexts remain messy worldwide, he hopes that empathy is understood as more than just encouraging people to feel connected to others in history. He wants us to understand its cognitive dimension, meaning that we grapple with 'the very self-conception of the history discipline' and engage in 'empathetic inquiry'.[24]

It is my argument in this chapter that family historians have largely discovered the uses of empathy and the value of 'empathetic inquiry', without necessarily being directed by historians, although some studied history at school and at an advanced level at university. This discovery provides them with purpose for the future. As we have already seen, these researchers are also undoubtedly historically conscious.

The term historical consciousness emerged in the 1990s to emphasize how people related to the past, the ways in which they made sense of the relationship between past, present and future, and how they understood the uses of history in their lives.[25] Protagonists of historical consciousness remained committed to the ethical project of the teaching of history and encouraging active citizenship. As Seixas reminds us with regards to students in the school classroom,

> The education of students as historical agents operating in their own historical moment means this: that they understand the impossibility of knowing once and for all *the* story of which they might be a part, and yet have the tools to steer

between mindless pie-in-the-sky utopianism *and* deadly despair as they shape themselves into the historical agents of their own futures.[26]

As with empathy, in recent years there has been considerable debate about the utility of the concept of historical consciousness as a concept. Some suggest it is 'too complex and too vague' to be useful.[27] However, scholars of education understand historical consciousness as key to the construction of moral citizenship. Being able to reflect well on past events enables individuals to better engage with others in the present and future. If people understand how pasts are plural, how different people shaped the past, they are better aware of how they might change the present and future.[28]

It is clear to me, as the discussion below will demonstrate, that many of my respondents believe that their research and the concomitant growth of their historical knowledge has led them to foster empathy for their ancestors as well as disadvantaged people in the present. As I suggested earlier, there is a strong link between family history research, community engagement and myriad forms of voluntary activity that contrasts with assumptions about family historians as insular, conservative and inward looking. Respondents articulate a profound affective connection to their family histories that leads them to better understand local, national and world history and the varied contexts of their ancestors' lives. Through this process they learn the differences between the contemporary world and those in the past. Gail Benjafield now feels 'more worldly-wise' because of her research.[29] Brenda Turner has a 'better understanding of why my family, all its branches, went to Canada. In some cases, it was from desperation ... We are all the same. Canada is a nation of immigrants, with a very small Aboriginal population. Much like Australia. All of us came here for the same reasons. Freedom and opportunity. It doesn't matter what you believe for God's sakes. We're all the same.'[30] Others have learned through their research about the relationship between past and present. Brenda Lee is fascinated by 'the impact that history has on the present, something that I didn't understand before.'[31]

In *Why History Matters*, John Tosh tells us that 'the most valuable objective of history teaching is to enable young people to situate themselves in time, to recognise the centrality of change and development in accounting for the world around them, to grasp the merits – and the drawbacks – of historical comparison, and to draw on the past for a richer sense of the possibilities in the future.'[32] This objective holds true not just for young people but for history learners of all ages, which is why it is so necessary to extol the benefits of family history research to others.

Figure 5a Image of Australian Lebanese Historical Society collaborative workshop, History House, Sydney, January 2019 © Tanya Evans.

Figure 5b Image of Australian Lebanese Historical Society collaborative workshop, History House, Sydney, January 2019 © Tanya Evans.

Figure 6 Image of Australian Lebanese Historical Society collaborative workshop, History House, Sydney, January 2019 © Tanya Evans.

In surveys, workshops, conversations and interviews, family historians tell me how they have developed empathy through the process of research and how it has changed their understanding of familial and social structures, in the past as well as the present. This development is revealed in the data I have gathered in surveys and recordings, but it is also shared conversationally and informally before, during and after official data gathering and via those online social media communications about family history which follow these workshops. These informal ongoing educative exchanges are one of the many benefits of this form of historical research. I relish the opportunities I have to engage with those who participate in my research because I can learn so much more about the impact of history learning upon their lives. Participants tell me that that their research has made them more active citizens, and led to an increasing involvement in their local, national and global communities because of their education. The form of citizenship they participate in, articulate and enable is one focused on participatory democracy in our pluralist societies – where people learn about their rights and responsibilities, to work well with others, to share knowledge, skills and resources for the greater good of their communities.

These communities include their families, localities, nations, as well as the global family history network. This research reveals how family history communities, that gather, communicate and collaborate online, locally, nationally and globally enable and model this important participatory work and form of citizenship. As Keith Barton reminds us, 'In a deliberative democracy, individuals don't simply pursue their own material gain or advancement, or seek increased freedom of liberty for their own communities; rather, they seek to contribute to the health of the multiple communities they belong to and intersect with'.[33]

Thirst for knowledge

In previous chapters, we have seen that family historians often have an excellent grasp of the use and value of different historical sources and are aware of how to ask and answer historical questions. For many of these family historians, the research process has significantly expanded their knowledge and scope and changed their understanding of world history and politics. Carolyn Jones suggests that while she does not 'think it has led me to think about my life differently … it has certainly made me think about my place in the world differently. With ancestors coming from so many different places it's made me realise that "my world" is much larger than just Australia. My family has a footprint all over the place'.[34] The discovery of new knowledge has fed the thirst for more about diverse people, places and the world.

Carole Whelan has discovered that the more she learns 'the more I am able to connect events in different countries'.[35] Mary Jane finds that 'through my experience of family history, I am more inclined to look at all aspects of history when studying one ancestor or one event in my family … [it] has helped me to reflect on my personal values and ethics. For example, the fact that my ancestors valued the land on which they raised their crops led me to learn about ecology and the environment'. Since she began her research, Mary Jane has 'been paying more attention to all these structures and systems and trying to understand how they shaped and influenced my ancestors and how they shaped and influenced society'.[36] Research enables individuals to connect themselves to much wider systems and structures and a better understanding of the world in which they live. BG's Canadian Aboriginal daughter is adopted, and this has encouraged her 'to look into Canada's own problems with our treatment of our aboriginal history. As well, my husband's family have what are called Home Children here, kids sent from England to be labourers in Canada in the late nineteenth century.

That led to more research.'[37] Research has revealed histories and circumstances about which they knew nothing from official sources of history and their school education system. Gail Lewis believes that her research has 'allowed me to meet and interact with many people I would never have met otherwise and has honed my interest in learning more about the people and places that feature in that.'[38] Glenna Morrison discovered that 'research into humble beginnings as well as privileged lives leads you to an appreciation of perspectives and a more thorough understanding of how some things come about ... If you understand where some views are coming from, you are more likely to give them proper consideration. Empathy is sometimes a stretch but it is a goal.'[39] For MP, 'I definitely appreciate and understand my previous generation's choices and decisions. I am conscious now when I see world events the impact that will have on future generations. It has made me more aware and more compassionate.'[40] Like Karin Davis who found that as 'time went on and my interviews and research uncovered more – I did come to have a far better knowledge of how global and national issues impacted my family – and their attitudes'.[41]

Family history allowed Maureen Cooney to be led 'to a new understanding of the world, enhanced my (limited) travel and introduced me to people who have helped me enormously. I hope I have helped at least one person, somewhere, to know more about their place in history.'[42] Tracey Treloar is 'empowered by knowledge, greater understanding of myself through knowing my ancestors, by knowing my place in the world (how I fit in to places and the world community) ... I'm sorry that many in history have been forced to change. So long as there is no harm in a person's belief or perspective, it is better for society to have diversity of thought and experience. This is how new societies like Australia grow and develop.'[43] This thirst for knowledge and its sating has fuelled the capacity of researchers to feel empathy and to share their knowledge to encourage the same response in others.

Empathy

In her history of the concept of empathy, Susan Lanzoni suggests that it 'challenges us to stretch the limits of the self, but more audaciously, the understanding of our humanness'.[44] It is clear from the evidence presented so far that family history research enables these respondents to locate themselves in the wider world, broadening their sense of self and society. Knowing fine well that the world does not merely revolve around themselves or their immediate family, they are compelled to think beyond the individual as they conceptualize their place in the world.

Robyn Tassicker thinks that she is 'more tolerant and accepting now, and so am more able to listen without judging'.[45] Karin Tonks discovered that 'interviewing, visiting and being a part of family history research has taught me patience (a little), empathy and a historical understanding I never knew I even lacked before I began'.[46] Ken McKinlay has found that his research has led him 'to broaden my views and forced me to not look at history through the lens of my own ethics and morality'.[47] Carolyn Jones's research has 'taught me to be much more tolerant. We don't know other people's stories or how they got to where they are, but I suspect in a lot of cases, their journeys have been just as difficult'.[48] These are people who have learned to walk in other people's shoes, time and time again when learning about their ancestors and others.

While Paul Bloom urges us to stop pinning our hopes on empathy if we are seriously committed to social change and urges us to learn the benefits of rational compassion, he does acknowledge the utility of getting inside people's heads to figure out what they are thinking and the good that may come from 'the capacity to understand others'.[49] He wants people to stop insisting on the value of empathy as a moral good in itself and to get them thinking deeply about why they feel the way that they do, how they might reject their gut feelings, to be surprised by new knowledge and to use this to commit to social change and justice.[50] It is my argument in this chapter that these valuable processes are precisely what results from sustained family historical research and the discussions family historians have with others about their findings.

That said, there is sometimes a slippage between how these family historians articulate compassion and empathy that can trouble those scholars who insist on their clear distinction as emotional categories.[51] For example, Paul Bloom would rather people value and aim for compassion and concern over empathy.[52] Family history researchers certainly talk frequently about the compassion they experience because of their research. Through her study CA 'became aware of how much compassion I have for others in difficulty ... I believe I understand my mother much better after finding out about her father's life'. Her compassion shifts between her family members as well as strangers. She 'feels much more compassionate ... as a result of finding out various problems my grandparents had ... empathy is a key component of how I see my ancestors now'.[53] RG's research has been motivated by compassion 'because revealing the past reveals pain, and we can't just barge on after our own goals with no consideration for the feelings of others ... Empathy is vastly important to me; I hope I manage it at most times'.[54]

While critics of the concept of empathy insist that people always tend to 'look after their own',[55] family historians reveal, as we have already seen, how blood is not always thicker than water. Through their research they learn about their own families, those of other people and sometimes even complete strangers. Such knowledge encourages them to try to think like others, in time periods, families, nations and contexts very different from their own. This awareness is what classroom teachers are trying to develop when they engender empathetic reactions amongst their pupils, in the context of teaching them to think historically. In Bloom's terms, these family historians demonstrate that they are capable of 'rational compassion,' whereby empathy can be a result of in-depth historical study, making the world better as a result of their knowledge and action upon it.

In all, the research process gives its practitioners agency. Mary Holland found that her research made her 'see the world in a different light … and have more empathy for other people. We are none of us, singular – we are all of one family or another even just the "family of the world".'[56] Karin Davis has also found that her research 'has made me much more understanding of what is sometimes termed people's "shortcomings" … it should give us a great sense of being part of an imperfect community and the empathy to deal with that on a daily basis.'[57] JA has found that 'doing family research has probably helped clarify my own values/ ethics. You also start to see things less "black and white" and become aware of the nuances of behavior, conduct, manners etc. of people.'[58]

Jackie Bobich has found herself 'much more empathetic to migrants and more inclined to want to lend a hand.'[59] Janelle Collins thinks

it's helped me to learn more compassion & acceptance of other people's circumstances, and it highlights to me what a privileged life I have just because of when & where I was born … I think it's helped me be less judgmental about other people's circumstances because my own ancestors went through many trials of their own, which personalizes their events for me … the breadth of my family's experiences had broadened my understanding of their lives, and helped me become more accepting & tolerant.[60]

Janine McMinn has also become 'more tolerant of those less fortunate ie poverty, refugees, oppressive regimes … I will also try and educate those who don't understand how an individual might make the decisions they do.'[61] SM is now 'more conscious of the need to walk in another's shoes – to attempt to understand the historical context of people's actions.'[62] Unlike some scholars whose work I discussed earlier, SM is convinced of the value of walking in other people's shoes.

Robyn Tassicker believes

that my family history work has resulted in my thinking about my life differently – greater insights, more accepting, more humble and becoming part of the interconnectedness of the global human family ... I think that I am more tolerant and accepting now, and so am more able to listen without judging. I can also accept and respect others who are not interested or even hostile to my approaches, as we all have our own agendas and timing is often very important.[63]

Shane O'Neil thinks that 'anything that deepens your humanity, cultivates understanding and appreciation of different journeys and starting points' is a good thing.[64]

These researchers relate in detail how they have been transformed by their research: intellectually, emotionally and politically. Carole Turner describes herself as

more compassionate now; less likely to focus on the scandal and more on the circumstances that brought them to that place. I feel empathy for their hardships and their human natures that I lacked in my youth ... Genealogists are privy to the whole gamut of human experiences – tragedy, secrets, joy, achievements. There are times to listen and times to speak. Everyone is deserving of empathy.[65]

Deb McAuslan suggests,

Crap happens in history, but being kind and supportive of others is the best we can do to make change ... I don't have any First Nations ancestry but know that going to lectures that are not your usual interest helps people grow ... This was about 20 years ago, but was the beginning of my seeing the horrors that indigenous peoples had suffered at our hands.[66]

Dee Leamey feels that her research gave her 'the gift of empathy which led me into Counselling'. It has also made her more tolerant 'to others' life style and choices.' Discovering the persecution of her Huguenot ancestors and those of her Jewish husband's family encouraged her to become a counsellor.[67]

Lilian Magill feels like she is 'a more empathetic person now because I have researched the lives of so many real people whose lives were not necessarily famous or perfect'.[68] Antonia Jones feels like 'we all have a lot of empathy for each other'.[69] Barbara Hearn found that 'having an isolated gay member of my parent's generation helped me be far more aware of how prejudice affects people now'. She has discovered that, 'I am able to undercut prejudices I am faced with by drawing on my family history e.g. I and my brother were the first in my family to go to university but some people think we have come through a privileged life and so cannot understand class struggle etc. Family history sorts that out. I appreciate how advantaged I am as a woman when I discovered what my predecessors had to go through.'[70] Betty O'Neill has 'always been a supporter of asylum seekers and refugees and am appalled at the way we as Australians or rather our government policies, treat people seeking refuge from war torn countries and from violence. This work has reinforced the importance of showing compassion and human decency to those in need of protection and support.'[71]

Many of these family historians are using their own family histories to interrogate national historical myths and storytelling, to produce new versions of the past that include their family's stories and the life stories of those marginalized by official histories, including the poor, people of colour and women. Traditional archival research combined with new DNA technology allows an investigation of communities previously erased or marginalized by archiving practices. This investigation is often combined with a crucial sense of connection and an empathetic response. The emotional work that family history allows here is not only an insight into lives that had been forgotten, but also a recognition of the difficulties faced by former generations. There is also a profound sense of connection, an affective historical practice and an awareness of contemporary privilege that parallels this process. This work allows for new ways of thinking about the past, and indeed enables an educative sense of engagement with difficult narratives that people then feel compelled to act upon.

Social confidence

Others have found that their knowledge has allowed them to develop greater social confidence. We have seen before that knowledge about the tough past lives of their ancestors is a source of strength for contemporary family historians. Young family historian BL has found that her work has 'enabled me to compare my life to those before me, and this helps me get through certain situations.'[72] She is not alone. Stephanie Hume deeply respects her ancestors and is 'in awe sometimes of the challenges they faced'.[73] Alison Madden found that her research 'has certainly made me very determined to take on what I didn't always think I was capable of'.[74] Brenda Turner 'feels grounded physically in ways I did not feel before' and 'has more nerve than I ever thought I had'.[75] These women are using their research to galvanize them in the present and to encourage them to act. We have seen how Harriet Jones is inspired by the bravery and hardships that especially the women in her family endured. She regularly returns to these stories 'when I think my life is challenging to help me get some perspective and inspiration'.[76] Mary Jane thinks that 'if my pioneer ancestors could create a home out of the wilderness and raise a large family without modern conveniences, I should be able to overcome the problems I encounter'.[77] If Brenda Lee is 'having a "pity party" (complaining because life it not as good as it should be), I can think of them and what they did to give me the life I have today. It is empowering'.[78] Barbara Hearn's research has given her 'a sense of place and freedom and allows me to talk about issues differently, like class and social mobility'.[79] Her research 'has helped to improve my self-confidence. Here is a subject I can talk knowledgably about. At school and in the workplace I had no interest in fashion, music or gossip, so I often felt left out. Now I can discuss family history with my peers and anyone else who shows an interest'.[80] Hannah Frost has also found that her research has given her 'a confidence in terms of knowledge about the family and the wider world that I wouldn't otherwise have'.[81] At a time when the neoliberal consensus limits many people's capacity for political understanding and action, family history is providing an important conduit to political awareness.[82]

This sense of social confidence and empowerment is crucial to family history research, but it also highlights a regularly expressed disconnect between 'then' and 'now'. The growth of family history can be understood as part of the 'boom' in the writing and publication of memoir and life-writing that has swept the globe since the turn of the century.[83] This is part of a broader process involving individuals using historical research and knowledge to understand present-day issues that are both personal and political. Working with family historians has shown that in response to contemporary political turmoil, individuals around the world are using their family histories to reframe an understanding of citizenship. They are interested in the familial, communal and social, and have no wish to live their lives as atomized individuals. The use of evidence and reflection is key to their practice and it is this skill that enhances their knowledge and empathic response.

Social change

Retz shows how, in the wake of the publication of E.P. Thompson's classic *The Making of the British Working Class* and scholarship contributed by other social historians during the 1970s, one effect of Thompson et al.'s work was to show 'how real people in real contexts were agents in their own making'.[84] These social historians of the 1960s and 70s revealed how historical reading, learning and reflection had the potential to reveal people's agency to themselves. It is my argument in this chapter that historical reading and reflection about one's family history enables researchers to discover their own agency and to gain some control over their lives. While some may not have realized its potential, the examples given in this chapter provide ample evidence that this can be the case.

NM has developed empathy for the struggles of her ancestors after discovering the conditions in which they lived.[85] Others, like her, aim to use this knowledge and understanding to change lives, especially the lives of the disadvantaged, in the present. This happens on a familial level, challenging the views of family members and sharing their research discoveries, but it also happens on a broader social level as well. AM feels as though her research has empowered her, becoming 'more informed and aware has enabled me to challenge some attitudes and get others to THINK [her emphasis] about the viewpoints they have and where they came from; and encourage them to be more tolerant and accepting of others'.[86] Brenda Lee believes that family history research empowers and transforms her:

It has given me a much broader perspective on life and our place in the world. I believe I was raised with limiting views on who I am, where I belong. History (with some help from maturity) has definitely changed my perspective ... That our past doesn't define us, but it can empower us. That we are equal to every human being in this world and are substandard to nobody ... It has made me believe that I am capable of making a difference in my community and that I have a responsibility to do so if I can. I realize the importance of community for a person's mental health and upbringing after seeing examples of it through history.[87]

Researchers like Brenda are then using this knowledge to shape the communities within which they participate for the better. Glenna Morrison found that family history brought the subject alive for her

I understand the power of studying history and I wish there were some way to help others learn from it ... I have watched others chase higher salaries, enhanced reputations and come to realise that these things really don't matter to me. I want to devote my time to learning about the past and sharing that information with others who care. I want to set the record straight.[88]

Deb McAuslan believes that her 'research has empowered me to challenge judgement of others'.[89] Following a childhood in which she was dominated by 'men and very posh debutante women', former social worker Barbara Hearn feels that 'knowing my history affirmed I was in a different league but could move about and my position would be determined by effort not by birth'.[90]

PC has also been politicized by his research, suggesting 'it hasn't just changed my sense of history, it has fundamentally changed my sense of identity, which has had implications for my current political and cultural outlook on life. I no longer learn about kings and queens, I learn about those who bled for them'. This has made him much more politically active on a range of levels – including campaigning for Scottish independence from the UK and after Brexit he applied for an Irish passport to protect his EU citizenship status 'both events are absolutely attributable in part to the sense of identity through which I now see myself as a result of my ancestral research. I have also put myself forward to stand for election next year in Scotland at local government level. My ancestry has connected me to the past, and helped focus me towards contributing to the future'. He remains supportive of the rights of minorities, including linguistic minorities, refugees and asylum seekers 'of whom we are not welcoming anything like enough'.[91] His sentiments are shared by many others. That said, other respondents told me that they have always been politically involved and contributed to their communities. Family history had not changed them in this way.[92] Gail Lewis, for instance, feels like 'I've already contributed and continue to contribute more than enough'.[93] Others feel a little more jaded about the potential of future progress. Dawn Springett does not 'have as much patience now to try and improve the world'.[94]

In contrast, Brenda Turner's research enabled her to reject 'the ethics of my entire close family. I am talking about the ethics they showed not the ones they would have admitted'. Her research has empowered her because

> it has taught me an awful lot about courage. It has taught me, no, re-enforced for me, that the red-necked way I was raised, with my father hating anyone who didn't look exactly like him, a white skinned Scot, such as being French speaking or Korean or Chinese or African, is complete bullshit. Hells bell's they just want what we wanted when we all went to Canada: to a safe, secure place to work hard and raise a family and try to become successful.[95]

Peter Keeda believes that 'by understanding my family's journey, I better understand issue such as prejudice, immigration, refugees and social integration'.[96] AM has discovered that 'being more informed and aware has enabled me to challenge some attitudes and get others to THINK about the viewpoints they have and where they came from; and encourage them to be more tolerant and accepting of others'.[97] HB learned a lot about the rise and fall of religious dissent and nonconformity over the twenty-five years he has been researching his family history and this has made him 'less tolerant of religious bigotry and fundamentalism' and likely to encourage others to challenge discrimination on a number of levels.[98]

Family history research has undoubtedly politicized these researchers. BL's research

> makes me want to make something of myself, to leave an impact on the world. There are many people in my family that have dozens even hundreds of records etc on them. Then there are others where their life followed them to the grave, and they leave nothing. I don't want my life to mean nothing, and to be forgotten, I want to make change.[99]

Marilyn Myers has become more involved in environmental issues because 'family history has shown me how small the world is and how dependent upon each other we are … Had I learned earlier the effect individuals have on the events of history I would have contributed more to Australian political life instead of sitting back and grumbling. I am pleased to have stepped outside a sense of powerlessness in my life, but also to have stepped into acceptance of my limited place in the world.'[100]

Not all these researchers are optimistic about the potential for their research and efforts to bring about social and political change. However, only 2 out of 136 of my respondents stated that they have been left more despondent than agentic as a result of their family history labour. David Dobson's research has made him aware of how 'man continues not to learn by his mistakes while the noble principle of public service is often lost to self-interest or bias'.[101] Robyn Dryen is 'disheartened when those who have researched intolerance and persecution exhibit the same intolerance and racism towards others'.[102]

Conclusion

While Obama may have reminded us in 2006 that we live in a world that demands we be selfish, the evidence presented in this chapter suggests otherwise. Granted, we are prompted every day by commentators, politicians and the media that we should eschew empathy because it makes us weak as individuals, families and nations. In these times of great global need, we are urged to protect our own and to prioritize ourselves and our immediate family. In marked contrast to these encouragements towards selfish conduct, family historians reject such pressures and use their research to challenge their own and other people's less tolerant and expansive views of the world. Their research teaches them not only about the discipline of history and how to think historically but to become active agents armed with such knowledge. They use this understanding to learn about their families and the families of others in the past, to acquire knowledge of disadvantage and to bring about social change on both small and large scales. This is not to suggest that I do not appreciate the limits of empathy outlined recently by psychologists and philosophers. Heck – we should always debate the finer points of how we and others might best attempt to change the world, but I do not think that the critique holds for the work that family historians have done and are doing. There is no doubt in my mind of the powerful experience of empathy among family history researchers and its impact on individual lives and society. Family historians use their scholarship to exercise the 'reasoned deliberation' psychologists hope we can use to contribute to the world around us.[103] As Pamela Cox suggests in her preface to this Bloomsbury series of books on 'New Social and Cultural History': 'To experience empathy is to experience an expansive, cosmopolitan and sceptical disposition. Some might say it is social history's creed'.[104] It is for this reason that we need to champion the work of family historians and to encourage others, both young and old, to engage with the practice of family history research. Scholars might also recognize and utilize the radical political potential of these forms of gathering, communication and collaboration about the past as well as their affective impact. Family historians provide an important humanist model for scholars committed to the civic purposes of universities and the political implications of their scholarship.[105]As were many social historians in the 1970s and thereafter, it is vital that we remain optimistic about history's relevance for the present and our potential to change the world for the better, both now and in the future.[106]

'I don't want my life to mean nothing': The future of family history

So far in the book we have seen how many family historians use their research to improve their lives and work in the present. The book has outlined the personal, public and political effects of their research and here we now turn to some of the cultural effects. This chapter also focuses on how family historians imagine the future of family history. As Susan Hinds, born in 1953 in Lidcombe but now living in Tasmania, reminds us, 'the more that have this knowledge, the less chance it gets lost'.[1] As this chapter shows, the products of family history can take many different forms, including written, oral and material types. It builds on some of the affective relationships that family historians have with the documents and objects associated with their research and the emotions attached to the diverse products they create using their family histories.

Here we are building on the increasing scholarly interest in emotions and material culture, albeit with a predominant scholarly focus, so far, on the medieval and early modern period.[2] Laura King's work on family archives and autobiography brings us into the twentieth century and she has revealed through her innovative and collaborative research with family historians and creative practitioners – the productive emotional attachments that family historians have to their possessions and what we might learn by analysing these and engaging with them creatively.[3]

I have been fascinated by family historians' belongings for several years. Here I explore how people have thought about their legacies from the nineteenth century through to the present and how they think about them today. A few years ago, I wrote about the material culture of families who travelled between Britain and Australia in the late eighteenth and early nineteenth century.[4] I drew on printed, oral, pictorial and material sources: diaries, memoirs, letters and objects belonging to a variety of cultural institutions including the Museum of Childhood in Perth, Museum Victoria, the Powerhouse Museum (PHM) in Sydney and the Historic Houses Trust (HHT, now Sydney Living Museums) of New South Wales, as well as those discovered within private collections, to explore some of the meanings of objects brought by families from Britain to Australia.[5] I argued that a focus on material culture enriches our understanding of the economic, social and cultural history of the family in late-eighteenth- and nineteenth-century Britain and Australia.[6] Evidence of what families brought with them on their journeys is not extensive, but I focussed on these objects to explore some of the meanings, synchronic as well as diachronic, of these items and the role they have played in the construction of family histories in Australia. Collecting the biographies of these belongings, rare though they are and unusual because they have survived and/or come to light, and linking them to their family histories and journeys, enriches our understanding of the history of the family in the late eighteenth and nineteenth century. It also allows us to examine their influence on the construction of public and private memory in post-settlement Australia. I argued that different family members created their own cultural scripts to construct and relate their family histories and played diverse roles in the memorialization of their genealogy. The same is true of contemporary family histories and the creative forms they might take.

Up until recently, the preservation of family histories through the safeguarding of diaries, journals and objects, often linked with the construction and sharing of family trees, has often lain in the hands of women. Objects have played a particularly important part in the construction of genealogies by women.[7] Some scholars have suggested that diaries, portraits, paintings and large objects of obvious economic value tended to be passed down the male line and were often displayed publicly but I argued that more intimate familial objects, of perhaps less obvious economic value, have been deliberately passed down the maternal line of families and usually kept within the home.[8] Women's roles within their family cultural economies were far from passive. Few women made wills, but some used the law to ensure that their property passed to those they wanted, often female relatives and friends.[9] While elite women could use objects 'to convey a multitude of meanings, from fashion, taste, and style to wealth and status, history and lineage, and from science, education, political allegiance, and religious conviction to personality, relationships, memory and mortality' most colonial women used them to 'sustain a specifically matrilineal family history'.[10] Like many processes that occurred within private contexts, they are difficult to uncover and therefore remain often under- and unvalued.

Collating, analysing and displaying objects of this material culture collected across the centuries allows us to fill in some of the silences about the experiences of women and children in the extant written sources, the diaries and letters mostly penned by men rather than women and belonging to the elite rather than the poor. A focus on objects allows us to acknowledge the agency of women within the family and to explore and analyse their role in the material as well as emotional economies of families as they constructed family histories in diverse forms.

A focus on material culture enables us to challenge conventional histories of the family that ignore or downplay the contribution of unmarried members and women and to move our narrative focus away from the normative marital unit. It allows us to address the historical neglect of women who did not marry and have children and to acknowledge that they were often the guardians of their family's history in their 'search for a permanent place in the family narrative'.[11] Several museum collections that I have researched, including Pauline Riley's in the Museum of Western Australia, Margery Harvey's quilts, one of which is held by Megan Martin who works for the Historic Houses Trust (now Sydney Living Museums), Florence Faithfull's belongings in the National Museum of Australia and Eliza Marsden Hassell's collection of family clothes in the Powerhouse Museum exist today due to the hard work of these nineteenth-century women who never married or mothered, preserving their family histories. Without children themselves, these women consciously, sub- or unconsciously placed themselves as integral to the family story by controlling its narrative and description and by inserting a counter-narrative in their family trees. By forcing their families to acknowledge the deviation from the linear 'birth, marriage, children, death' construction, these never-married women situated themselves into the family story which gave them one strategy to make sense of their lives as individuals but also provided them with a means to represent themselves to their relatives and the wider social and cultural world. It enabled them to validate their lives within a society deeply anxious about family formation and reproduction. These cultural pressures are as powerful in the twenty-first century as they were in the nineteenth and the centuries before and after.

Most of the quilts on the Australian National Quilt Register were passed down the maternal lines of families establishing 'a female lineage in which the women became the proprietors of their oral and textile history'.[12] They were often made to mark moments in the life cycle including marriages, births and deaths, times when families transformed and restructured, and given as gifts to celebrate or mourn these moments in people's lives.[13] Tracing the movement of objects through families allows us to appreciate the complex construction of family life, historical change and continuity, the varieties of family forms, both then and now and the ways in which the construction and representation of the family reached between public and private worlds. In the process, they provided their daughters, granddaughters and others with proof, material and oral, of their crucial contribution to their family's story. When family historians in contemporary Australia, Canada and Britain treasure the possessions of their ancestors, they are thinking long and hard about how that family, and themselves, will be remembered in the future.

Legacy and generativity

Psychologists have examined the positive impact that individuals gain from crafting a legacy to leave for the generations that follow them, hoping to influence the world in positive ways.[14] Family history plays an important role in this process, whether consciously or not, allowing individuals to benefit as well as others.[15] Susan Moore and her psychologist collaborators who have examined the motivations of family historians in their recent book reveal the generative possibilities of family history in their survey research. Following Erickson's theory of psychosocial development, as people age, they become increasingly concerned about the knowledge and skills that will follow them and how people might remember them once they are gone. The process involves thinking beyond the self and one's impact on the world around them. While parenting plays a significant role in people's understanding and experience of generativity, others use family history, the development of their professional identities as well as voluntary and community labour to develop their social contributions and to build the foundations of their legacy. Psychologists suggest that attention to generativity has a profoundly positive impact on people's mental and physical health.[16]

Louise Blake wrote her PhD thesis on women who lived on the Victorian goldfields east of Melbourne in the late nineteenth century but was initially drawn to history through her family stories. Her example helps to link my research on colonial material culture and family history with this research. She became a family historian in the late 1980s when she was in her late teens but became captivated by family history through the efforts of her maternal grandmother who had built a family archive.

> She kept A LOT of things from her childhood and adulthood, as well as material culture belonging to other members of her family. The collection includes photographs and slides, artwork, china, souvenirs, clothing, autograph books,

cards, scrapbooks, books, newspapers, diaries, letters, small items of furniture, archival records, and family history files.

After training in heritage and becoming a consultant professional historian, one of the ways in which Louise has come to terms with not having children herself is by working hard on preserving and telling the stories of women in her family tree.[17] Astutely conscious of the invisibility of women and marginalized groups in our histories, with training in the interpretation of material culture she was aware of and could state the significance of her great-grandmother's scrapbook which was compiled in the 1880s. This scrapbook, belonging to her paternal great-grandmother, has now been deposited with Museum Victoria and digitized for the use of future researchers. Louise was delighted to learn recently that a Victorian PhD student has been using it as part of her research on colonial childhood.[18] Louise is now committed to teaching family historians how to interpret, preserve and share the material culture of their family histories so that they will last far into the future.

Louise has learned a lot through her research about how Australian motherhood has changed over time, but it is also changing the way in which she thinks about her role as a woman in society today.[19] She demonstrates that there is a significant connection between the practice of family history and childlessness. These women, and some men, are using history to work through the gendered expectations of society, with regards to women's need to mother, and to challenge them. They are determined to look beyond children as their only legacy, detailing the lives of mothers in the past to insist on the revaluation of women's labour in the present.

My family history survey respondents provide ample evidence of reflections about legacy. Verity Morris encapsulates concerns about generativity beautifully, 'As you get older you often think about what your legacy could be, and if you have made even a tiny bit of difference. My research has had such a positive response from many family members, which results in spurring me on to achieve more.'[20] Dawn Springett feels that 'by giving my family members an identity I am keeping their stories alive.'[21] Carole Whelan has discovered through her research that 'it is my personal role to write down my families' stories for the younger generations. If I don't do it, then these stories will be lost and the younger generation will not have the pride in what their ancestors accomplished.'[22] For LG her research has taught her that 'I think that it was vital to my belief that history has to be shared, and that it is important for a sense of belonging and identity, and cannot be hoarded like a treasure.'[23] Mary Holland feels 'motivated to leave behind an organized genealogy for present and future family'.[24] When reflecting on the value of his family history work Walt Crites found that reflecting on my survey questions helped him understand the positive impact his research had upon him and others.[25] So many of these researchers understand how important it is to convince younger generations of the value of their work so that it survives into the future and is reshaped by the generations that follow.

Kate Hurst, in the North of England, feels compelled to encourage younger people to become involved with family history.

> One thing that I have become really keen on is challenging the perception that family history is something that only older/retired people do; the more I have engaged with other family historians, the more I have begun to think that there must be ways to make the pastime appeal to younger generations, and I am really keen to try to encourage people to do this.
>
> For the past year, I have been approaching schools to ask whether it would be possible to visit schools to talk to History students, to show how they can apply the skills they are learning to researching their ancestors and to show that it doesn't have to be 'boring', but instead can take whichever path each person feels is best for their purposes.[26]

Kate and others are committed to teaching as many people as possible, including family as well as others, about the value of family history. In 1983 Ron Sinclair became a family historian because he 'read an article in a Sydney newspaper about the increase in the number of family historians and that made up my mind to find out my ancestry so that I could pass it on to my children'.[27] As discussed previously, local, community family history societies and organizations are deeply concerned about their aging membership and are passionate about constructing creative ways for young people to become excited about family history research. Janelle Collins feels like her research is her 'life's purpose … being the family storyteller & knowledge keeper has shown me that it's my calling & also what I can contribute to the community to help others know how to do the same for their families'.[28]

It seems that this form of generativity is especially significant for family historians who are not parents. Like women who never married and had children in large nineteenth-century families, as discussed above, they make their mark on the family tree in alternative ways. They use family history to cement their legacies within their families, to question assumptions about having children and to teach others about the varied and valuable roles that individuals play within family structures. NM aims to be a good ancestor. Because I don't have children, I have formally asked one of my nieces to be the custodian of my family history research. She is not that interested in family history research at this stage in her life but she understands its importance and has agreed to take care of my research and pass it onto someone else in the family after I'm gone. Conducting family history research has helped me to see that I am part of a huge melting pot of people. I now see the links between me and others in more intricate ways. Instead of thinking I come from a small family (my parents + 3 children), I think of myself as part of a huge family that includes thousands and thousands (possibly millions) of ancestors in the past and just as many descendants in the future. My family history research has helped me to feel less sad about not having children. Instead of seeing myself as one of the only people in my current family as having no children, I now see myself as one of the custodians and explorers of our family's history.[29]

Family history research has given MN a sense of purpose in her family.

Research has made others more aware of the value of childless ancestors eager to record their family histories. Kath Robinson felt obliged to become a family historian due to the efforts of a single, childless aunt. She

became interested in family history in 1996 following the death of my father's unmarried sister aged 80. The task of clearing her house fell to me as I was her last remaining close relation. She was a great hoarder and we found many old photographs, newspaper cuttings – mainly obituaries and memorial cards. I had never heard of half the people the cards and obituaries related to and still have no idea who half the people in the photographs are! I started to look into my family history, initially out of curiosity and found to my surprise from the census records that my father's sister was one of 10 children! This was what fired my interest in family history – I have been researching ever since.[30]

Respondents are committed to revealing the lives of their ancestors, determined to get others to value their significance. Like Tracey Treloar who has

no children of my own, so in some ways my ancestors have become my children. The revelation/exposure/recognition of them and their histories will be my legacy, a contribution to my family's community and the general history of who we are. I am also keen to assist others in their family history research, thereby assisting the greater community to create a fuller, rounder history of man.[31]

We heard from Julie Poulter at the start of this book, when she told us that 'family history research is almost my favourite thing in the world to do! I have decided to not have children, and as a result have much more time to devote to the family history cause! This will be my legacy.'[32] However, it is not only childless women who are committed to preserving the varied forms of their family histories. It has given others' lives a purpose that was lacking in the past. JM wants to 'leave behind something which I hope will be of interest to quite a few people, and I've put in the "hard yards". It has given me a purpose.'[33] Patsy Trench thinks that 'by recording the family history I hope I'm contributing to an increased understanding of our family background for generations to come'.[34] Dee Leamey told me that she 'would take it a stage further and say I truly believe I was guided to write their stories. Why should their time on earth be unrecorded? Family history in a sense is conferring immortality. What a privilege to be able to do this! This has been my life's work and I have loved every moment!'[35] Janelle Collins 'loves being the person that people ask for information from. It makes me feel intelligent & important. I love being the memory-keeper for my family, like I'm doing a really important job on behalf of others.'[36] Pamela Fane feels the same way:

> Now that I am researching all of my lines and we are in the age of the computer sometimes I feel overwhelmed with the sheer volume of information that I have and angst about how I can get it all in some semblance of order and preserve it, not for my uninterested family, but people who may come along in the future and be grateful for the facts, the photos and the stories.[37]

This concern with legacy has fuelled my desire to hold collaborative workshops with family historians since 2016 so that I can encourage them to think beyond researching, to stop just gathering data and keeping it among themselves. I suggest suitable options and outputs for their research. This means I have encouraged them to think about writing and publishing works of creative non-fiction, blogs, websites, etc., but also how best to preserve their family histories and to share them with others. It is important that they share and disseminate their research more widely so that others might learn from it and others should value their labour and efforts. As I have suggested throughout this book, it is vital that people outside of family history communities understand the significance of this work. These passionate collaborators need no persuasion and others need to learn from their example.

Creative responses to thinking about legacy and the forms memories might take encourages some family historians to engage thoughtfully and imaginatively with different ways to represent and record family histories. The turn to digital formats has been transformational for many contemporary family historians. Online platforms provided by Ancestry.com and Findmypast.com are clearly popular, but researchers are also turning to other online platforms including Reliving (allowing families to construct digital family trees, undertake oral history interviews and advise how to store memorabilia), MiLife (allowing families to store all their documents and stories digitally) and Traditions of the Ancestors (encouraging diverse groups and communities to record and celebrate their heritage so that others can learn from them).[38] This process also encourages researchers to better appreciate the value of material forms of family history and to learn more about the significance of material culture. This also enables them to better explain its value to others, especially family members keen to throw possessions away rather than to horde them.

Material culture of family history

As we have seen, there is a long history of the memorialization of families taking place in written, oral and material forms. Family historians and others need to understand the strengths and weaknesses of these different forms of history and the various methods that structure them. All of us need to think creatively about how we might construct and present our historical knowledge and what sources we use to piece together our learning. This is a subject I expand upon in the epilogue with the help of my British colleague and family history collaborator, Jerome de Groot. There have been several examples so far of family historians' enjoyment of the materiality of their research. We have also read of researchers' resentment paying Ancestry's fees to undertake research and how some 'traditional' family historians wish more recent converts might discover the joys of archival research rather than just focusing on the online databases of knowledge available to them via personal computers in their own homes. This is, of course, something felt keenly by academic, so-called 'traditional' historians as well. Perhaps this is unfair, as historian Carolyn Steedman has suggested when discussing the

> agitation and resentment I feel when paying a personal subscription to a commercial Internet database provider, or for-profit genealogy company. Such companies provide (among other material) baptism, marriage, and burial details extracted from the parish records held in UK county record offices. 'They're *our* records!' you cry. 'I don't see why I should pay to look at them!' But of course, looking at or consulting them (which you could do for free if, for example, you took the train to Shropshire Archives) is not what you're paying for. Payment is for their transcription, digitization, and the online search facility. Access to

the physical repositories which hold records of national and local government and administration is free, and also public, in that local record offices (and the National Archives at Kew and the National Archives of Scotland in Edinburgh) are funded out of tax revenues, local and national. The private family archive at Scone Palace charges for moving the Murray papers, not for consulting them; I had no right to the parsimonious resentment I feel every time I catch sight of my personal monthly subscription to Ancestry.co.uk, for I was not myself paying for transportation to Edinburgh. In these several ways, the records themselves are cut loose from their many contexts, and you, being not at home, are cut loose from your own. In a situation like this, far away, and in another country, you are inclined to hear voices.[39]

All of us need to pay more attention to the materiality of our research, how the data we research is collected and presented and the diverse outputs we might produce using it. My survey did not ask questions about the material culture of family history research, but several researchers shared details on objects, photos and ephemera. Some wrote about the delight they took in working through materials associated with family archiving and creating materials that would last into the future, memorializing their ancestors. These outputs took a variety of forms including cookbooks, self-published books and photo albums. I discussed researcher's relationships with photographs in Chapter 3, but family historians have emotional responses to most of the material culture associated with their research. CA became a family historian because her 'uncle was very advanced in his family history research and showed me his work in progress. I was really in love with the old photos and artefacts (family books etc.) that he had.'[40] When Shane O'Neil was a child:

> Family artefacts in our home fascinated me as well as the stories my mother told me of her childhood and family life, and the special significance she attached to these things … I am indebted to my mother for her early story telling, her fragments of memoir, her investment in me as the family researcher and custodian, and her diligence in keeping and annotating (at my request) most of the photos I have inherited.[41]

Several of my informants have dedicated an enormous amount of energy and money to carefully presenting and preserving the family archive. Richard Reid is a trained public historian, but his archive boxes (mostly inherited from his father) are a delight to behold (pictured in Figure 7) and many others can learn from his example. These treasure boxes contain thousands of negatives of pictures from the 1920s, 30s, 40s and 50s that Richard and his sister aim to scan.[42] Similarly,

Figure 7a Richard Reid, family archive © Richard Reid.

Figure 7b Richard Reid, family archive © Richard Reid.

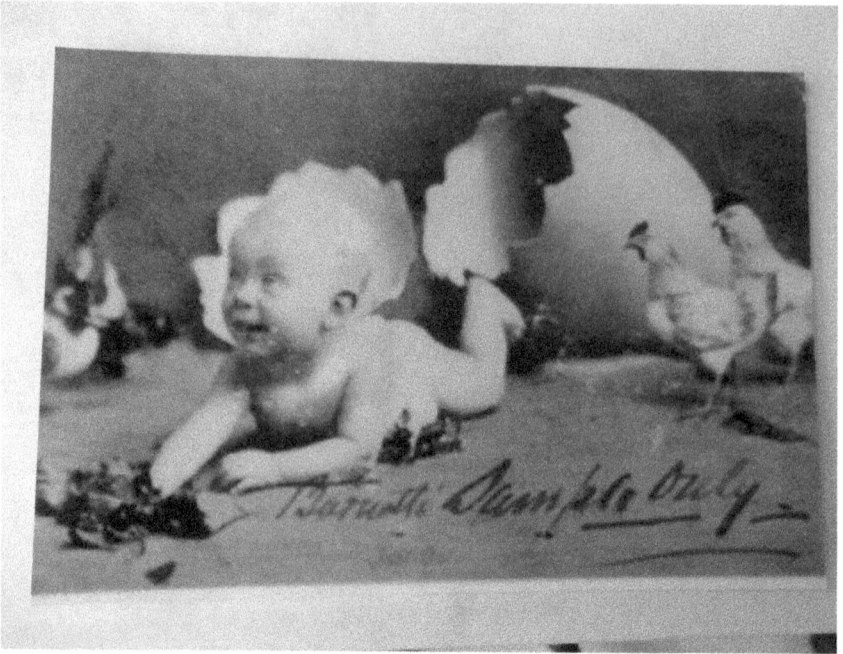
Figure 8 Anne Coote's postcard (credit Anne Coote).

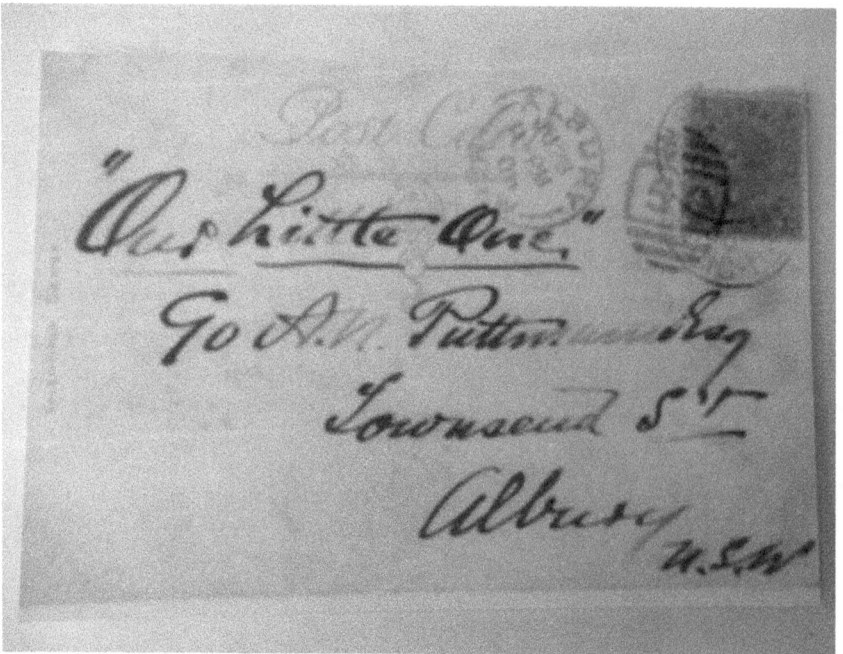
Figure 9 The reverse of Anne Coote's postcard (credit Anne Coote).

Dianne Mitchell has dedicated her retirement to working through her family archive because she feels 'a burden and obligation relating to our personal family history. I have 3 archive boxes of information, letters, photos, documents that I know will be thrown out if I don't consolidate and write up these smaller lives.'[43]

Family historians often treasure these diverse relics of their family's past. Public historian and keen family historian, Anne Coote has a range of objects in her possession related to her family history research, but most are paper based, including a postcard sent by her maternal grandmother to Anne's grandfather about her new baby, Anne's uncle; and her great-grandfather's ticket for his voyage to Australia in 1854. There is also a lock of hair, a toddler's shoe, once belonging to an older sister of her husband. The child died on the voyage out from Scotland to Australia and was buried at sea near the Great Australian Bight. Fortunate family historians list similar objects and it is important that we reflect on these material reminders of our family's past to remind ourselves and others of their value and how we might use them to help us to learn about past worlds.

Family bibles

Ten years ago, I spoke to undergraduate students about my research on family history in the tertiary classroom and asked if they had family members who were family historians. Some would roll their eyes and sigh about the irrelevance of such pursuits and how boring family members were if they undertook this work. In recent years this easy dismissal of family historian relatives has been replaced with a passion for the potential offered by such an intimate, tactile conduit to the past. I have learned that Aboriginal and multicultural students in particular are using family history to connect with grandparents and to learn about their family's non-Anglo-Australian heritage. These stories have only recently been aired in school classrooms and students have become more comfortable talking about them amongst their peers.

One former student of mine, Greer Gamble, in her late twenties, is an enthusiastic family historian who first forayed into family history when she heard some stories about her great-grandfather's war service and discovered his records online. She also understood that family history might allow her to connect with her father because he became more interested in his own father's war service. Learning about social history had made her 'question the relevance of the intellectual and cultural histories I had previously been drawn to ... Focussing on ordinary people confronted me with the question of just how

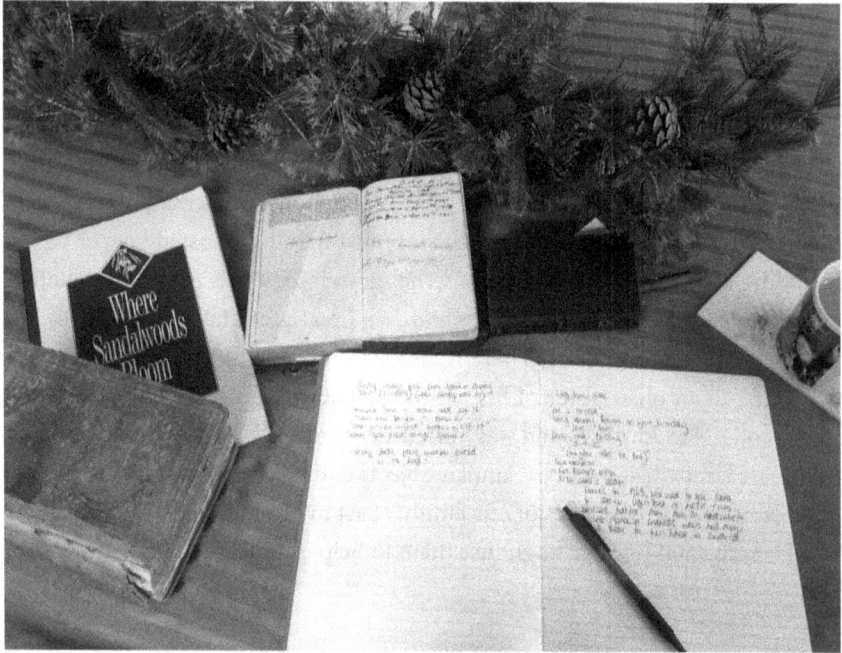

Figure 10 Greer Gamble's Family Bibles © Greer Gamble.

relevant the sorts of cosmopolitan zeitgeists I had read about in my intellectual history research were to the actual, often illiterate, figures who people our past'. She believes that our focus on written documents means that we know so little about these illiterate people Greer writes about and it makes her 'determined to think about new, less textual, ways of researching and writing history'.[44] She has discovered that her research has allowed her to become closer to family members and given them subjects of mutual interest to talk about. One of the objects she is attracted to the most is one of her family's bibles.

Greer loves her great-great-grandmother Hannah Hunter's bible and the bible belonging to her great Aunty Jean (pictured here)

> Irreligious myself, I don't value the Bibles for the same reasons Jean and Hannah valued them; I value them because Jean and Hannah valued them. The once-pristine pages of these cloth-bound tomes brought my relatives closer to their God, and made them feel part of something bigger. And as I run my fingers down the fraying leather spine of my great-great-grandmother's bible and read her heartfelt inscription, I feel part of something bigger, too.

Family bibles have long been understood as treasure troves by family historians, for religious and non-religious alike. There is a profitable online trade in family bibles and family historians are often key to tracking these down to help solve mysteries in their family trees, as well as the family trees of others.[45] The Society of Australian Genealogists based in Sydney established a volunteer project to try to reunite donated orphan bibles with their contemporary familial descendants. Few have been returned and the Society struggles to find the space to store them.[46] Although a burgeoning literature exists on the meanings of family bibles for medieval and early modern individuals, very little has been written on their meanings for contemporaries.[47] I hope to encourage further research in this area by briefly discussing their significance here. While writing this chapter I asked my Twitter historian friends and acquaintances what they knew about the meanings of family bibles. The question resulted in a blog post authored by British historian Kate Gibson revealing some of the uses family bibles were put to in eighteenth-century Britain and what they reveal about lay religious belief and practice. This showed that family bibles have long been used by families to record births, deaths and marriages, and were passed down the generations to help keep memories alive. Religious objects like these were deemed to have an immortality that would far outlive the names of people contained within their

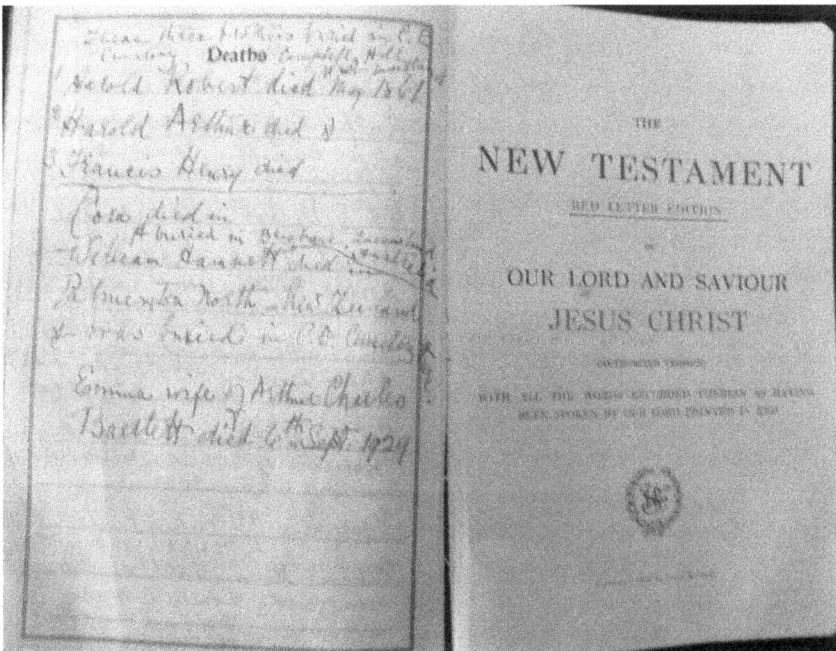

Figure 11 Orphan Family Bibles © Tanya Evans (credit Society of Australian Genealogists).

Figure 12 Family Historians at a Cemetery (credit Society of Australian Genealogists).

pages.[48] Indeed, for many individuals in the early modern past, their wishes seem to have come true. Using bibles and other evidence, contemporary family historians are unearthing and humanizing these individuals, who have often been long forgotten. However, there are many bibles still requiring homes with contemporary families and the Society of Australian Genealogists have a long list they hope to pass on to others.

Though they might not be revered as religious objects, family bibles have a sacred significance for contemporary researchers who value their non-religious uses and the information they impart. Doreen Leamey was propelled to become a family historian by the discovery of her family bible:

> When I was about 3-5 years old when I found this 'old' book (the family bible) in my favourite haunt under the stairs. I did not know what it was but loved it because it was old. Anything old intrigued me.
>
> Then when I started school I loved my first history book 'little folks of long ago'. I still have it now. I am 77! It began a life time love of history.
>
> ... there were names in it said to be family members and it had been given to my mother by my father's maternal grandmother on her death bed. At that time my father would not talk of his mother who died of TB when he was 7. I carried

her middle name so was always drawn to find out more about her and her short life, leaving three children of which my father was the eldest.

I was very close to my mother's mother who lived to 97 so very intrigued to know more about the other grandmother who died so long and whose name I bore. Strangely enough by giving the bible to my mother who was not related to her she sent it via her to the one family member who would document her family as she had begun to do. The more I do family history and the more the intensity of the connection I feel with my roots, the more I feel this was not coincidental.[49]

She felt compelled to solve the mystery the bible contained and from there her passion for research grew. It is this she believes that led her to become a lifelong family historian passionate about chasing leads in her family tree.

Tracey Treloar has worked with family historians at many levels and nationally she 'tracked down the branch of our family who had the family bible, met them and went together to view the bible (now at the state library of nsw)'. She loves sharing her research with others.

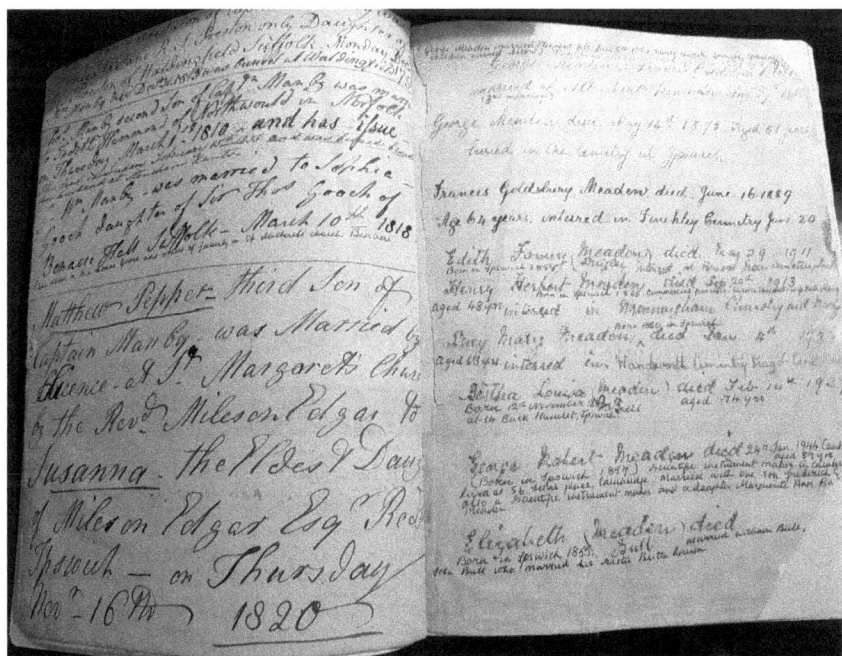

Figure 13a Doreen Leamey's Bible © Doreen Leamey.

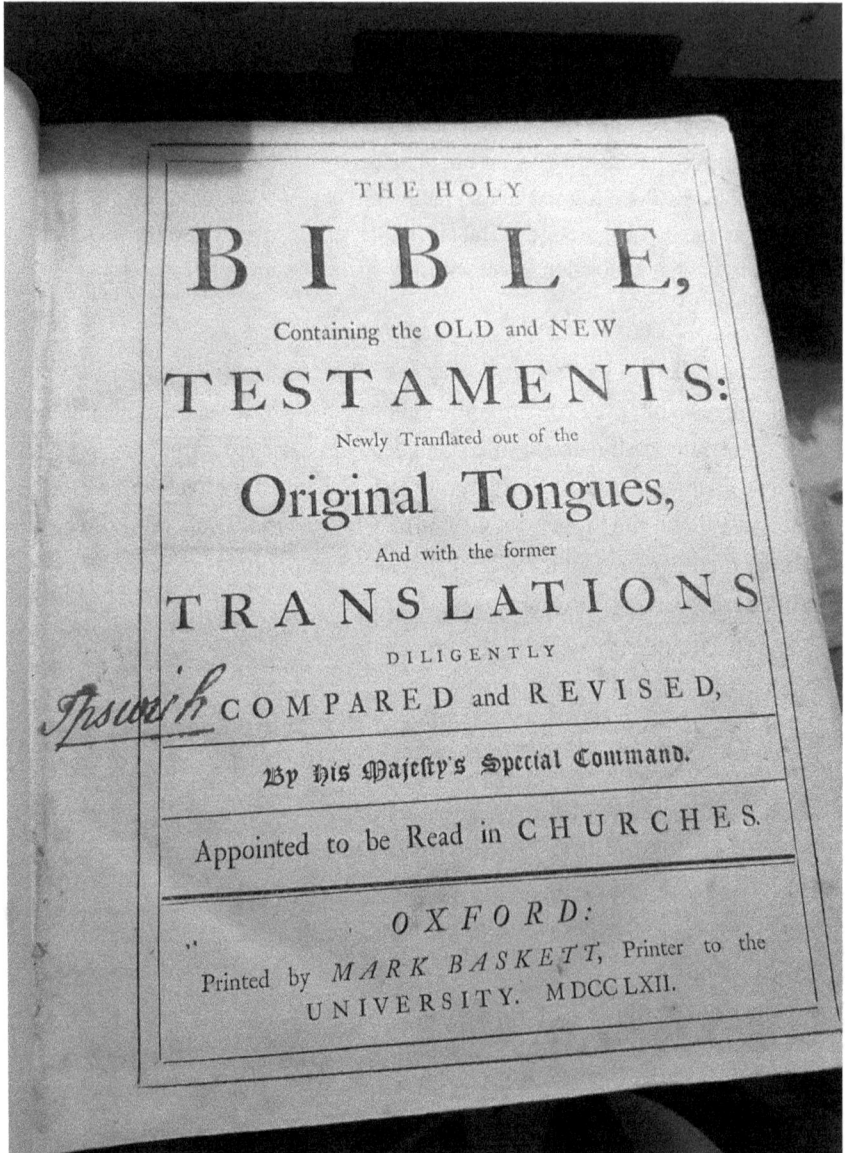

Figure 13b Doreen Leamey's Bible © Doreen Leamey.

I feel it is the only way to make progress in family history research. The inheritance lottery means that only some family members gain access to documents, photos and memorabilia – but in actuality, access to these should belong to all those whose ancestors are involved. I actually feel it's my duty to

Figure 14 Doreen Leamey on a cruise (credit Doreen Leamey).

share everything I have, and the finds I have uncovered through my research – thereby connecting my kin, and providing accurate information for all those struggling to sift through the thousands and thousands of records that may or may not pertain to their family.[50]

TR came into possession of his family bible in 1968 and this spurred him on to researching his great-grandfather's Irish family line.[51] Kath Robertson's research benefited enormously when she came into possession of a family bible:

> I have had contact with someone descended from my mother's family who inherited a family Bible. In that Bible the original owner recorded the dates and times of birth of all of his children. From this I have learned that this family had 2 additional children who do not appear on the Census records as they only lived a few hours after birth![52]

HN became a family historian after he dug out a bible to corroborate some information passed on from someone else.

> A distant cousin, Grant Hardie, I never knew existed emailed me out of the blue. He had come across something I had posted in an internet forum connected with another of my interests, motor racing and its history. He had already been researching our family history for many years and had recognized details about my father. That prompted me to dig out a family bible I had inherited from an aunt. It turned out to contain notes from her research into our family history in the 1960s. These overlapped extensively with Grant's information. We shared what we had and I got the bug.[53]

A family bible also spurred Peggy Beckett to begin her family history research:

> I grew up hearing about, but not believing, my maternal grandmother's aristocratic ancestors. When I inherited the pages from the family bible (which dates back to 1720) I realized that most of what she'd told me was probably true, so I set out to research the family and find out more.[54]

Alison Woolf, a Committee member and long-term volunteer at the Society of Australian Genealogists (SAG) in Sydney, also treasures her family bible. She was responsible for organizing SAG's project to reunite families with their bibles in the Society's possession, discussed above. She has one containing inscriptions from the late 1600s to the early 1900s, which provides her with the basis of the family tree that has been in her family's possession for many, many years. Alison spent years working her way through each almost invisible to the pencil entry gathering paper evidence to root each person in her family's past. She collected another family bible by surprise. Almost twenty years ago she received an email from someone trawling eBay who found she might be related to someone noted and after some googling discovered her public tree on Rootsweb and made contact to inform her. Within ten minutes her husband purchased the bible for an extortionate sum for which she felt 'not one moment of regret'. She believes her bibles contain both mystery and emotion.

> Why do we feel so emotionally involved with an artefact which we know our ancestor has touched? It appears a general human response, not something we imagine in advance; an overwhelming feeling of awe as we make the connection to the past, and as the awe passes and we examine our prize we may be lucky enough to find the solution to a mystery, or a mystery waiting for a solution … do not ever miss the chance to examine a family bible.[55]

Our global community of family historians collect similar familiar objects, revere their ancestors' possessions and work hard to produce material legacies for future generations to reveal along with the stories of their ancestors. Family history research using material culture enables researchers to establish a much more powerful connection to the past than an engagement with academic history alone.

Photo albums

Others spend many years constructing family photo albums and take enormous pleasure in distributing them as gifts to relatives, to engage their audiences and convince others of the value of their work. Shane O'Neil has spent a lot of time and money crafting photo albums and is a little bemused that her efforts are not valued more highly:

> With the help of a photographer friend, I put together a high quality replica of a photo album our mother made of the first 18 years of marriage with photos from 1946 up until 1963 when my brother was 17; I was 12 and my sister 7. My plan was to have this produced as a beautiful gift for my brother's children and also my sister's so they could see how their father and mother respectively looked and grew during their own childhood.
>
> I paid my friend a considerable sum to restore the photos before I spent more money to have 10 photo albums produced by Albumworks. Over the last 12 months, I have progressively been giving the albums to my brother's children and also to my sister and her children. The silence is almost deafening. I really don't know what the recipients think of the gift, what they have done with it, whether they will ever look at it. A simple 'thank you' would be nice. I am puzzled by this lack of response especially in light of the time, effort and money both my friend and I put into this project. She contributed a great deal because if I had paid her

for all her hours, she would have earned something like $2 or $3 an hour.[56]

She remains puzzled as to why her family is not more grateful for these gifts. She hopes that maybe one day they will learn to treasure them like she does.

Cookbooks

As a keen cook myself, I take enormous delight seeing family historians memorialize their family histories using food. Several of our family historians treasure family recipes that they then use to construct family cookbooks that stretch across time – memorializing several generations of the same family and their taste in food. This allows researchers to concentrate on and celebrate the lives of women in their family trees and gives value to more of this mostly invisible domestic labour in the past. Canadian Alison Madden made contact:

> With a distant cousin via a posting she made on Ancestry and we found we lived fairly close to each other. We decided to meet up, she indicated another cousin was also interested in the family history, I mentioned my recently deceased cousin and her mother and one thing led to another. We met up for the first time in 2010 and continue to meet about once every month or two to work on research and share our stories. We put together a 200 page cookbook of old family recipes as well as some of our own favourites. The old recipes I scanned were either handwritten or typed, we put in a brief family trees for all the contributors, photos, and somehow I became chief editor, printer, etc. I learned way more about Word! I also invested in a high tech scanner, cold laminator, and much more equipment. That was a huge project but very satisfying, having sold over 60 copies simply by word of mouth. And all that equipment has really paid off as well now that the private archive project has landed in my lap.[57]

Debra McAuslan has been doing her family history for over thirty years and she loved compiling a recipe book for her children:

> I believe I have a duty to help in a leadership role to encourage others to become interested in their family history. I incorporated family history into a cookbook for my daughter. I typed out recipes … with the story of why they became part of our heritage/tradition. I then added the picture of the person, whether it was my great grandmother, grandmother, great Aunts, Aunts, mother and sisters to accompany the recipe. I have made photobooks for my sisters and my children … starting with them and going backwards in ancestors and their stories. So I

see myself as the family historian and it pushes me to find creative ways to share my passion with others.[58]

Gemma Beswick works as an executive assistant for a heritage consultancy in Sydney. She is currently undertaking a Diploma in Family History at the Society of Australian Genealogists and aims to use her great-great grandmother's cookbook to form the basis of her major project. These manuscript cookbooks are her most 'prized items' amongst her family's archives. She regularly makes things for her family using the books. She is a young family historian, aged thirty-four, and has worked on her mysterious family history for many years.

Figure 15 Gemma Beswick with her great-great grandmother's cookbook
© Tanya Evans.

She shares her passion with her mother who often accompanies her on research trips and travel to significant family history sites.[59]

Food is crucial to familial memorialization, especially among migrant families. It is certainly one of the most familiar ways settler migrant nations engage with their multicultural populations. Scholars have questioned whether engaging with ethnic food means that people are less racist and more multiculturally aware.[60] However, many families remain committed to preserving certain dishes and traditions which are passed down carefully through the generations. Chinese Australian Justina Lui, now in her early thirties, is understood as her family's family historian. Her family arrived in Victoria in the late nineteenth century, after travelling via San Francisco looking for farm work. This initial journey prompted a period of familial chain migration. Her role has become more significant as her cousins have married non-Chinese people and many of their partners do not understand the family's complex structure and history. She speaks Cantonese while most of her cousins do not. Her family stories are shared with families in the United States and Canada, and many of them travel to Melbourne each year to listen and share in the telling. She enjoys her role instructing wider family in their history and customs. To facilitate this, each year the large family gather and visits the cemetery in Melbourne where all their family has been buried since the late nineteenth century. Some traditional Cantonese rituals are adhered to while others are not.

> We take a whole pig, cakes, boiled eggs, drinks, rice wine and we have a picnic with the dead. It has become a day long activity … It is a chance for the whole family to come together and reminisce about the past, the people now gone, stories of life back then, and also to catch up with everyone and what they are up to now. The younger kids are in charge of folding the bouillons while the adults do the burning. As older relatives pass away, the younger ones must learn how to make the cakes and take a bigger role in organising the event.

Justina wants to create a bank of Chinese stories and rituals for her immediate cousins who are now starting families themselves. It is for this reason that material culture is so important to her research. She wants to use photographs and objects to piece together stories of migration and settlement and reveal how her ancestors had 'fully formed lives' behind the pictures. She says that while her family participates in complex family rituals the younger generations do not actually believe in them. They are important for storytelling, but not for fulfilling spiritual or religious needs. Through her research and these rituals Justina has gained a much deeper understanding of Australian and Chinese culture and how to keep them alive for future generations of her family.[61]

Other family historians are committed to producing short and long books based on the family histories to share with familial members. TR:

> A couple of years ago I wrote down, in a narrative form, what I had learned of the history of our family from the 16th century to the late 20th. I did this for the benefit of my children and grandchildren, present and future, thinking they might never access my various computer databases but they might read a short book. I had never before tried a project or exercise like that before and although the work was only about 60 pages long its completion gave me a great sense of accomplishment and satisfaction.[62]

There is no doubt that these forms of research have enabled these historians to understand the value and significance of family heirlooms. JA:

> I think more now about keeping personal records and writing my story for the next generation. I am also more aware of items that I inherited which might be of interest to a museum or library eg photographs of school classes, theatre programs from the 1920s.[63]

This clearly has value for families but also wider communities. Larger audiences are better reached via blogs and websites rather than via books shared mostly among family members. I have encouraged many family historians I meet with to start drafting blog posts and writing online to share their work before thinking about longer, self-published books with likely more limited audiences.

Blogs and websites

We have seen throughout the book how important blogs, websites and social media have become for sharing family history research and information. Educationalists Dana Saxon and Christine Sleeter in the United States have grasped the possibilities of family history for transforming the lives of the disadvantaged, encouraging people to learn about their family histories and to share them online.[64] Sleeter has written extensively, much of it online as part of her blog, about the ways in which she approaches her life history for personal as well as for educational purposes. She encourages all her students, future and current teachers, to explore their own histories in order to better understand cultural privilege so that they might become more accomplished teachers. She believes that encouraging people to explore the multiple ways in which people construct their subject positions over time enables them to better understand 'institutionalized power relationships'. For Sleeter who grew up with 'an unproblematic, unified sense of myself as White' learning about her European and African ancestry has troubled her understanding of self. She has become aware that her grandparents had silenced their history of family poverty and blackness because they wanted to lay claim to middle class status. Her family had claimed Cherokee ancestry to explain their black skin and to eventually transition as white.[65] Like many of the family historians who feature in this book, she hopes others might learn from her example.

Art

In late 2014, Nethery Whylie dropped me an email from the United States. She is in her fifties, a professional librarian, student of history and an artist now living in Colorado, on the edge of the Rocky Mountains. She told me she had recently completed her Master of Fine Arts. She wanted to thank me and kindly acknowledge my *History Workshop Article* on family history, which she used in her work.[66] She told me how she used her art as a method of conducting and communicating historical research and creating new knowledge. Her research was focused upon female identity in the historical American west, and she wanted to work through the history of her great aunts who raised her mother after she was abandoned. She used her family history and surviving photographs to disrupt her own understanding of her family history; the archive passed down from her deceased mother revealed snippets of some of the stories those aunts had never shared. She used these great-aunts as a case study of early-twentieth-century women living without men, in largely unconventional lives, outside the bounds of patriarchal relations in the American West. Her research revealed how 'my great-aunts didn't live the circumscribed lives I would have thought' in 'small-town Oklahoma'.[67]

Her final work was titled 'She's not who you thought she was' and was displayed in New York and Berlin. The Berlin website's description of her exhibition described how her 'work with my images of my ancestresses and the struggle over the right to define "womenhood" in the American West led me to belief in the power of family history to be disruptive of preconceived historical assumptions if allowed to speak for itself. This was 'an experiment in disrupting my reading of family photographs. Photographs of female relatives from 1910– 1930 in Oklahoma, USA, are paired with texts intended to open rather than close the reading of the photo'.[68] She and I hope that family historians and creative practitioners can use her example to inform their own work and to toy with potential outputs for their research.

Conclusion

This focus on the material culture of family history and the creative products that might be produced using research should excite us about the future of family history. They remind us of the agency that research produces when knowledge and expertise is constructed, reflected upon and then shared creatively. Our family historians tell us how much their research empowers them. As Janine McMinn suggests, 'while our ancestors have had an influence on our genes we can, and do, have a lot of individual influence'.[69] The examples above remind us that we are not powerless in shaping the course of our lives. Psychologists Merrill and Fivush suggest that intergenerational narratives and family histories shared orally in families are positively related to identity development and well-being in adolescents.[70] Ample research confirms that everyone benefits when older generations share their memories and family history with younger generations. This is one of the reasons why the family historians who feature in this book hope to persuade more young people of the value of their historical endeavour. Brenda Lee is well aware that her research 'has helped me to understand how I became who I am. My family's history played a big part in the person I developed into. As an adult, I took my personal development further through education and life experience to become who I am today.' She 'would love to see Family History and Genealogy placed in the curriculum for high schools. If kids could understand where they came from and what has influenced them to be who they are, they will have a healthier view of themselves and the world and be better prepared for life'.[71]

For this and many other reasons, I hope to encourage family historians to be as wild and creative as possible when thinking about what to do with the histories of their families. As Raphael Samuel urged us in the 1980s and 90s – let us celebrate history as a social form of knowledge and encourage as many people as possible to sit at the history table and to tell their stories.[72] The sharing of bibles, photo albums, cookbooks, blog posts, websites and other creative forms provides vital social platforms for family historians to establish their expertise and to disseminate their work. They are crucial to the construction of the emotional communities that sustain their work and encourage the field to grow far into the future.

Epilogue

I suggested at the start of this book that family history allows vast numbers of people to think historically and to produce distinctive forms of historical understanding that challenge academic monopoly of historical knowledge.[1] Except, of course, as we must have learned by now, most people do not learn about the past from academic historians. They learn most of what they know about history through family members, television, museums and independent research. Few academics monopolize historical knowledge outside of tertiary institutions and scholarly communities. Many people, even those who have undertaken university degrees, have little knowledge or understanding of what it is that scholars do and rarely engage with or value their knowledge, expertise, authority and scholarly contributions. Therefore, it is crucial that scholars pay more attention to the public. As Pinto and Taithe suggest, of course generations of historians have been doing this for hundreds of years, but everyone needs to learn that

> it is not just the imparting of history by historians that is important, but also, and perhaps primarily, the democratization of the production of history – and engaging with the new producers and consumers of history (especially its consumer–producers) is for us the battlefield in which to counter the problems arising from the commodification of history and the welcomed demise of the ivory tower.[2]

Many socially progressive historians fantasize about using their research to change the world. If we have any hope of doing so, we need to work a lot harder at gaining the respect of others outside the university sector by explaining what we actually do more effectively. One of the ways we might do this is by collaborating with 'ordinary people' passionate about history. In this case, family historians.

I hope I have made clear throughout the book how the benefits of collaborating with family historians include fostering lifelong learning and pedagogical innovation inside and outside the academy, promoting the transfer of knowledge between generations, expanding audiences for history, emphasizing the value of history, as well as encouraging social inclusion. This has benefits for individuals as well as society and facilitates the democratization of history. It is for this reason that family historians should be friends with social and public historians. This practice is key to communicating our historical knowledge and its value for all citizens who live across the world today.

We know that historical knowledge and broad humanistic understanding are vital to the future of democratic self-government. The discipline of history teaches us independent, critical thinking, knowledge and understanding of individuals and the world in which we live, in the past as well as the present.[3] However, the contemporary world seems to have largely lost sight of these values and a commitment to their significance in our education and everyday lives. I like to hope that millions of family historians all over the world can help us persuade non-believers, primarily focussed on individuals and the market, of the importance of historical knowledge and understanding. I hope they reveal that it is better to think about how individuals might contribute best to societies on a reciprocal basis, understand the complexity of lives, to respect others and to empathize with those less fortunate than themselves. For this to happen, no matter what our education level and expertise is, we must all remain in touch with our emotions and remain active learners throughout our, hopefully, long lives. An active participation and emotional engagement in classrooms as well as in public is vital for encouraging people to understand the world through other people's eyes.

Along with others I have argued that family historians demonstrate, if not explicitly, Stephane Levesque's 'procedural concepts' of history. Students of family history learn how to practice and think critically about history, about how it is made, by moving between the different stages of learning about historical significance, continuity and change, progress and decline, evidence and historical empathy. Understanding the craft of history is crucial to this process. Moving through these concepts allows students to actively engage with their historical knowledge and not just to passively accept 'facts' and 'stories' on their own terms. It is my argument that this results in an understanding among individuals of their own historical agency – their capacity to change themselves and the world.[4] This form of lifelong learning, appropriate to all stages of the life cycle, teaches us that there is always more to learn about being a good citizen. Education in citizenship is crucial when it seems to be failing within the school system and elsewhere in many parts of the world.[5]

Family history enables people to better understand difference, in terms of class, race, gender and ethnicities. It urges them to understand other parts of the world and much more about the diverse people who live there. Researchers learn how to move with ease between the micro and macro. Undertaking their research, gathering and processing their data teaches family historians how to see and understand the world from the viewpoint of others. It prepares them for plural existences and empathetic concern. It reveals the circumstances of those who live in poverty and how they might control their plight. It outlines the power relations of class, race and gender that structure personal and professional lives in the past and present and how they might be challenged. It produces understanding about the lives of people who were discriminated in the past and why that was wrong and allows contemporaries to challenge these stereotypes. It teaches people that the stories we tell about our lives can be shaped in different ways and how they might be effectively disrupted and challenged. It reveals the disjuncture between official/national storytelling about the past with family folklore and memory. Collectively family historians show how important careful research and critical thinking are to all of us. They teach us how important it is to think for ourselves and to reflect on the meaning of our lives and the lives of others. They also reveal the benefits of working as a community with a shared end goal – to learn more about family life, social and cultural contexts in the past as well as now. They urge us all to examine our lives and think about our impact on the world as well as how best to work well with others.

In January 2019 with British colleagues led by Laura King and Nick Barratt, I helped establish the #HistoriansCollaborate network. This aims to be a 'collaborative network for family, local, social and community histories'. We want to encourage a network of scholars working in the Arts across the UK and Australia on community collaborative projects especially those working with family, local and community historians. Each one of us seeks to challenge the hierarchies and boundaries that exist between family historians, academic and other historians in the Galleries Libraries and Museum sector and elsewhere that prevent meaningful dialogue between us. We have established a set of online seminars that will take place in 2021, through the Institute of Historical Research's seminar programme, continuing our conversations and collaborations between diverse producers and consumers of family history around the world.[6]

This epilogue suggests some ways the future of family history collaboration might take shape and the possibilities of co-production considering how we can continue to seriously and usefully engage with this strongly defined and self-governing group of researchers. As this book argues, family historians all over the world provide models for socially engaged research for us all, academics and non-academics alike. Drawing on parts of an article co-written with Jerome de Groot and Matthew Stallard this epilogue points to a range of possible new research outputs and engagement as suggested in the previous chapter. These contexts are co-produced because they have been developed in discussion and debate with the family history community and a global network of scholars of family history which we argue is crucial for productive exchange moving forward. This book has suggested we need to better understand and showcase the approaches of this particular group of historical scholars. I have shown how family history is a politically, historically, ethically engaged practice. There are consequences and challenges of serious engagement with this community to mainstream historical practice.

Family historians are an incredibly large, diverse, complex set of researchers. We need to work closely with them on specific projects as outlined above and below so that both parties gain a clear sense of practice, approach, methodology and the historiographical implications of the kind of collaborative, engaged and confronting work that is being done in this field. Such work should be as open-ended as possible and possibly without 'outputs', at least as they are understood by academics. As I have demonstrated, scholars who hope to use their work for political effects, as we do, have much to learn from these humanist family historians as demonstrated in this book.

As we have seen, public history and family history is often maligned for debasing historical scholarship with its focus on eliciting emotional responses to the past.[7] Family historians take enormous pleasure in their work. This takes many forms including the pleasure of 'the chase', delight in the process of research and the joy of communicating their historical knowledge with others. It is possible that scholars need to rediscover and better articulate a sense of pleasure when undertaking their work. Scholars have a different affective relationship to their work but there is the potential to learn from family historians how these affective relationships and responses might make the process and impact of research more pleasurable, more profound, perhaps confronting but also more exciting. Instead of some academics dismissing emotional involvement as having nothing to do with serious historical study, as researchers, we all need to probe our own affective engagements with our subjects, outline its impact on our processes of research, and to make the emotions of our work clearer to multiple audiences when discussing its theoretical and methodological framework and implications.[8] We use the data gathered from our engagements with family historians to reiterate the political consequences and educative effects of these affective relationships and responses to the past for different groups of researchers and how these groups might come together.

It seems clear that historians should be engaging more self-consciously with their research participants as well as non-academic history researchers in their scholarly area and to better document these relationships.[9] Historians need to build time into their public history projects to converse with diverse researchers and to make a serious commitment to engagement as equal participants. As researchers, it is important for us to understand others' motivations for participating in our projects and what they hope to gain from them. It is clear to us that many of these researchers hope to maintain an ongoing relationship with scholars, to read the fruits of our research, for us to share our outputs with them and to continue our conversations about history and the contemporary world. We need to work harder at sharing the fruits of our labour with non-scholarly audiences. Our efforts are wasted if our scholarship sits behind paywalls and few people engage with it.

Furthermore, we need to think carefully about co-working and co-production in this context, the ethics of engaging with these groups.[10] Rather than simply impose models of 'history', 'evidence', 'argument', 'critique' and 'knowledge' we need to develop ways of articulating this in partnership and dialogue, especially when engaging with non-mainstreamed groups.[11] This is a space to hear, discuss and learn from the practical and theoretical interventions of family historians. The wider purpose is to consider the implications of this type of engagement, and to think about models for how this might open up a more inclusive and respectful historical discipline for the future.[12]

The #HistoriansCollaborate network and other projects have begun tentatively to provide models for bringing in non-mainstream and non-tertiary sector voices to challenge normative versions of history.[13] Working in collaboration with family historians, archivists, museum professionals, diverse genealogical organizations, local and community history organizations will lead to recognition of their challenge to historiographical norms. Such work includes focus groups and collaborative discussions rather than traditional conference proceedings.

It is still surprising how little involvement non-academic audiences have in the development of conferences, research workshops and symposia. Involving family historians genuinely in planning and discussion is key. Scholars need to move away from 'showing and telling' to listening productively as many public historians have done for decades.[14] Successful examples include the 'Related Histories' conference held at the National Library of Australia in late November

2017,[15] the symposia de Groot and Evans organized in Manchester 2017 and Sydney 2018,[16] Laura King's workshop in Leeds 2018[17] and the work currently being undertaken by the 'Inheriting the Family' AHRC-funded network based in Britain and Australia especially within their History Harvests.[18] History Harvests and workshops have been co-planned with non-academic partners to ensure all groups are represented and given a platform to speak.

We have included skills and historiography sharing in workshops involving family and local historians. In particular are three workshops in 2019 that brought family, academic, local and community historians and leaders to discuss their work, reading and to share their skills. In August 2019 in Orange, regional New South Wales, participants were asked to attend the workshop with details of their family history research and to bring along one object related to this. The aim was to encourage participants to present their research to local audiences using the resources of the local library, family, local history and museum community. The audience was keen to discover appropriate reading material, where they could learn new skills with regards to research and writing and how to publish their work. Feedback was overwhelmingly positive.

Rather than articles hidden behind paywalls, it is important to explore new ways of transmitting knowledge: podcasts, social media posts, videos, usable software, co-produced online and physical exhibitions, crowd-sourced data production, for example. There are numerous global examples of family historians blogging about their work to share their passion for history with as wide an audience as possible but also to make clear the politics behind their practice. See for example the website of the Hipster Historian who wants to make 'family history more intersectional and accessible to all'.[19] Academics have much to learn from their example as communicators.

This book concludes by embracing the pluralism of family history forms and creative outputs, suggesting scholars can learn from all of them. We want to break down social and cultural boundaries and include everyone in that process. I aim to practice what I preach. Once this book is put to bed, I will begin work in earnest on an Australian Research Council-funded collaborative Linkage project titled 'History, heritage and environmental change in a deindustrialized landscape'. At two sites called Ruined Castle and Nellie's Glen in the rugged Jamison and Megalong Valleys near Katoomba in the Blue Mountains in New South Wales lie the neglected remains of a shale-mining village. Archaeological elements identified during a pilot study undertaken in 2018 include twenty structures, attesting to habitation between 1880 and 1914. These preliminary results demonstrate the potential insights offered by a comprehensive, in-depth study of the site's tangible and intangible cultural heritage. Recent bushfires in the mountains make this research both timely and urgent.[20] As such, the years ahead provides a unique opportunity to work with our partners – the National Parks and Wildlife Service (NPWS), the Blue Mountains World Heritage Institute (BMWHI) and two NSW-based heritage consultancies – to produce a test case assessing the impact of bushfires on heritage sites, while also providing resources for industrial heritage conservation, education and cultural heritage tourism in the context of environmental change for the local community. Family, local and community historians are key to this project.

Our overarching goal is to advance scholarly and cross-generational knowledge about everyday life in a relatively isolated industrial community and the long-term impact of its deindustrialization and ruination by giving flesh and voice to the people who inhabited and laboured in this place. To fulfil this goal, our multidisciplinary, collaborative scholarly and community-based inquiry connects identified and as-yet-undiscovered archaeological evidence with intangible heritage contained in historical sources to tease out interconnections between work, family, community, gender, transiency and migration over time. To investigate these links, our team proposes to collect and synthesize archival records, oral evidence, archaeological remains and memorabilia held by members of the local community. We will translate the evidence not solely into datasets and scholarly publications, but also documentary and multimedia stories, heritage listing applications with management plans, accessible narratives and multimedia content for walking tours, school excursion kits, and online exhibits and other public-facing resources, furthered by development of a software platform to facilitate content delivery for educational purposes and tourism. Such outputs can make a significant contribution to conservation of industrial heritage and cultural heritage tourism thereby helping our Partner Organizations' (POs) fulfil their heritage responsibilities and public outreach needs, while also producing educational content for other stakeholders and end users, including community members, tourists and school children. My continued collaborations with family historians will make clear the 'impact' of history and how crucial it is to all of us.

Appendix – Survey and Interview Questions

Questions for Oral History Project: Keeping it in the Family? Family History and Historical Consciousness in Australia, England and Canada from 1900 to the present

Name:
Date:
Employment (if employed):

1. When were you born and where did you grow up?
2. When did you become a family historian?
3. Why did you become a family historian?
4. What was your understanding of history at the time?
5. Has your understanding of history changed over time?
6. How do you understand the relationship between family history and the history of your nation/the globe?
7. How has your research and discoveries made you feel?
8. Has this depended upon the discovery being unearthed?
9. Does your research and findings make you feel proud/sad/ angry/shameful/ happy? If so, why and in what ways?
10. Have you had any other emotional responses to your research?
11. Has your emotional relationship with your family history changed over time and depending upon who or what you were researching?
12. How have other members of your family responded to your work? Have those responses been emotional? If so, in what ways?
13. Do you think emotional responses to family history have changed over time? If so, how and in what ways?
14. For example the discovery of secrets and lies, skeletons in the closet like bigamy, mixed race ancestry and illegitimacy used to be thought of as shameful. Society constructed these categories in particular ways in different historical contexts. Do you think this is true today?

    If not, why not?
    If so, why?

15. Do you think that your research **empowers** you in particular ways?
16. How do you understand the **politics** of family history research?
17. How do you relate to other members of the family history community?
18. How do you understand that community? Is it local, national or global?
19. Has your research challenged the way that you think about the history of the family or national history more broadly?
20. Has it changed the way in which you understand your nation's history?
21. How do you feel about academic historians?
22. Do you admire their work, or do you question it?
23. Do you feel respected by academic historians when you 'do' family history?
24. Do you like the idea of partnering with academic historians – what are the pros and cons, do you think?
25. Are your collaborations with family historians usually enjoyable or not?
26. Can you detail these for me – are these collaborations, exchanges of information taking place on a local, regional, national or global level?
27. Is this something you value in your work – sharing your information with others and gaining from their insights and research?
28. Has feminism, racism or other political beliefs informed your work at all?
29. I was wondering if you feel like your research has transformed you? Has it encouraged you to think about your life differently? Has it led you to think about your place in the world in different ways?
30. How has your experience of family history changed the way in which you understand the discipline of history?
31. Has it helped you to better understand yourself and what you are capable of? If so, in what ways?
32. Has it helped you to reflect on what motivates you/your personal values/ ethics. If so, in what ways?
33. Has it led you to reflect on what you want to do to contribute to the community. If so, in what ways?
34. Has it helped you to understand and appreciate diversity (in culture, background, experience, perspectives). If so, in what ways?
35. Has it helped you to (better) understand organisational, social and/or political structures and systems? If so, in what ways?
36. Has it helped you to develop your interpersonal (communication, listening and empathy) skills? If so, in what ways?
37. Is there something else you would like to reflect on?

Notes

Introduction

1   Robyn Fivush, 'The Development of Autobiographical Memory', *Annual Review of Psychology*, 62 (2011): 559–82 and Robyn Fivush and Catherine A. Haden, *Autobiographical Memory and the Construction of a Narrative Self: Development and Cultural Perspectives* (Mahwah, New Jersey: Psychology Press, Lawrence Erlbaum Associates, 2003).

2   Paul Ashton and Paula Hamilton, *History at the Crossroads: Australians and the Past* (Ultimo: Halstead Press, 2003), 135; Paul Ashton and Paula Hamilton (eds.), 'Australians and the Past', *Australian Cultural History*, Special Issue, 22, 2003.

3   Frank Mort, 'Foreword', in Sasha Handley, Rohan McWilliam and Lucy Noakes (eds.), *New Directions in Social and Cultural History* (London: Bloomsbury, 2018), xv.

4   Paul Ashton and Meg Foster, 'Public Histories', in Sasha Handley, Rohan McWilliam and Lucy Noakes (eds.), *New Directions in Social and Cultural History* (London: Bloomsbury, 2018), 156. Martha Nussbaum, *Not for Profit: Why Democracy Needs the Humanities* (New Haven: Princeton University Press, 2010).

5   For further discussion of some of these ideas also, see Pedro Ramos Pinto and Bertrand Taithe (eds.), *The Impact of History? Histories at the Beginning of the Twentieth Century* (Abingdon and New York: Routledge, 2015).

6   This is the focus of Jerome De Groot's current work: https://www.alc.manchester. ac.uk/english/research/projects/double-helix-history/ and https://www.youtube. com/watch?v=6V9Ndi_yINg (accessed 28 May 2021).

7   Tanya Evans, 'Who Do You Think You Are? Historical Television Consultancy', *Australian Historical Studies* 46, no. 3 (2015): 454–67.

8   John Spurway, 'The Growth of Family History', *Push* 27 (1989): 53–112.

9   Tanya Evans, 'Secrets and Lies: The Radical Potential of Family History', *History Workshop Journal* 71 (2011): 49–73. It is now refreshing to see the increased number of PhD theses using 'traditional' historical research techniques combined with family history research see https://sag.org.au/event-4050592?fbclid=IwAR0vJc_OS1K7vyRg_jquL1LQmFBzeAb8RxGQ3BEkJ1bfCp_uH5fA6iFL_Is (accessed 11 December 2020).

10 Margaret Conrad, Kadriye Ercikan, Gerald Friesen, Jocelyn Letourneau, Delphin Muise, David Northrup and Peter Seixas, *Canadians and Their Pasts* (Toronto: University of Toronto Press, 2013).

11 For a taster, see Tanya Evans and Jerome De Groot (eds.), Special Issue on Family History, *International Public History* (Berlin: De Gruyter, 2019).

12 Quoted at a Symposium on Family History held at Macquarie University September 15th-16th 2014.

13 Thanks to Martyn Killion for sharing this information, 28 January 2021.

14 Noeline Kyle, 'Genealogy', in Graeme Davison, John Hirst and Stuart Macintyre (eds.), *The Oxford Companion to Australian History* (Oxford: Oxford University Press, [1998] 2001), 280–1. See also Graeme Davison, 'Ancestors: The Broken Lineage of Family History', in his *The Use and Abuse of Australian History* (Sydney: Allen and Unwin, 2000), 80.

15 Davison, 'Ancestors', 83.

16 Babette Smith, 'Molesworth Lives? A Reply to Some Reviewers of *Australia's Birthstain*', *Journal of Australian Colonial History* 11 (2009): 229 and David Roberts quoted in 'Sons and Daughters of the Southern Cross', *Sydney Morning Herald* 10–11 (Oct. 2009): 5.

17 Evans, 'Secrets and Lies' and Tanya Evans, Jerome De Groot and Matthew Stallard, 'I don't even trust what I read in the history books': family history and the future of co-production and collaboration' Article under review.

18 Wendy Bottero, 'Practising Family History: Identity as a Category of Social Practice', *British Journal of Sociology* 66, no. 3 (2015): 534–66, https://doi.org/10.1111/1468-4446.12133; Anne-Marie Kramer, 'Kinship, Affinity and Connectedness: Exploring the Role of Genealogy in Personal Lives', *Sociology*, 45 (2011): 379–95, https://doi.org/10.1177/0038038511399622.

19 Christine Nash, 'Genealogical Identities', *Environment and Planning D: Society and Space* 20 (2002): 27–52; Christine Nash, *Genetic Geographies: The Trouble with Ancestry* (Minnesota: Minnesota University Press, 2015).

20 Tanya Evans, *Fractured Families: Life on the Margins in Colonial New South Wales* (Sydney: New South Press, 2015).

21 Including Manchester City Library, North Sydney Stanton Library, Orange City Library and Gallery, Australian Lebanese Historical Society, Australian Jewish Genealogical Society and the Society of Australian Genealogists.

22 Tanya Evans and Jerome De Groot, 'Emerging Studies in Family History', in *International Public History* (Berlin: De Gruyter, 2019).

23 https://historianscollaborate.com/ (accessed 28 January 2021).

24 https://www.history.ac.uk/partnership-seminars/historians-across-boundaries-collaborative-historical-research (accessed 28 January 2021).

25 Peter Hobbins, 'Public History: Exploring Productive Relationships with Partner Practitioners', November 2018, http://www.phansw.org.au/public-history-exploring-productive-relationships-with-partner-practitioners.

26 Christine Kenneally, *The Invisible History of the Human Race: How DNA and History Shape Our Identities and Our Futures* (Melbourne: Black Inc, 2014).

27 https://genealogyalacarte.ca/wp-content/uploads/2019/04/Facebook-for-Canadian-Genealogy-May-2019.pdf (last accessed 21 September 2020).

28 Helen Little, 'Genealogy as a Theatre of Self-Identity: A Study of Genealogy as a Cultural Practice within Britain since c. 1850', PhD thesis, University of Glasgow, 2010.

29 Francois Weil, *Family Trees: A History of Genealogy in America* (Cambridge: Harvard University Press, 2013).

30 Alex Haley, *Roots: The Saga of an American Family* (New York: Doubleday, 1976).

31 Weil, *Family Trees* and Jerome de Groot, *Consuming History: Historians and Heritage in Contemporary Popular Culture* (London: Routledge, 2009).

32 https://findingaway.auctr.edu/AAFHA.asp and https://www.aahgs.org/ (both accessed 23 November 2020).

33 Jerome De Groot, 'On Genealogy', *The Public Historian* 37, no. 3 (2015): 102–27.

34 Federation of Family History Societies, https://www.familyhistoryfederation.com/about 2016; Australian Federation of Family History Organisations Inc., 2004, https://affho.org/#:~:text=AFFHO%20was%20established%20in%201978,or%20territory%20and%20New%20Zealand.

35 Martha Sear, 'A Thousand Different Hands: History in communities', in Anna Clark and Paul Ashton (eds.), *Australian History Now* (Sydney: New South, 2013), 198–214.

36 Reid, 'The Development', 20. https://www.tvguide.com/tvshows/ancestors-in-the-attic/episodes/472273/; https://web.archive.org/web/20111004102343/http://www.ontarioroots.com/index.html?%2Fcontent%2F01%2Fmenu_01_01.html.

37 Roy Rosenweig and David Thelan, *The Presence of the Past: Popular Uses of History in American Life* (New York: Columbia University Press, 1998), 3.

38 Paul Ashton and Paula Hamilton, *History at the Crossroads: Australians and the Past* (Ultimo, NSW: Halstead Press, 2010), 135; Conrad et al., *Canadians and Their Pasts*.

39 Anna Clark, *Private Lives, Public History* (Melbourne: Melbourne University Press, 2016), 6.

40 See my 'Secrets and Lies: The Radical Potential of Family History', *History Workshop Journal*, 71 (Spring 2011): 49–73.

41 A team of academics based at the University of Newcastle and journalists working for *The Guardian* newspaper created a fantastic online resource revealing the history of Frontier wars across Australia -wars that many families were deeply imbricated within: https://www.theguardian.com/australia-news/series/the-killing-times; (accessed 4 September 2020).https://www.theguardian.com/australia-news/2019/mar/06/descended-from-both-sides-of-queenslands-bloody-massacres (accessed 4 September 2020). The project won a NSW Premier's History Award in 2019: https://www.newcastle.edu.au/newsroom/faculty-of-education-and-arts/

massacre-map-and-guardian-australia-partnership-project-wins-premiers-history-award (accessed 23 November 2020).

42 Richard Evans, 'Review of *Who do you think you are?*' *History Australia* 5: 3, December 2008. See also Peter Sherlock, 'Colonial Memories: the Hungerfords of Farley', (unpublished paper), p. 24. Thanks to Peter for sharing this paper with me.

43 Victoria Haskins, 'Beyond Complicity: Questions and Issues for White Women in Aboriginal History', *Australian Humanities Review* 39 (September 2006): 5.

44 Babette Smith, *A Cargo of Women: Susannah Watson and the Convicts of the Princess Royal* (Crows Nest: Allen and Unwin, 1988); *Australia's Birthstain: the Startling Legacy of the Convict Era* (Crows Nest: Allen and Unwin, 2008).

45 On the impact of anti-transportation campaigns, see Kirsten McKenzie, *Scandal in the Colonies* (Melbourne: Melbourne University Press, 2004), 152 and James Boyce, *Van Diemen's Land: A History* (Melbourne: Black Inc., 2008).

46 Smith, *Australia's Birthstain*, Introduction.

47 Roberts quoted in 'Sons and Daughters', 5. See also Ashley Barnwell, 'From Convict Shame to Convict Chic: Intergenerational Family Memory and Family Histories', *Journal of Family History* 12, no. 4 (2017): 398–411.

48 See Lucy Frost and Hamish Maxwell-Stewart (eds.), *Chain Letters: Narrating Convict Lives* (Melbourne: Melbourne University Press, 2001). Many of the authors in this volume acknowledge the help of family historians in their work. See also Trudy Cowley, *A Drift of Derwent Ducks: Lives of the 200 Female Irish Convicts Transported on the Australasia from Dublin to Hobart in 1849* (New Town, 2005); and Alison Alexander, *Tasmania's Convicts: How Felons Built a Free Society* (Sydney: Allen and Unwin, 2010).

49 The island was mostly untouched by the large-scale immigration that we associate with Australia's construction as a nation, and even today its population is only 500,000.

50 Alexander, *Tasmania's Convicts,* 3; Robyn Eastley, 'Using the Records of the Tasmanian Convict Department', *Tasmanian Historical Studies,* 9, 2004.

51 Lucy Frost, 'The Politics of Writing Convict Lives: Academic Research, State Archives and Family History', *Life Writing* 8, no. 1 (2011): 19–33.

52 http://www.foundersandsurvivors.org/.

53 Portia Robinson, *The Hatch and Brood of Time: A Study of the First Generation of Native-Born White Australians 1788–1828* (vol. 1, Melbourne: Melbourne University Press, 1984); Grace Karskens, *The Rocks: Life in Early Sydney* (Melbourne: Melbourne University Press, 1997). See also Trevor McClaughlin, *Barefoot and Pregnant? Irish Famine Orphans in Australia* (Melbourne: Genealogical Society of Victoria, 1991).

54 Victoria Haskins, 'Beyond Complicity'; and Cassandra Pybus, 'The Old Commodore: A Transnational Life', in *Transnational Ties: Australian Lives in*

the World, ed. Desley Deacon, Penny Russell and Angela Woollacott (Australian National University E Press: Canberra, 2008). Pybus used micro-history and biography for her work on Billy Blue, African-American convict who travelled the world before settling in New South Wales. He befriended the great and the good of early Sydney but sank into poverty once his patron, Governor Macquarie, left the colony. She also uses family history in her latest book *Truganini* (Crows Nest: Allen and Unwin, 2019).

55   https://www.ucl.ac.uk/lbs/ and https://www.abc.net.au/religion/australia-and-the-dark-legacy-of-slave-ownership/12744288 (both accessed 23 November 2020).

56   Jane McCabe, *Race, Tea and Colonial Re-Settlement* (London: Bloomsbury, 2017), Judith Bennett and Angela Wanhalla (ed.), *Mother's Darlings of the South Pacific: The Children of Indigenous Women and US Servicemen World War II* (Honolulu: University of Hawaii Press, 2016), Alice Echols, *Shortfall: Family Secrets, Financial Collapse and a Hidden History of Banking in America* (New York: The New Press, 2017); Rachel Buchanon, *Ko Taranaki Te Maunga* (Wellington: Bridget Waters Books, 2018). For recent discussion on the dismissal of family history and the aims of the #HistoriansCollaborate network, see Mike Esbester, 'Thoughts on Collaboration: The Start of a Manifesto', http://www.railwayaccidents.port.ac.uk/thoughts-on-collaboration-the-start-of-a-manifesto/ and https://nataliepithers.wixsite.com/historianscollab (accessed 26 September 2019).

57   Graeme Davison, *Lost Relations: Fortunes of My Family in Australia's Golden Age* (Sydney: Allen and Unwin, 2015).

58   Penny Russell, 'Travelling Steerage: Class, Commerce, Religion and Family in Colonial Sydney', *Journal of Australian Studies* 38, no. 4 (2014): 383–95.

59   Paul Irish, *Hidden in Plain View: The Aboriginal People of Coastal Sydney* (Sydney: New South, 2017); Michael Bennett, *Pathfinders: A History of Aboriginal Trackers in NSW* (Sydney: New South, 2020); Betty O'Neil, *The Other Side of Absence: Discovering My Father's Secrets* (Sydney: Simon and Shuster, 2020); Alana Piper, 'Did They See It Coming? How Fortune-telling Took Hold in Australia – with Women as Clients and Criminals', *The Conversation*, 3 February 2020. Alana is co-authoring a book on Mary Scales with descendant Samedhi Driscoll; Marian Lorrison, 'Love and Other Bruises: Passion and Yearning in a Time of Social Transformation', PhD thesis, Macquarie University, 2020.

60   Bettina Bradbury, *Caroline's Dilemma: A Colonial Inheritance Saga* (Sydney: New South Publishing, 2019). These are questions asked and explored at this Webinar hosted by the Society of Australian Genealogists on 187th December 2020: https://sag.org.au/event-4050592?fbclid=IwAR0vJc_OS1K7vyRg_jquL1LQmFBzeAb8RxGQ3BEkJ1bfCp_uH5fA6iFL_Is. A Special Issue of the journal *Life Writing* is planned on this theme due for publication in late 2022/early 2023.

61 Erica Cervini, PhD, Victoria University, 2019. She has published this as a book, *Yizkor for Rose: A Life Lost and Found*, (2020). Readers may also be interested listening to an interview with Erica on ABC Radio National's program *Life Matters*: https://www.abc.net.au/radionational/programs/lifematters/how-your-family-history-could-enrich-us-all/12497166 (accessed 23 November 2020).

62 Louise Blake, 'Women and Community on the Upper Goulburn Goldfields', Monash University PhD thesis, 2019. For another example of a family history PhD thesis, see: Jennifer Barrera, 'The Millers: Historical Analysis of an Early Australian Colonial Family' Federation University 2020.

63 Shauna Bostock Smith, 'From Colonisation to My Generation: An Aboriginal Historian's Family Research from Past to Present', ANU PhD thesis 2020.

64 For a flavour, see: https://historianscollaborate.com/events/ (accessed 28 May 2021).

65 For an account of the rise of family history in England, see Simon Titley-Bayes, 'Family History in England, c. 1945–2005: Culture, Identity and (Im)mortality', unpublished PhD Thesis, University of York (2006).

66 http://www.sog.org.uk/about/history-of-the-society/ (accessed 23 November 2020). Simon Titley-Bayes, 'Family History', 28.

67 https://www.familyhistoryfederation.com/; https://www.findmypast.com.au/articles/federation-of-family-history-societies-members (accessed 23 November 2020). Maggie Loughran, 'History of Genealogy/Family History', *Making History: The Changing Face of the Profession in Britain*, (2008) https://archives.history.ac.uk/makinghistory/resources/articles/family_history.html.

68 http://www.one-name.org/guild.html (accessed 23 November 2020). See also Jules Hudson and Nick Barratt, 'The Rise and Rise of Family History', *History Today* 57, no. 4 (2007): 20–1.

69 Alison Light, *Common People: The History of an English Family* (London: Penguin, 2014), 255.

70 Carmen Calill, *Oh, Happy Day, Those Times and These Times* (London: Penguin, 2020).

71 Alison Baxter, 'Debatable Lands: Exploring the Boundaries of Fiction and Nonfiction through Family History', Oxford Brookes PhD Thesis (2019). She has published her book *A Cornish Cargo: The Untold History of a Victorian Seafaring Family* (2020).

72 Laura King and Jessica Hammett, 'Family Historians and Historians of the Family: The Value of Collaboration', Paul Ashton, Tanya Evans and Paula Hamilton (eds.), *Making Histories Public* (Berlin: De Gruyter, 2020), 237–51.

73 https://www.irishfamilyhistorycentre.com/article/expert-workshop-child-incarceration-in-19th-century-dublin-by-aoife-oconnor (accessed 23 November 2020).

74 http://acriminalrecord.org/about/ (accessed 23 November 2020).

75   Joseph Amato, *Jacob's Well: A Case for Rethinking Family History* (Minnesota: Minnesota Historical Press, 2008), 234.

76   Christine Kenneally, *The Invisible History*, 314 and Jerome de Groot and Matthew Stallard, "'Things Are Coming Out That Are Questionable, We Never Knew About": DNA and the New Family History', *Journal of Family History* 45, no. 3 (2020), https://sites.manchester.ac.uk/double-helix-history/author/mfatsjd2/; Keith Wailoo, Alondra Nelson and Catherine Lee, *Genetics and the Unsettled Past: The Collision of DNA, Race and History* (New Brunswick: Rutgers University Press, 2012).

77   Amato, *Jacob's Well*.

78   Jack Hodgkins, *Broken Ground* (Toronto: Emblem Editions, 1998); Caroline-Isabelle Caron, *Se Creer des Ancestres: Un Parcours Genealogique Nord-American XIX-XX seicles* (Quebec: Septentrion, 2006) and Alice Munro, *Open Secrets: Stories* (Toronto: Vintage, 1995) and *The Beggar Maid: The Story of Flo and Rose* (Toronto: Vintage, 1991).

79   John Reid, 'The Development and Transformation of Canadian Genealogy', in Randy Boswell (ed.), *The Personal Past: History, Identity and the Genealogical Impulse* (Canadian Issues, Association of Canadian Studies, Spring-Summer, 2020), 17–21. See his blog: https://anglo-celtic-connections.blogspot.com/2020/.

80   Ron Lambert, 'A Study of Genealogists and Family Historians', *Global Genealogy*, http://globalgenealogy.com/globalgazette/gazrr/gazrr20.htm (accessed 4 September 2020).

81   Leighann Neilson, 'Why Are Canadians Researching Their Family History?', Boswell et al., *The Personal Past*, 22–5; Del Muise, 'Heritage Omnivores: Canadian Baby Boomers at Home and in Public' (unpublished paper). Del Muise, 'Why Start in Family History', *Genealogy in Canada*, http://genealogyincanada.blogspot.ca/search/What%20Makes%20%20A%20Genealogist%20Start. (accessed 13 March 2017).

82   Heather Devine, *The People Who Own Themselves: Aboriginal Ethnogenesis in a Canadian Family, 1660-1900* (Alberta: University of Calgary Press, 2004).

83   Clark, *Private Lives, Public History*.

84   Del Muise, 'Heritage Omnivores: Canadian Baby Boomers at Home and in Public' (unpublished paper).

85   Angus Baxter, *In Search of Your Roots: A Guide for Canadians Seeking Their Ancestors* (Toronto: Macmillan, 1977).

86   Reid, 'The Development', 19.

87   Conrad et al., *Canadians and Their Pasts, The Pasts Collective*, esp. Chapter 4 'Family History in a Globalizing World'. See also Margaret Conrad, M., Dubé, N., Northrup, D., & Owre, K., "'I Want to Know My Bloodline": New Brunswickers and Their Pasts', *Journal of New Brunswick Studies / Revue d'études Sur Le Nouveau-Brunswick, 1,* 2010. For more detail on the Canadians and Their Pasts

project, see: http://www.canadiansandtheirpasts.ca/. Randy Boswell et al., *The Personal Past: History, Identity and the Genealogical Impulse* (Association of Canadian Studies, Spring/Summer 2020).

88   Conrad et al., 'I want to know my bloodline', 9. See also Devine, *The People Who Own Themselves;* Jane Badets, 'Who Am I? Reflections on Measuring Ethnic Ancestry in Canada,' Boswell et al., *The Personal Past,* 26–32.

89   Jean Teillet, 'Indigenization: How Genealogy and DNA Justify Race Shifting in Eastern Canada', Boswell et al., *The Personal Past,* 40–3.

90   See also family historian Tracy Arial's plea for more academics to collaborate, 'How Genealogy Improves Historical Study', in Boswell et al., *The Personal Past,* 67–70.

91   Paul Basu, *Route Metaphors of 'Roots Tourism' in the Scottish Highland Diaspora* (London: Routledge, 2004); Carla Almeida Santos and Grace Yan, 'Genealogical Tourism: A Phenomenological Examination', *Journal of Travel Research* 49, no. 1 (2010): 56–67; Gary McCain and Nina M. Ray, 'Legacy Tourism: The Search for Personal Meaning in Heritage Travel', *Tourism Management* 24, no. 6 (2003): 713–17; Carol A. Kidron, 'Being There Together: Dark Family Tourism and the Emotive Experience of Co-presence in the Holocaust Past', *Annals of Tourism Research* 41 (2013): 175–94 https://www.familytreemagazine.com/premium/genealogy-insider-genealogy-tourism/; https://www.businessdestinations.com/relax/an-interest-in-genealogy-is-fuelling-heritage-tourism/; https://www.familysearch.org/blog/en/heritage-tourism/; https://familytreetours.com/ (all accessed 21 September 2020).

92   https://tracesmagazine.com.au/ (accessed 7 January 2020).

93   See also De Groot, Stallard and Evans, 'I don't even trust now', 2020.

94   Elizabeth Yakel, 'Seeking Information, Seeking Connections, Seeking Meaning: Genealogists and Family Historians', *Information Research* 10, no. 1 (2004); Amy Smith, 'Family Webs' The Impact of Women's Genealogy Research on Family Communication', PhD thesis, Bowling Green State University, 2008, p. 7.

95   Conrad et al., 'I want to know my bloodline', 10.

96   Penny Summerfield, 'Mass-Observation: Social Research or Social Movement?' *Journal of Contemporary History* 20, no. 3 (1985): 439–52. doi:10.1177/002200948502000306 and her *Histories of the Self: Personal Narratives and Historical Practice* (Abingdon: Routledge, 2019).

97   For a recent twitter discussion on this among historians working on family history started by Hannah Barker, see: https://twitter.com/Ordinary_Times/status/1320103618746384384 (accessed 16 October 2020).

98   Email correspondence with Marg Doherty, Secretary of the Australian Federation of Family History Organizations 20 August 2020. Similar data is reported from the Society of Australian Genealogists.

99   Australian Survey Response Kay Daniels, No specific date, 2016.

100 Australian Survey Response, Kay Spence, 2016.

Chapter 1

1   Including Jane Mccabe, Race, *Tea and Colonial Re-Settlement* (London: Bloomsbury, 2017), Judith Bennett and Angela Wanhalla (ed.), *Mother's Darlings of the South Pacific: The Children of Indigenous Women and US Servicemen World War II* (Honolulu: University of Hawaii Press, 2016), Alice Echols, *Shortfall: Family Secrets, Financial Collapse and a Hidden History of Banking in America* (New York: The New Press, 2017); Rachel Buchanon, *Ko Taranaki Te Maunga* (Wellington: BWB Texts, 2018).

2   Bonnie Smith, *The Gender of History: Men, Women and Historical Practice* (Cambridge: Harvard University Press, 1998); Mary Spongberg, *Writing Women's History since the Renaissance* (New York: Palgrave, 2002), 75.

3   Joan Thirsk, 'Women, Local and Family Historians', in David Hey (ed.), *The Oxford Companion to Local and Family History* (Oxford: Oxford University Press, [1996] 2008); Daniel Woolf, 'A Feminine Past? Gender, Genre, and Historical Knowledge in England 1500–1800', *American Historical Review* (June 1997): 645–79.

4   Martin Bashforth, nd. 'What is Radical about Family History, Part 1', https://bashforth.wordpress.com/politics/what-is-radical-about-family-history-part-1/; Alison Light, 'Genealogy Is Not History's Poor Relation', *The Guardian*, accessed October 12, 2020, https://www.theguardian.com/books/2014/oct/11/genealogy-not-historys-poor-relation-family.

5   On the History Workshop Movement, see Sophie Scott-Brown, *The Histories of Raphael Samuel: A Portrait of a People's Historian* (Canberra: Australian National University E Press, 2017).

6   Alan Booth, 'Making Teaching Public: The Scholarship of Teaching and Learning in History in Perspective', in David Ludvigsson (ed.), *Enhancing Student Learning in History: Perspectives on University History Teaching* (Opuscula Historica Upsaliersia, 48, 2012); Sam Wineburg, *Historical Thinking and Other Unnatural Acts* (Philadelphia: Temple University Press, 2001), http://historicalthinkingmatters.org/why/.

7   This is her website: https://www.quirkycharacters.com.au/about.html.

8   Email communication with Julie Poulter, 26 April 2016.

9   Geof Eley, *A Crooked Line: From Cultural History to the History of Society* (Ann Arbor: University of Michigan Press, 2005).

10   https://fabians.org.uk/about-us/our-history/ (accessed 24 November 2020) Bernard Shaw, *The Fabian Society: Its Early History* (London: Franklin Classics, (1892), 2018).

11   Pat Thane, 'Asa Briggs, Baron Briggs of Lewes, 1921–2016'; http://socialhistory.org.uk/2017/04/19/pat-thane-on-asa-briggs/.

12   Eric Evans, Social History Society, 2016; http://socialhistory.org.uk/wp-content/uploads/2018/01/Evans-speech.pdf (accessed 17 September 2018); Miles Taylor, 2016,

Social History Society; http://socialhistory.org.uk/wp-content/uploads/2018/01/Taylor-speech.pdf, (accessed 17 September 2018).

13 https://www.campop.geog.cam.ac.uk/ (accessed 24 November 2020).

14 Barbara Taylor, 'History Workshop Journal', *Making History: The Changing Face of the Profession in Britain* (Institute of Historical Research online source, 2008), https://archives.history.ac.uk/makinghistory/resources/articles/HWJ.html.

15 Frank Bongiorno, 'Asa Briggs and the Remaking of Australian Historiography', in Miles Taylor (ed.), *The Age of Asa: Lord Briggs, Public Life and History in Britain since 1945* (Basingstoke: Palgrave, 2015), 90–107.

16 Pat Thane, 'Asa Briggs, Baron Briggs of Lewes, 1921–2016'; http://socialhistory.org.uk/2017/04/19/pat-thane-on-asa-briggs/.

17 *Social History*, https://socialhistory.org.uk/about/our-history/ (accessed 11 April 2018); https://www.theguardian.com/society/2010/aug/10/keith-nield-obituary (accessed 24 November 2020).

18 Ruth Harris, and Lyndal Roper, 'Introduction to a Special Issue Marking Olwen Hufton's Intellectual Contribution to History', *Past and Present*, Vol. 1, January 1–11, 2006.

19 James Vernon, 'Who's Afraid of the Linguistic Turn: The Politics of Social History and Its Discontents', *Social History* 19, no. 1 (1994): 81–97; Anna Green and Kathleen Troup, *Houses of History: A Critical Reader in Twentieth-Century History and Theory* (New York: New York University Press, 1999), 34.

20 Social History Society, https://socialhistory.org.uk/about/people/thane/ (accessed 11 April 2018).

21 Bongiorno, 'Asa Briggs and the Remaking of Australian Historiography', 90–107.

22 Bongiorno, 'Asa Briggs and the Remaking of Australian Historiography'.

23 Bicentennial History Research Project, http://archivescollection.anu.edu.au/index.php/bicentennial-history-project-research-school-of-social-sciences (accessed 27 April 2018).

24 Frank Bongiorno, '"Real Solemn History" and Its Discontents: Australian Political History and the Challenge of Social History', *Australian Journal of Politics and History* 56, no. 1 (2010): 6, 20, 12.

25 Bongiorno, 'Asa Briggs and the Remaking of Australian Historiography', 97.

26 Green and Troup, *Houses of History*, 336.

27 Prominent Melbournian professors Andrew May and Graeme Davison are exceptions.

28 University of New England, https://www.une.edu.au/study/study-options/study-areas/history-and-political-science/local-family-and-applied-history (accessed 8 June 2018).

29 University of Tasmania, http://www.utas.edu.au/arts-law-education/study/diploma-of-family-history (accessed 8 June 2018) and Kristyn Harman, 'The Transformative Power of Digital Humanities when Teaching Family History Online', *Journal of*

University Teaching and Learning Practice 15, no. 3 (2018), https://ro.uow.edu.au/jutlp/vol15/iss3/7/ (accessed 26 September 2018).

30	James Opp and John Walsh (eds.), *Home, Work and Play: Situating Canadian Social History* (Oxford: Oxford University Press, Third Volume 2015), Introduction.

31	See also David Gagan and H.E. Turner, 'Social History in Canada: A Report on the State of the Art', *Archivaria*, 1982, 14 January, 27–52, 35.

32	Gregory Kealey, 'The Writing of Social History in English Canada, 1970–1984', *Social History*, Oct 1985, vol. 10, no. 3, North American Issue, 347–65. See also Gagan and Turner, 'Social History in Canada: A Report on the State of the Art', 27–52.

33	Kealey, 'The Writing of Social History in English-Canada, 1970–1984', 348. Thanks to Del Muise and James Opp for sharing their perspectives on the institutionalization of social history in Canada.

34	Franca Iacovetta, 'Springsteen's 'Working on a Dream' and Remembering Thirty Years of Activist Collaborations in Canadian Labour and Social History', *Left History*, Spring/Summer 2017, The University of Toronto, 5–26, 28.

35	*Social History/Histoire Sociale* https://muse.jhu.edu/journal/440 was established in 1968, https://www.hssh.ca/about-us/#anchor-journalhistory (accessed 25 November 2020); *Acadiensis* was established in 1971, https://www.acadiensis.ca/; *Urban History Review* was established in 1972, https://www.erudit.org/en/journals/uhr/; *Labour/Letravail* was established in 1976, http://www.lltjournal.ca/index.php/llt.

36	https://utorontopress.com/us/books/by-series/canadian-social-history-series (accessed 24 November 2020). On Greg Kealey's contribution see: https://www.unb.ca/faculty/emeritus/honorees/fredericton/htol/gregkealey1.html (accessed 25 November 2020). For more details on the establishment of the journals, see Kealey 'The Writing of Social History', 352. For details on the University of Toronto's social history series, see Kealey, 'The Writing', 363.

37	Franca Iacovetta, 'Springsteen's 'Working on a Dream' and Remembering Thirty Years of Activist Collaborations in Canadian Labour and Social History', *Left History*, Spring/Summer 2017, The University of Toronto, 5–26; Christopher Dummitt and Michael Dawson, *Contesting Clio's Craft: New Directions and Debates in Canadian History* (London: Institute for the Study of the Americas, University of London, 2009), Introduction.

38	Graeme Davison, 'Paradigms of Public History', *Australian Historical Studies* 24: 96, 4–15, 4. See also his '"Yarning in the Street": The Evolution of Australian Public History' in Stuart Macintyre, Lenore Layman and Jenny Gregory (eds.), *A Historian for All Seasons: Essays for Geoffrey Bolton* (Clayton: Monash University Publishing, 2017), 71–97.

39	Graeme Davison, 'Public History', *Oxford Companion to Australian History,* 538.

40	Ludmilla Jordanova, 'Public History' in her *History in Practice* (London: Bloomsbury, 2006 [2000]), 141 and Paul Ashton and Meg Foster, 'Public histories', in Handley et al., *New Directions in Social and Cultural History*, 153. For a defence of the professional historian, see James Gardner, 'Trust, Risk and Public History: A View from the United States', *Public History Review* 17 (2010): 53.

41 Paul Ashton and Meg Foster, 'Public Histories' in Handley et al., *New Directions*, 151–70.

42 Ashton and Foster, 'Public Histories', 153.

43 Mark Donnelly, 'Public History in Britain: Repossessing the Past', in Ashton and Trapeznik, *What Is Public History Globally*, 24–35, 25.

44 On the development of public history in Britain see Mark Donnelly, 'Public History in Britain: Repossessing the Past', in Ashton and Trapeznik, *What Is Public History Globally*, 24–35. Thomas Cauvin has compiled a map of public history programs offered around the world: https://www.google.com/maps/d/viewer?mid=1ZhqyOd B0BcJScyhKsjsTRo9V3Ps2mS2q&ll=16.943502516528437%2C0&z=2 (accessed 26 November 2020).

45 Lisa Murray and Mark Dunn, 'Public History in Australia', in Paul Ashton and Alex Trapeznik (eds.), *What Is Public History Globally?* (Bloomsbury, 2019), 13.

46 Graeme Davison, 'Public History', in Graeme Davison, John Hirst and Stuart Macintyre (eds.), *Oxford Companion to Australian History* (South Melbourne: Oxford University Press, 2001), 538.

47 David Dean and John Walsh, 'Some Reflections on Public History in Canada Today', *International Public History*, January 2020, https://www.degruyter.com/ view/journals/iph/2/2/article-20190021.xml. Michael Dove and Michelle Hamilton, 'Public History in Canada: Public Service or Public Service?', in Ashton and Trapeznik (eds.), *What Is History Globally?*, 37–49.

48 Shirley Tillotson, 'The Canadian Historical Review at 100 years', *Canadian Historical Review* 100, no. 3 (September 2019): 315–48, 323, 356.

49 Davison, 'Public History'.

50 Paul Ashton and Paula Hamilton, '"At Home with the Past: Initial Findings from the Survey"', *Australian Cultural History* 23 (2003): 27, 6. This was based on an American survey by Roy Rosenzweig and David Thelan, *The Presence of the Past: Popular Uses of History in American Life* (New York: Colombia University Press, 1998).

51 See Ashton and Hamilton, '"At Home with the Past"', 27, 6 and their "Connecting with History: Australians and Their Pasts"', in Kean and Ashton, *People and Their Pasts*, 23–42.

52 Margaret Conrad et al., *Canadians and Their Pasts* (University of Toronto Press, 2013), 13.

53 Raphael Samuel, *Theatres of Memory: Past and Present in Contemporary Culture* (London: Verso, 1994), 8. For Samuel's contribution to public history, see Hilda Kean, 'Public History and Raphael Samuel: A Forgotten Radical Pedagogy?', *Public History Review* 11 (2004): 51.

54 Michael Frisch, *A Shared Authority: Essays on the Craft and Meaning of Oral and Public History* (New York: State University of New York Press, 1990).

55 Including, Ann Curthoys, 'Crossing Over: Academic and Popular History', *Australasian Journal of Popular Culture* 1, no. 1 (2012): 718; Anna Clark, 'Ordinary People's History', *Journal of Australian Studies* 9, no. 1 (2012): 201–16; Hilda Kean and Paul Ashton, *People and Their Pasts: Public History Today* (Houndmills, Basingstoke: Palgrave Macmillan, 2008); Hilda Kean, Paul Martin, and Sally J. Morgan (eds.), *Seeing History: Public History in Britain Now* (London: Francis Bootle, 2000); Jerome De Groot, 'Genealogy, Hobby, Politics and Science', in his *Consuming History: Historians and Heritage in Contemporary Popular Culture* (London: Routledge, 2009).

56 Evans, *Fractured Families*, Intro.

57 Tanya Evans, 'Secrets and Lies: The Radical Potential of Family History', *History Workshop Journal.*

58 Lyndal Roper, *Oedipus and the Devil: Witchcraft, Sexuality and Religion in Early Modern Europe* (Abingdon: Routledge, 1994).

59 Clare Hemmings, 'Invoking Affect: Cultural Theory and the Ontological Turn', *Cultural Studies*, 19, 5 September 2005, 548–67; Barbara Rosenwein, 'Worrying about Emotions in History', *American Historical Review* 107, no. 3 (June 2002): 821–45.

60 Ute Frevert, *Emotions in History* (Budapest: Central University Press, 2011).

61 Joanna Bourke, 'Fear and Anxiety: Writing about Emotion in Modern History', *History Workshop Journal* 55 (2003): 111–33.

62 Sally Newman, '"The Freshman Malady": Rethinking the Ontology of the "Crush"', *Rethinking History* 16, no. 2 (2012): 279–301; Katie Barclay, 'Falling in Love with the Dead', *Rethinking History* 22, no. 4 (2018): 459–73.

63 Emily Robinson, 'Touching the Void: Affective History and the Impossible', *Rethinking History* 14, no. 4 (2010): 503–20, 517, 504.

64 Sara Ahmed, *The Cultural Politics of Emotions* (Edinburgh: Edinburgh University Press, 2004), 3.

65 'Jan Plamper conversation with Reddy, Rosenwein and Stearns', *History and Theory* 49, no. 2 (May 2010): 237–65, 262 and Peter Stearns, 'History of Emotions' in *Handbook of Emotions* 3rd ed. Michael Lewis, Jeannette Haviland-Jones and Lisa Feldman Barrett (2008).

66 Plamper, 'The History of Emotions', 262, 263. Peter Stearns founded *The Journal of Social History* in 1967, in the United States.

67 Jan Plamper, William Reddy, Barbara Rosenwein and Peter Stearns, 'The History of Emotions: An Interview with William Reddy, Barbara Rosenwein and Peter Stearns', *History and Theory* 49, no. 2 (May 2010): 237–65.

68 'Jan Plamper in conversation with Reddy, Rosenwein and Stearns', *History and Theory* 49, no. 2 (May 2010): 237–65, 263 and Barbara Rosenwein and Riccardo Cristiani, *What Is the History of the Emotions?* (Cambridge: Polity Press, 2018).

69 For an excellent summary of the work of all these scholars which is outside the scope of this book, see Rob Boddice, *The History of Emotions* (Manchester: Manchester University Press, 2018).

70 Barbara Rosenwein, 'Worrying about Emotions in History', Review Essay, *American Historical Association* 107, no. 3 (June 2002): 821–45; Barbara Rosenwein and Riccardo Cristiani, *What Is the History of the Emotions?* (Cambridge: Polity Press, 2018), Chapter 2 and Jan Plamper, *The History of Emotions: An Introduction* (Oxford: Oxford University Press, 2015), 252.

71 Jorma Kalela, 'Making History: The Historian and the Uses of the Past', in Hilda Kean and Paul Martin (eds.), *The Public History Reader* (Oxon: Routledge, 2013), 108.

72 Steven High, 'Sharing Authority in Writing Canadian History: The Case of Oral History' in Dummitt and Dawson's, *Contesting Clio's Craft*, 21–6.

73 Michael Kammen, 'Carl Becker Redivivus: Or, Is Everyone Really a Historian?', *History and Theory* 39, no. 2 (2000): 230–42, 234.

74 Australian Survey Response, 3 December 2016.

75 Australian Survey Response, No specific date given, 2016.

76 Australian Survey Response, No specific date given, 2016.

77 Australian Survey Response, Specific Date NG, 2016.

78 Canadian Survey Response, No specific date given, 2016.

79 Canadian Survey Response, Anon., 6th September 2016.

80 Australian Survey Response, 29th June 2016.

81 Canadian Survey Response, 5th September 2016.

82 Australian Survey Response, September 2016.

83 Australian Survey Response, 7th November 2016.

84 Australian Survey Response, 8th November 2016.

85 Australian Survey Response 16th October 2016.

86 Canadian Survey Response, 28th September 2016.

87 Australian Survey Response, CA 20 July 2016.

88 Australian Survey Response, Liam Roberts, 23rd September 2016.

89 Australian Survey Response, Julie Jones, 25th August 2016.

90 Canadian Survey Response, Ken McKinlay, 22nd September 2016. See also British Survey Response, 16th October 2016.

91 Canadian Survey Response, 5th September 2016.

92 British Survey Response, Hannah Frost, 12th September 2016.

93 British Survey Response, Hannah Frost, 12th September 2016.

94 British Survey Response, Hannah Frost, 12th September 2016.

95 British Survey Response, Helen Jenkins, 26th September 2016.

96 British Survey Response, Kate Hurst, 22nd September 2016.

97 Australian Survey Response, 16th October 2016. For more specific mentions of social history, see also Australian Survey Response, Patsy Trench, 2016; Australian

Survey Response, Julie Jones, 25th August 2016; Australian Survey Response, Janine McMinn, 2016. Canadian Survey Response, Rick Tank, 25th September 2016; Canadian Survey Response, Peggy Chaman, 30th August 2016; British Survey Response, Barbara Hearn, 9 October 2016.

98 British Survey Response, PC, 22nd September 2016. See also Australian Survey Response, Kerry Waight, 12th September 2016; Australian Survey Response, Shane O'Neil, 25th November 2016.

Chapter 2

1   Brenda Lee Canadian Survey Response, 5th September 2016.
2   Lynn Abrams, *Oral History Theory* (Abingdon: Routledge, 2016), http://www. auswhn.org.au/blog/oral-history/; Joan Sangster, 'Telling Our Stories: Feminist Debates and the Use of Oral History', *Women's History Review* 3, no. 1 (1994): 5–28, DOI:10.1080/09612029400200046.
3   Elizabeth Reese, Catherine Haden, and Robyn Fivush, 'Mother-child Conversations about the Past: Relationships of Style and Memory Over Time', *Cognitive Development* 8, no. 4 (1993): 403–30.; R. Fivush, 'Maternal Reminiscing Style and Children's Developing Understanding of Self and Emotion', *Clin Soc Work J* 35 (2007): 37–46. https://doi.org/10.1007/s10615-006-0065-1 https://doi.org/10.1016/ S0885-2014(05)80002-4; Fivush, 'Maternal Reminiscing Style and Children's Developing Understanding of Self and Emotion'.
4   Liz Gloyn, Vicky Crewe, and Laura King, 'Ties That Bind: Materiality, Identity, and the Life Course in the "Things" That Families Keep', *Journal of Family History* 43, no. 2 (2018): 157–76.
5   Paula Hamilton and Kate Darian Smith, 'Memory and History in Twenty-First Century Australia: A Survey of the Field', *Memory Studies* 5, no. 3 (2013): 370–83.
6   Wendy Bottero, 'Practising Family History: "Identity" as a Category of Social Practice', *The British Journal of Sociology* 66, no. 3(2015): 534–56, Anne-Marie Kramer, 'Kinship, Affinity and Connectedness: Exploring the Role of Genealogy in Personal Lives', *Sociology* 45, no. 3(2011): 379–95; Catherine Nash, 'Genealogical Identities', *Environment and Planning D: Society and Space* 20, no. 1 (2002): 27–52.
7   Catherine Nash, '"They're Family!": Cultural Geographies of Relatedness in Popular Genealogy', in Sara Armed, Anne-Marie Fortier and Mimi Sheller (eds.), *Uprootings/Regroundings: Questions of Home and Migration* (Oxford and New York: Berg, 2003), 179–203, 194.
8   Frigga Haug et al., *Female Sexualisation: A Collective Work of Memory* (London: E. Carter, Trans, Verso, 1987).

9   Jenny Onyx and Jennie Small, 'Memory-Work: The Method', *Qualitative Inquiry* 7, no. 6 (2001): 773–86, https://doi.org/10.1177/107780040100700608. See also Evans, de Groot, Stallard, 'I don't even trust'.

10 Christine Ingleton, 'The Use of Memory-Work to Explore the Role of Emotions in Learning', *Research and Development in Higher Education* 16 (1994): 265–71.

11 See Chapter One pp. Alison Madden, Canadian Survey Response, 29th August 2016. See also Donald Davis's Canadian Survey Response, 28th September 2016; Barbara Barclay's, Australian Survey Response, 16th October 2016; Brenda Lee, Canadian Survey Response, 5th September 2016.

12 RG, Canadian Survey Response, 29th August 2016.

13 Australian Survey Response, 16th October 2016.

14 See the first History Hour twitter discussion among the #HistoriansCollaborate network https://twitter.com/search?q=%23HistoriansCollaborate&src=typed_query (accessed 21st January 2021).

15 Shane O'Neil, 25th November 2016. See also Mary Jane's, Canadian Survey Response, 27th September 2016.

16 KD, English Survey Response, 17th October 2016.

17 Kate Hurst, English Survey Response, September 22nd 2016.

18 BL, Australian Survey Response, September 2016.

19 Shane O'Neil, Australian Survey Response, 25th November 2016. See also Mary Jane S. Canadian Survey Response, 27th September 2016.

20 Australian Survey Response, 16th October 2016. See also Candy Hawkins, Australian Survey Response, 8th October 2016.

21 Helen Jenkins, English Survey Response, 26th September 2016.

22 Betty O'Neill, Australian Survey Response, 21st August 2016. Her memoir was published in August 2020: *The Other Side of Absence: Discovering My Father's Secrets* (Ventura Press). See also Glenna Morrison's, Canadian Survey Response 1st September 2016; and Anne Cavanagh's, Australian Survey Response, 20th July 2016.

23 RG, Canadian Survey Response, 29th August 2016.

24 Barry Cobb, Australian Survey Response, 3rd October 2016.

25 Donald Davis, Canadian Survey Response, 28th September 2016.

26 Peggy Beckett, English Survey Response, 25th September 2016.

27 Mary Jane, Canadian Survey Response, 27th September 2016.

28 Brenda Lee, Canadian Survey Response, 5th September 2016.

29 TR, Canadian Survey Response, 25th September 2016; see also Matthew Benson's Canadian Survey Response, 26th September 2016; Pamela Fane, Canadian Survey Response, 8th October 2016; Peggy Chapman, Canadian Survey Response, 30th August 2016; Walter Crites, Canadian Survey Response, 3rd September 2016; Alan Bruce Campbell, Survey Response, 9th September 2016; Barbara Barclay, Australian Survey Response, 16th October 2016; Betty O'Neil, Australian Survey Response, 21st August 2016.

30 Glenna Morrison, Canadian Survey Response, 1st September 2016.

31 Justina Lui, email correspondence with the author, 12th September 2016; Justina Lui in discussion during an oral history interview with the author, 17th November 2016.

32 Peter Keeda, Australian Survey Response, 8th November 2016.

33 See also John Shrimski's Australian Jewish Genealogical Society Survey Response, 7th November 2016; Robin Dryen, Australian Jewish Genealogical Society Survey Response, 3rd December 2016.

34 John Shrimski's Australian Jewish Genealogical Society Survey Response, 7th November 2016. See also Peter Keeda's Australian Jewish Genealogical Society Survey Response, 2016.

35 Australian Survey Response, Dani Haski, 2nd September 2016.

36 www.coasit.org.au (accessed 11th December 2020).

37 Interview with Maria Linders 14th September 2016.

38 Canadian Survey Response, Brenda Lee, 6th September 2016.

39 Shurlee Swain and Nell Musgrove, 'We Are The Stories We Tell About Ourselves: Child Welfare Records and the Construction of Identity Among Australians Who, as Children, Experienced Out-Of-Home "Care"', *Archives and Manuscripts* 40 (2012): 1, 4–14, https://doi.org/10.1080/01576895.2012.668840. See also Delyth Edwards, *Cultural, Autobiographical and Absent Memories of Orphanhood: The Girls of Nazareth House Remember* (Cham, Switzerland: Palgrave, 2017).

40 Ashley Barnwell, 'Hidden Heirlooms: Keeping Family Secrets across Generations', *Journal of Sociology* 54, no. 3 (2017): 446–60.

41 Carol Smart, 'Families, Secrets, Memories', *Sociology* 45, no. 4 (2011): 539–53; Barnwell, 'Hidden Heirlooms'.

42 Jerome De Groot and Matthew Stallard, '"Things Are Coming Out That Are Questionable, We Never Knew About": DNA and the New Family History', *Journal of Family History* 45, no. 3 (2020): 274–94, 287.

43 Survey Response, Dianne Johnstone, 12th November 2016; talk following a presentation by the author and follow-up email communication with the author Nov 2016.

44 Ashley Barnwell, 'Family Secrets and the Slow Violence of Social Stigma', *Sociology* 53, no. 6 (2019): 1111–26, 1112.

45 See also Tanya Evans, 'Discovering Violence in the Family', in *Gender Violence in Australia: Historical Perspectives*, ed. Alana Piper and Ana Stevenson (Clayton, VIC: Monash University Publishing, 2019), 20–33.

46 Debra McAuslan, Canadian Survey Response, 29th September 2016, Brenda Lee, Canadian Survey Response, 5th September 2016. Linda Reid, Canadian Survey Response, 31st August 2016, Walter Crites, Canadian Survey Response, 3rd September 2016.

47   Irene Blackburn, Survey Response, 15th October 2016.

48   Gillian Rose, *Doing Family Photography: The Domestic, the Public and the Politics of Sentiment* (Farnham, Surrey UK: Ashgate, 2010), 8–9.

49   John Gillis, *A World of Their Own Making: A History of Myth and Ritual in Family Life* (Oxford: Oxford University Press, 1997), xvi.

50   Ruth Finnegan, 'Family Myths, Memories and Interviewing,' in *The Oral History Reader*, Robert Perks and Alistair Thompson (eds.), (New York: Routledge, 2006, 2nd ed), 180; Rapheal Samuel and Paul Thompson (ed.), *The Myths We Live By* (London: Routledge, 1990); Gillis, *A World of Their Own Making*; Penny Tinckler, 'Photo-Interviews: Listening to Talk About Photos,' in *Using Photographs in Social and Historical Research* (London: SAGE, 2014), https://dx.doi.org/10.4135/9781446288016.n9.

51   Asri Erll, 'Locating Family in Cultural Memory Studies,' *Journal of Comparative Family Studies* 42, no. 3, Families and Memories: Continuity and Social Change (May-June 2011), 303–18, 306.

52   Ibid., 306.

53   See also Evans, de Groot, Stallard, 'I Don't Even Trust'.

54   See also Paul Basu, *Highland Homecomings: Genealogy and Heritage Tourism in the Scottish Diaspora* (London: Routledge, 2007).

55   Carole Whelan, Canadian Survey Response, 4th September 2016.

56   Barbara Hearn, English Survey Response, 9th October 2016.

57   See also Anna Clark, *Private Lives, Public History* (Carlton, VIC: Melbourne University Press, 2016) and Tanya Evans and Anna Clark, 'Family History and Transnational Historical Consciousness,' in Anna Clark, Anne Rees and Alecia Simmonds (eds.), *Transnationalism, Nationalism and Australian History* (Singapore: Palgrave Macmillan, 2017), 167–78, https://doi.org/10.1007/978-981-10-5017-6_11.

Chapter 3

1   Australian Survey Response, Harriet Jones, 6th August 2016.

2   British Survey Response, 17th October 2016.

3   Australian Survey Response, John Stanhope, 10th November 2016.

4   Australian Survey May, vol. Response John Bennett, 26th September 2016.

5   On emotions and gender, see Peter Read, 'Before Rockets and Aeroplanes': Family History', *At Home with the Past, Australian Cultural History*, no. 23 (2003): 131–42, 133. Jan Plamper, William Reddy, Barbara Rosenwein and Peter Stearns, 'The History of Emotions: An Interview with William Reddy, Barbara Rosenwein and Peter Stearns', May, vol. 49, no. 2 (2010): 237–65.

6   Canadian Survey Response, Matthew Benson, 26th September 2016.

7   British Survey Response, 26th September 2016.

8   Bernard Gammerl, 'Can You Feel Your Research Results: How Do Deal with and Gain Insights from Emotions Generated during Oral History Interviews', in H. Flam and J. Kleres (eds.), *Methods of Exploring Emotions* (Abingdon: Routledge, 2015).

9   Australian Survey Response, Jane Harding, 6th August 2016.

10 British Survey Response, MP, 22nd September 2016. See also, Australian Survey Response, BL 22nd September 2016; Australian Survey Response, AM, 24th September 2016; Australian Survey Response, MN (anon) NG; Australian Survey Response, JM, 10th October 2016. See also Canadian Survey Response, Tina L Davis, 12th September 2016; Carole Turner, Australian Survey Response, NG; Canadian Survey Response, Gail Lewis, 30th August 2016; Canadian Survey Response, Donald Davis, 28th September 2016; Australian Survey Response, Betty O'Neill, 21st August 2016.

11 Australian Survey Response, Catherine Ong, 15th July 2016.

12 For a sociological perspective, see Anne-Marie Kramer, 'Kinship, Affinity and Connectedness: Exploring the Role of Genealogy in Personal Lives', *Sociology* 45 (2011): 379–95.

13 Judith Butler, *The Psychic Life of Power: Theories in Subjection* (Redwood City: Stanford, 1997); Lauren Berlant, *The Queen of America Goes to Washington City Essays on Recognition and Sexual Difference* (Durham: Duke University Press, 1997).

14 Steph Lawler, 'Rules of Engagement: Habitus, Power and Resistance', *Sociological Review, Special Issue: Feminism after Bourdieu*, edited by Lisa Adkins and Beverley Skeggs, volume 52, Issue 2 (October, 2004): 110–28, 111.

15 John Bynner, 'Whatever Happened to Lifelong Learning? And Does It Matter', *Journal of the British Academy*, 2017, https://www.britac.ac.uk/sites/default/files/03%20Bynner%201836.pdf.

16 Robert Stebbins, *Serious Leisure* (London: Transaction Publishers, 2007).

17 Wendy Bottero, 'Practising Family History: 'identity as a category of social practice', *British Journal of Sociology* 66, no. 3 (2015): 534–66 and Wendy Bottero, 'Who Do You Think They Were? How Family Historians Make Sense of Social Position and Inequality in the Past', *British Journal of Sociology* 63, no. 1 (2012): 54–74.

18 Jerome De Groot, 'On Genealogy', *The Public Historian* 37, no. 3 (2015): 102–27.

19 Barbara Barclay, Australian Survey Response, 5th September 2016.

20 Jeanette Tsoulos, Australian Survey Response, 5th October 2016.

21 Australian Survey Response, CA, 20th July 2016.

22 Canadian Survey Response, Deb McAuslan, 29th September 2016.

23 Australian Survey Response, Helen Dell, 24th September 2016. See also Australian Survey Response, Robyn Tassicker, 11th October 2016; Australian Survey Response, Julanne Henessey, 13th October 2016; Canadian Survey Response, RG, 29th August 2016; Australian Survey Response, Lilian Magill, 12th July 2016.

24 Australian Survey Response, Lilian Magill, 12th July 2016.

25 Australian Survey Response, Harriet Jones, 6th August 2016; See also, Australian Survey Response, HG, 24th August 2016. See also, British Survey Response, Dea Leamey, 28th September 2016.

26 See also Amy Smith, 'Family Webs: The Impact of Women's Genealogy Research on Family Communication', PhD thesis, Graduate College of Bowling Green State University, 2008. Her research was based on interviews with twenty-two family historians.

27 Australian Survey Response, NM, 2016

28 Australian Survey Response, Kay Spence, Specific date not given, 2016.

29 Barbara Hearn, Survey Response, 9th October 2016.

30 https://www.google.co.uk/amp/s/www.bbc.com/news/uk-england-london-54886813.amp (accessed 28th May 2021).

31 https://www.education4change.org.uk/ (accessed 28th May 2021).

32 Peter Seixas (ed), *Theorizing Historical Consciousness* (Toronto: University of Toronto Press, 2006); Anna Clark and Tanya Evans, 'Family History and Transnational Historical Consciousness', in Anna Clark, Anne Rees and Alecia Simmonds (eds.), *Transnationalism, Nationalism and Australian History* (Basingstoke: Palgrave Macmillan, 2017), 167–78; Anna Clark, 'Inheriting the Past: Exploring Historical Consciousness across Generations', *Historical Encounters: A Journal of Historical Consciousness, Historical Cultures, and History Education* 1, no. 1 (2014): 88–102; Stephane Levesque, *Thinking Historically* (Toronto: University of Toronto Press, 2008).

33 Emma Shaw, "Life in the 'Past Lane': An Exploration of the motives and metahistorical understanding of family history researchers', PhD thesis, University of Newcastle, 2017; Emma Shaw, conference paper 'Family history as public pedagogy: learning to "do" and produce history in public spaces', paper presented at 'Related Histories' conference, 2017, National Library of Australia, 28th November; Peter Lee, 'History Teaching and the Philosophy of History', *History and Theory* XXII, no. 4(1983): 19–49; Alan Booth, 'Pedagogy and the Practice of Academic History in Late-Twentieth-century Britain', *Rethinking History: The Journal of Theory and Practice* 13, no. 3 (2009): 317–44.

34 British Survey Response, HSN, 15th September 2016.

35 Christine Clifford, Survey Response, 16th October 2016.

36 On the concern over numbers, see https://www.nytimes.com/2020/05/01/us/coronavirus-college-enrollment.html; https://www.theguardian.com/australia-news/2020/jun/19/incredibly-frustrating-australian-year-12-students-express-dismay-at-skyrocketing-fees-for-arts-degrees; https://www.theguardian.com/commentisfree/2020/jun/19/doubling-university-fees-for-the-arts-will-leave-australia-less-equipped-for-our-complex-world (all accessed 4th December 2020).

37 Tanya Evans, 'Enhancing Student Engagement through Flipping: A Case Study in Australian History', *The History Teacher*, Society for History Education affiliate of American Historical Association, 51, 4, August, 2018, 611–38.

38 Booth, 'Pedagogy and the Practice of Academic History in Late-Twentieth-century Britain', 317–44.

39 Adele Nye and Marnie Hughes-Warrington, Jill Roe, Penny Russell, Mark Peel, Desley Deacon, Amanda Laugeson and Paul Kiem, 'Historical Thinking in Higher Education', *History Australia*, 6:3, 2016, 73.1–73.16, 2016, DOI:10.2104/ha090073.

40 Noeline Kyle, 'Genealogy', in Graeme Davison, John Hirst and Stuart Macintyre (eds.), *The Oxford Companion to Australian History* (Oxford, [1998], 2001), 280–1.

41 Australian Survey Response, Ron Sinclair, 22nd August 2016.

42 Australian Survey Response, Irene Morgan, 23rd September 2016.

43 British Survey Response, Dea Leamey, 28th September 2016; See also, Australian Survey Response, Jenny Wilson, 25th July 2016; British Survey Response, Christine Clifford, 14th October 2016; Australian Survey Response, Marilyn Myers, NG.

44 Australian Survey Response, Irene Morgan, 23rd September 2016.

45 Canadian Survey Response, Glenna Morrison, 1st September 2016; Australian Survey Response, John Dean, 29th June 2016; Australian Survey Response, Ambra Sancin, 4th September 2016; Australian Survey Response, Julie Jones, 25th August 2016; Australian Survey Response, Karin Davis, 14th July 2016; Australian Survey Response, Pennie Griffiths, NG.

46 Australian Survey Response, Pennie Griffiths, NG.

47 Canadian Survey Response, Brenda Lee, 5th September 2016.

48 Canadian Survey Response, Donald Davis, 28th September 2016.

49 Canadian Survey Response, Mary Jane, 27th September 2016.

50 Australian Survey Response, LB, 23rd September 2016. For other mentions of pride, see Australian Survey Responses, Jenny Wilson, 25th July 2016; John Dean, 29th June 2016; Les De Belin, ND, MN; Thais Hardman, 25th September 2016; Caroline R, 2nd December 2016; Elizabeth Capelin, 3rd August 2016; Christine Hutchison, 2nd February 2017; TH, 11th October 2016; Catherine Ong, 15th July 2016; VM (anon) ng; Canadian: Marie Bentley Egglesfield, 12th January 2017.

51 Australian Survey Response, 30th September 2016. See also Canadian Survey Response, Linda Reid, 31st August 2016; Canadian Survey Response, LG, 6th September 2016; Canadian Survey Response, TR, 25th September 2016; Australian Survey Response, Ian Devenish, 12th October 2016; Australian Survey Response, Stephanie Hume, September 2016; British Survey Response, Jill Gregory, 26th September 2016; Australian Survey Response, 21st July 2016; Australian Survey Response, HG, 24th August 2016.

52 British Survey Response, Dea Leamey, 28th September 2016.

53 Australian Survey Response, Jenny Wilson, 25th July 2016.

54 Canadian Survey Response, Brenda Turner, ND.

55 Canadian Survey Response, RG, 29th August 2016.

56   Australian Survey Response, Tracey Treloar, 30th September 2016.

57   Australian Survey Response, HG, 24th August 2016.

58   Australian Survey Response, Ian Devenish, 12th October 2016.

59   Australian Survey Response, Jenny Wilson, 25th July 2016.

60   Australian Survey Response, CA, 20th July 2016.

61   Australian Survey Response, Marilyn Myers, NG.

62   British Survey Response, Jan Brown, 17th October 2016.

63   Australian Survey Response, AM, 24th September 2016.

64   Australian Survey Response, Maureen Cooney, NG.

65   British Survey Response, Irene Blackburn, 15th October 2016.

66   Canadian Survey Response, Carole Whelan, 4th September 2016.

67   British Survey Response, Christine Clifford, 14th October 2016. See also Australian Survey Responses, Candy Hawkins, 8th October 2016; Helen Dell, 24th September 2016; Jackie Bobich, 27th September 2016; Australian Survey Response, Lilian Magill, 12th July 2016.

68   Australian Survey Response, CA, 20th July 2016.

69   Australian Survey Response, Antonia Jones, 10th October 2016.

70   Canadian Survey Response, Brenda Lee, 5th September 2016.

71   Australian Survey Response, Betty O'Neill, 21st August 2016.

72   Australian Survey Response, Dawn Spriggett, 21st December 2016.

73   Deb McAuslan, Canadian Survey Response, 29th September 2016.

74   RG, Canadian Survey Response, 29th August 2016.

75   Carolyn Jones, Australian Survey Response, date NG.

76   Australian Survey Response, 16th October 2016.

77   Australian Survey Response, Michelle Goldsmith, 30th August 2016.

78   Peter Stearns, *Shame: A Brief History* (Champain: University of Illinois Press, 2017), 90.

79   Barbara H. Rosenwein and Riccardo Cristiani, *What Is the History of Emotions?* (Cambridge: Polity Press, 2018).

80   Stearns, *The Revival of Shame,* in *Shame: A Brief History,* p. 99. John Demos (as cited in C. Z. Stearns & Stearns, 1988, 69–86). See also Deborah Cohen, *Family Secrets: Shame and Privacy in Modern Britain* (Oxford: Oxford University Press, 2013) and Pat Thane and Tanya Evans, *Sinners, Scroungers, Saints: Unmarried Motherhood in Twentieth-Century England* (Oxford: Oxford University Press, 2012).

81   Australian Survey Response, 1st October 2016.

82   Peter Stearns, *Shame: A Brief History,* 76.

83   Australian Survey Response, Ian Devenish, 12th October 2016.

84   Stearns, *Shame,* 120.

85   Australian Survey Response, Barry Cobb, 3rd October 2016.

86   Australian Survey Response, J. Brian Hardaker, 26th September 2016.

87   Australian Survey Response, Carolyn Jones, no date, 2016.

88 Canadian Survey Response, Alison Madden, 29th August 2016.

89 British Survey Response, PC, 22nd September 2016.

90 Australian Survey Response, Patsy Trench, NG, 2016.

91 Canadian Survey Response, Debra McAuslan, 29th September 2016. See also Canadian Survey Response, Gail Benjafield, 2nd September 2016.

92 Australian Survey Responses, Betty O'Neil, 21st August 2016; Quotation from the response from Jane Harding, 6th August 2016; John Bennett, 26th September 2016; Julanne Henessey, 13th October 2016; Kerry Waight, 12th September 2016.

93 Rebecca Curtin, 'Australian families suffering "silent war" of domestic violence says advocate', *ABC News*, 18 May 2016.

94 Wendy O'Brien and Kate Fitz-Gibbon, '"Silent victims": Royal Commission recommends better protections for child victims of family violence', *The Conversation*, 1 April 2016.

95 https://www.theguardian.com/society/2020/dec/01/the-worst-year-domestic-violence-soars-in-australia-during-covid-19 (accessed 4th December 2020).

96 'Hear them speak', *The Guardian Labs*, accessed 19 December 2017, https://www.theguardian.com/nab-more-that-matters/ng-interactive/2017/dec/07/hear-them-speak-victims-of-domestic-violence-share-their-stories#/.

97 Sarah Wendt, 'Why don't we speak up when we see signs of domestic violence?' *The Conversation*, 1 October 2014.

98 Australian Survey Response, 24th August 2016.

99 Family & Community Services NSW, 'Focus topic: Under-reporting of domestic violence assaults', *Women in NSW* (NSW Government, 2013); 'Fact file: Domestic violence in Australia', *ABC News*, 15 April 2016.

100 Australian Survey Response, Caryn Paterson, date NG, 2016.

101 She's one of the few participants who has asked to be anonymized.

102 Margaret Nelly (anonymized), Survey Response, 2016.

103 Australian Survey Response, Karin Davis, 14th July 2016.

104 Australian Survey Response, Les De Belin, date NG 2016.

105 For more details, see Alana Piper and Ana Stephenson (eds.), *Gender Violence in Australia* (Basingstoke: Palgrave, 2019).

106 Sally Newman, 'The Freshman Malady': Rethinking the Ontology of the "Crush"', *Rethinking History* 16, no. 2 (2012): 279–301, 282.

107 Australian Survey Response, Barbara Barclay, 16th October 2016.

108 Australian Survey Response, Harriet Jones, 6th August 2016.

109 Australian Survey Response, Susan Hinds, 19th October 2016.

110 Australian Survey Response, Carol Turner, NG. See also Australian Survey Response, LB, 23rd September 2016; Australian Survey Response, Jeannette Tsoulos, 5th October 2016.

111 Nancy Chodorow, *The Reproduction of Mothering: Psychoanalysis and the Sociology of Mothering* (Oakland: University of California Press, 1978).

Chapter 4

1   Australian Survey Response, Carol Turner, Specific date not given, 2016.

2   Simon Michael Titley-Bayes, 'Family History Societies in England, c. 1945–2006, Culture, Identity and ImMortality', PhD thesis, University of York, 2006, 91.

3   Barbara Rosenwein, *Emotional Communities in the Middle Ages* (Ithaca, New Jersey: Cornell University Press, 2006), and Barbara Rogoff, 'Developing Understanding of the Idea of Communities of Learners', *Mind, Culture and Activity* 1, no. 4 (Fall 1994): 209–29. See also Rob Boddice on emotional communities in his, 'The History of Emotions' in Handley et al., *New Directions*, 49.

4   Barbara H. Rosenwein, and Riccardo Cristiani, *What Is the History of Emotions?* (Polity Press, 2018), 24.

5   Canadian Survey Response, Pamela Fane, 8th October 2016.

6   For further details on social capital, see John Field, *Social Capital*, Second Edition (London: Routledge, 2008).

7   British Survey Response, Jan Brown, 17th October 2016.

8   https://raogk.org/ (accessed 7th December 2020).

9   Amy Smith, '"Family Webs" The Impact of Women's Genealogy Research on Family communication', PhD thesis, Bowling Green State University, 2008, 39.

10 British Survey Response, Jan Brown, 17th October 2016.

11 British Survey Response, Irene Blackburn, 15th October 2016.

12 For further evidence using Australian survey data, see also Susan Moore, Doreen Rosenthal and Rebecca Robinson, *The Psychology of Family History* (Abingdon: Routledge, 2020), Chapter 5: 'Beyond the Self', 48–57.

13 Emma Shaw, 'Life in the Past Lane': An exploration of the motives and meta historical understanding of family history researchers., University of Newcastle (Australia) PhD thesis, 2018.

14 Henriette Roued-Cunliffe and Copeland, *Participatory Heritage* (London: Facet, 2017). Henriette Roued-Cunliffe, 'Visualising Historical Networks, Family Trees and Wikipedia', *Academic Quarter*, Volume 15. Autumn, 2017; Henriette Roued Cunlifee, 'Collection Building Amongst Heritage Amateurs', *Collection Building* 36, no. 3 (2017): 108–14.

15 Steph Lawler, 'Rules of Engagement: Habitus, Power and Resistance', in Lisa Adkins and Beverley Skeggs (eds.), *Sociological Review, Special Issue: Feminism after Bourdieu* (Oxford: Blackwell), vol. 52, Issue 2, October, 2004, 110–28.

16 John Field, 'Good for your soul? Adult learning and mental well-being', *International Journal of Lifelong Education* 28, no. 2 (2009): 175–91 on the benefits of life learning.

17 Pierre Bourdieu, 'The Forms of Capital', J.G. Richardson (ed.), *Handbook of Theory and Research for the Sociology of Education* (New York: Greenwood Press, 1986), 241–58; Field, *Social Capital*, 117–19.

18 Tanya Evans, 'Enhancing Student Engagement through Flipping: A Case Study in Australian History', *The History Teacher* 51, no. 4 (2018): 611–38.

19 For further example of successful pedagogy, see Alan Booth, 'Pedagogy and the Practice of Academic History in Late Twentieth-Century Britain', *Rethinking History* 13, no. 3 (2009): 317–44.

20 See also Amy Smith, '"Family Webs" The Impact of Women's Genealogy Research on Family communication', PhD thesis, Bowling Green State University, 2008, 8.

21 British Survey Response, Dee Leamy, 28th September 2016.

22 British Survey Response, Peggy Beckett, 25th September 2016.

23 Canadian Survey Response, Brenda Turner, ND. See also Canadian Survey Response, Deb McAuslan, 29th September 2016; Australian Survey Response, BL, 22nd September 2016.

24 Canadian Survey Response, Donald Davis, 28th September 2016.

25 Canadian Survey Response, Donald Davis, 28th September 2016. See also Canadian Survey Responses, Mary Jane, 27th September 2016; Gail Benjafield, 30th August 2016.

26 Canadian Survey Response, Ken McKinlay, 22nd September 2016. See also Canadian Survey Response, TR, 25th September 2016.

27 Moore et al., *The Psychology*, 50.

28 Canadian Survey Response, Anon., 6th September 2016. See also Canadian responses, Glenna Morrison, 1st September 2016; Ken McKinlay, 22nd September 2016.

29 Canadian Survey Response, Brenda Lee, 5th September 2016. See also Canadian Survey Responses, Matthew Benson, 26th September 2016; Pamela Fane, 8th October 2016.

30 Canadian Survey Response, Peggy Homans Chapman, 30th August 2016.

31 Australian Survey Response, Barbara Barclay, 16th October 2016.

32 Australian Survey Response, Caryn Patterson, ND. See also Karin Davis, 14th July 2016; Vicki Hilder, 2016.

33 Australian Survey Response, Shane O'Neil, 25th November 2016.

34 Canadian Survey Response, 29th September 2016.

35 Australian Survey Response, Caryn Patterson, ND. See also Australian Survey Response, anonymized (MN) and LB, 23rd September 2016, Robyn Tassicker, 11th October 2016.

36 Australian Survey Response, Jeannette Tsoulos, 5th October 2016. See also Australian Survey Response, Sharon Wheelock, Nd. See also Shane O'Neil, 25th November 2016; Stephanie Hume, September 2016; Thais Hardman, 25th September 2016; Tracey Treloar, 30th September 2016.

37 Australian Survey Response, Harriet Jones, 6th August 2016.

38 British Survey Response, Barbara Hearn, 9th October 2016.

39 British Survey Response, SA, 29th September 2016.

40 British Survey Response, Bob H, 25th September 2016. See also British Survey Response, Christine Clifford, 14th October 2016.

41 Australian Survey Response, Julie Jones, 25th August 2016.

42 Field, *Social Capital*, 119–25, quote 122.

43 Australian Survey Response, Jenny Wilson, 25th July 2016.

44 https://www.abc.net.au/news/2017-02-21/community-heritage-groups-at-risk-of-becoming-history/8289296; https://www.historians.org/publications-and-directories/perspectives-on-history/december-2012/the-future-of-local-historical-societies; https://anglo-celtic-connections.blogspot.com/2012/03/counteracting-decline-of-genealogical.html; https://australiascience.tv/community-groups-battle-volunteer-decline/ (accessed 4th December 2020).

45 British Survey Response, PC, 22nd September 2016.

46 Australian Survey Response, LB, 23rd September 2016.

47 Canadian Survey Response, Alison Madden, 29th August 2016.

48 Australian Survey Response, AM, 24th September 2016.

49 Canadian Survey Response, RG, 29th August 2016.

50 Canadian Survey Response, Brenda Turner, ND, 2016.

51 Canadian Survey Response, Carole Whelan, 4th September 2016.

52 Canadian Survey Response, Debra McAuslan, 29th September 2016.

53 Canadian Survey Response, Donald Davis, 28th September 2016.

54 Canadian Survey Response, Peggy Homans Chapman, 30th August 2016.

55 Smith, 'Family Webbs', 38–9.

56 Australian Survey Response, Lilian Magill, ND, 2016.

57 Australian Survey Response, anonymized, ND, 2016. See also Australian Survey Response, Vicki Hilder, ND, 2016. See also https://www.ancestry.com/corporate/blog/using-facebook-to-grow-your-family-tree/; https://www.gsq.org.au/event/using-social-media/ and https://www.familytreemagazine.com/resources/online/best-social-media-for-genealogy/ (all accessed 7th December 2020).

58 Canadian Survey Response, Richard Tank, 25th September 2016.

59 Australian Survey Response, BB, 16th October 2016. See also Australian Survey Response, Betty O'Neill, 21st August 2016; Carolyn Jones, ND, 2016.

60 Thanks to Laura Dundas for her work as a Macquarie University PACE student in Semester 2 2020.

61 For example, see for Canada: French-Canadian Legacy Podcast https://fclpodcast.com/; Digging Into the Past: Family History in Canada https://www.bac-lac.gc.ca/eng/news/podcasts/Pages/family-history-canada.aspx; Maple Stars and Stripes https://maplestarsandstripes.com/ and for Britain: BBC4 Tracing your roots https://www.bbc.co.uk/programmes/b006zbxm/episodes/downloads; Amateur Family History Podcast (UK) https://podcasts.apple.com/gb/podcast/amateur-family-history-podcast-uk/id1448636109.

62 Canadian Survey Response, Debra McAuslan, 29th September 2016.

63 Australian Survey Response, John Thomas Dean, 29th June 2016. See also Australian Survey Response, JM, 10th October 2016.

64 British Survey Response, Helen Jenkins, 26th September 2016.

65 British Survey Response, Irene Blackburn, 15th October 2016.

66 Australian Survey Response, Janelle Collins, ND, 2016.

67 British Survey Response, Kath Robinson, ND, 2016. See also Australian Survey Response, Les De Belin, ND, 2016.

68 Canadian Survey Response, Alison Madden, 29th August 2016.

69 Canadian Survey Response, RG, 29th August 2016.

70 Australian Survey Response, 16th October 2016.

71 Australian Survey Response, Harriet Jones, 6th August 2016.

72 Australian Survey Response, JM, 10th October 2016. See also Australian Survey Response, Stephanie Hume, September 2016; Tracey Treloar, 30th September 2016.

73 Australian Survey Response, Kay Spence, ND, 2016.

74 Canadian Survey Response, Peggy Chapman, 30th August 2016.

75 Australian Survey Response, Robyn Dryen, Australian Jewish Genealogical Society, 3rd December 2016.

76 https://support.ancestry.com.au/s/article/Brick-Wall-Solutions; https://www.familytreemagazine.com/strategies/true-genealogy-brick-walls/; https://www.findmypast.co.uk/content/expert-brick-wall; https://media.nationalarchives.gov.uk/index.php/brick-walls-and-lost-ancestors/; https://www.tracesmagazine.com.au/2015/12/ancestry-dna-testing-for-family-history-breaking-down-brick-walls-a-case-study/ (accessed 7th December 2020).

77 British Survey Response, MP, 22nd September 2016. See also Australian Survey Response, Julanne Hennessey, 13th October 2016; Julie Jones, 25th August 2016, Les De Belin, ND; Vicki Hilder, ND, 2016.

78 Australian Survey Response, Stephanie Hume, September 2016.

79 Canadian Survey Response, 28th September 2016.

80 British Survey Response, Kate Hurst, 22nd September 2016. See also British Survey Response, Kath Robinson, 2016.

81 Australian Survey Response, Robin Dryen, AJGS, 3rd December 2016.

82 https://www.theguardian.com/lifeandstyle/2014/apr/05/family-tree-apps-genealogy-laura-berry (accessed 7th December 2020).

83 Australian Survey Response, Harriet Jones, 6th August 2016.

84 British Survey Response, Janet Few, 22nd September 2016.

85 British Survey Response, Kate Hurst, 22nd September 2016.

86 British Survey Response, Kate Hurst, 22nd September 2016.

87 Canadian Survey Response, Mary Holland, 25th September 2016.

88 Australian Survey Response, Dawn Springett, 21st December 2016.

89 Australian Survey Response, Tracey Treloar, 30th September 2016.

90 Australian Survey Response, Kay Spence, ND, 2016.

91 Australian Survey Response, Harriet Jones, 6th August 2016.

92 British Survey Response, 22nd September 2016.

93 Canadian Survey Response, RG, 29th August 2016.

94 Australian Survey Response, Gail Wright, 1st October 2016.

95 Canadian Survey Response, Walter Crites, 3rd September 2016.

96 Australian Survey Response, Gail Wright, 1st October 2016.

97 British Survey Response, Hannah Frost, 12th September 2016.

98 For further discussion on the ethics of family history written by a family historian, see Penny Walters, *Ethical Dilemmas in Genealogy* (Self Published, San Bernardino, California, 2020). Ancestry.com also has a Message Board dedicated to 'Ethics in Family History' to guide researchers.

99 See also Ashley Barnwell, 'Keeping it secret: Revealing the secrets in your family history' (ed. K. Hyde) [Blog post]. December 15 2017; https://blogs.ancestry.co.uk/ancestry/2017/12/15/keeping-it-secret-revealing-the-secrets-in-your-family-history/.

100 https://www.cyndislist.com/etiquette/general/ (accessed 8.10.20). See also Moore et al., *The Psychology of Family History*, Chapter 9 'Ethical Dilemmas', 93–103.

101 British Survey Response, Christine Clifford, 14th October 2016.

102 British Survey Response, Jill Gregory, 26th September 2016.

103 Australian Survey Response, LB, 23rd September 2016.

104 Australian Survey Response, ND, 2016.

105 Australian Survey Response, Barry Cobb, 3rd October 2016.

106 Canadian Survey Response, Brenda Lee, 5th September 2016.

107 Canadian Survey Response, Gail Lewis, 30th August 2016.

108 Carol Smart, 'Families, Secrets, Memories', *Sociology* 45, no. 4 (2011): 539–53.

109 Australian Survey Response, CA, 20th July 2016.

110 Australian Survey Response, MJ, 10th October 2016.

111 Sian Lindley, 'Before I forget: From Personal Memory to Family History', *Human-Computer Interaction* 27, no. 1–2 (2012): 13–36.

112 Australian Survey Response, PS, 17th October 2016.

113 Ibid.

114 Canadian Survey Response, GL, 6th September 2016.

115 Australian Survey Response, Robyn Tassicker, 11th October 2016.

116 Australian Survey Response, SM, 16th October 2016.

117 Canadian Survey Response, Alan Campbell, 9th September 2016.

118 Australian Survey Response, Susan Hinds, 19th October 2016.

119 Australian Survey Response, Carole Turner, ND, 2016.

120 British Survey Response, Barbara Hearn, 9th October 2016.

121 Australian Survey Response, JA, 10th October 2016.

122 Australian Survey Response, Harriet Jones, 6th August 2016.

Chapter 5

1   https://www.theguardian.com/science/2013/jan/04/barack-obama-empathy-deficit (accessed 30th October 2020). Obama's speech on YouTube: https://www.youtube.com/watch?v=4md_A059JRc (accessed 30th October 2020). The transcript of Obama's speech to students at North Western University: https://www.northwestern.edu/newscenter/stories/2006/06/barack.html (accessed 30th October 2020).

2   British Survey Response, Kate Hurst, 22nd September 2016.

3   Peter De Seixas, *Theorizing Historical Consciousness* (Toronto: University of Toronto Press, 2006); Anna Clark, 'Inheriting the Past: Exploring Historical Consciousness across Generations', *Historical Encounters: A Journal of Historical Consciousness* 1, no. 1 (2014): 88–102; Stephane Levesque, *Thinking Historically* (Toronto: University of Toronto Press, 2008); Tanya Evans and Anna Clark, 'Family History and Transnational Historical Consciousness', in Anna Clark, Anne Rees and Alecia Simmonds (eds.), *Transnationalism, Nationalism and Australian History* (Basingstoke: Palgrave, 2017).

4   Australian Survey Response, Carol Turner, Specific date NG, 2016.

5   Jason Endacott, 'Reconsidering Affective Engagement in Historical Empathy', *Theory and Research in Social Education* 38, no. 1 (2010): 6–47, DOI:10.1080/0093 3104.2010.10473415 and Jason L. Endacott, 'Negotiating the Process of Historical Empathy', *Theory & Research in Social Education* 42, no. 1 (2014): 4–34, DOI:10.108 0/00933104.2013.826158.

6   Tyson Retz, *Empathy and History: Historical Understanding in Re-Enactment, Hermeneutics and Education* (New York and Oxford: Berghahn Books, 2018), 2–18; David Burchell, 'The Trouble with Empathy', *Griffith Review* (Winter 2005): 115–32. Inga Clendinnen, 'The History Question: Who Owns the Past', *Quarterly Essay*, September 2006; Paul Bloom, *Against Empathy: The Case for Rational Compassion* (London: Harper Collins, 2016) (Breithaupt, 2019).

7   Susan Lanzoni, *Empathy: A History* (New Haven: Yale University Press, 2018), 9; Hanna Roisin, 'The End of Empathy', NPR, April 15th 2019, https://www.npr.org/2019/04/15/712249664/the-end-of-empathy?fbclid=IwAR0p16X-C6-v3U0Ch-kck7ne6ryKwuxPity3o0OxirP2SCvraj-K60VW6o4; Burchell, 'The Trouble with Empathy', 115–32.

8   Rob Boddice, 'The History of the Emotions', in Handley et al., *New Directions*, 54–5.

9   Lanzoni, *Empathy*, 12.

10 Tyson Retz, Introduction, *Empathy and History*, 14.

11 Fritz Breithaupt, *The Dark Sides of Empathy* (Ithaca: Cornell University Press, 2019).

12 Lanzoni, *Empathy*, 15.

13 For a flavour, see: Ann Low-Beer, 'Empathy and History', *Teaching History* (1989): 8–12; Cairns, John, 'Some Reflections on Empathy in History', *Teaching History* (1989): 13–18; Tony Boddington, 'Empathy and the Teaching of History', *British Journal of Educational Studies* 28, no. 1 (1980): 13–19; Richard Harris and L. Foreman-Peck, '"Stepping into other peoples" Shoes': Teaching and Assessing Empathy in the Secondary History Curriculum', *International Journal of Historical Learning, Teaching and Research* 4, no. 2 (2004): 98–111; Endacott, 'Negotiating the Process of Historical Empathy', 42, 4–34.

14 Jason Endacott and Sarah Brooks, 'Historical Empathy: Perspectives and Responding to the Past', in *Wiley International Handbook of History Teaching and Learning* (Hoboken: Wiley Publishing, 2018).

15 Keith Barton, 'History, Humanistic Education and Participatory Democracy' in Ruth Sandwell (ed.), *To The Past: History Education, Public Memory and Citizenship in Canada* (Toronto: University of Toronto Press, 2006), 54–6.

16 Peter Lee, 'History Teaching and Philosophy of History', *History and Theory* 22, no. 4 (1983): 40. For a detailed account of Lee's impact on history education, see Retz, *Empathy and History*, Chapter Two, 'The Influence of the Philosophy of History' and Chapter Nine 'Competing Conceptions'.

17 Jason Endacott and Sarah Brooks, 'An Updated Theoretical and Practical Model of Historical Empathy', *Social Studies Research and Practice* 8 (2013): 41–58.

18 Retz, *Empathy and History*, Chapter 10 'Historical Thinking and Historical Consciousness', 3. See also Lévesque, *Thinking Historically*.

19 Sam Wineburg, *Historical Thinking*, xi; Levesque, *Historical Thinking*, 30.

20 Retz, *Empathy and History,* Intro, 6.

21 Peter Seixas (ed.), *Theorizing Historical Consciousness* (Toronto: University of Toronto Press, 2004) and Peter Seixas and Tom Morton, *The Big Six: Historical Thinking Concepts Student Book* (Calgary, Canada: Nelson, 2012).

22 Levesque, *Historical Thinking*, 28.

23 Ibid.

24 Retz, *Empathy and History*, Conclusion, final page.

25 Anna Clark and Carla Peck (eds.), *Contemplating Historical Consciousness: Notes from the Field* (New York and Oxford: Berghan Books, 2020); Silvia Edling, Heather Sharp, Jan Lofstrom and Niklas Ammert, 'The Good Citizen: Revisiting Moral Motivations for Introducing Historical Consciousness in History Education Drawing on the Writings of Gadamer', *Citizenship, Social and Economics Education* 19, no. 2 (2020): 133–50 and Silvia Edling, Heather Sharp, Jan Lofstrom and Niklas Ammert, 'Why Is Ethics Important in History Education? A Dialogue between the Various Ways of Understanding the Relationships between Ethics and Historical Consciousness', *Ethics and Education* 15, no. 3: 336–54.

26   Peter Seixas, 'Progress, Presence and Historical Consciousness: Confronting the
     Past, Present and Future in Postmodern Time', *Pedagogica Historica: International
     Journal of the History of Education* 48, no. 6 (2012): 859–72, 871.

27   Edling et al., 'The Good Citizen', 135.

28   Ibid., 133–50.

29   Canadian Survey Response, Gail Benjafield, 2nd September 2016.

30   Canadian Survey Response, Brenda Turner, ND, 2016.

31   Canadian Survey Response, Brenda Lee, 5th September 2016.

32   John Tosh, *Why History Matters* (Palgrave: Houndmills, 2008), 127, 65.

33   Barton, 'History, Humanistic Education, and Participatory Democracy', 54–6.

34   Australian Survey Response, Carolyn Jones, ND, 2016.

35   Canadian Survey Response, Carole Whelan, 4th September 2016.

36   Canadian Survey Response, Mary Jane, 27th September 2016.

37   Canadian Survey Response, BG, 2nd September 2016.

38   Canadian Survey Response, 30th August 2016. See also Glenna Morrison's Survey
     Response, 1st Sept 2016.

39   Canadian Survey Response, Glenna Morrison, 1st September 2016.

40   British Survey Response, MP, 22nd September 2016.

41   Australian Survey Response, Karin Davis, 14th July 2016.

42   Australian Survey Response, Maureen Cooney, ND, 2016.

43   Australian Survey Response, Tracey Treloar, 30th September 2016.

44   Lanzoni, E*mpathy*, 18.

45   Australian Survey Response, Robyn Tassicker, 11th October 2016.

46   Australian Survey Response, Karin Tonks, 14th July 2016.

47   Canadian Survey Response, Ken McKinlay, 22nd September 2016.

48   Australian Survey Response, Carolyn Jones, ND, 2016.

49   Bloom, *Against Empathy*, 3–4.

50   Ibid., 7.

51   Martha Nussbaum, 'Compassion: The Basic Social Emotion', *Social Philosophy and
     Policy* 13, no. 1 (1996): 27–58. doi:10.1017/S0265052500001515.

52   Bloom, *Against Empathy*, 23, 166.

53   Australian Survey Response, CA, 20th July 2016.

54   Canadian Survey Response, RG, 29th August 2016.

55   Bloom, *Against Empathy*, 94.

56   Canadian Survey Response, Mary Holland, 25th September 2016.

57   Australian Survey Response, Karin Davis, 14th July 2016.

58   Australian Survey Response, JA, 10th October 2016.

59   Australian Survey Response, Jackie Bobich, 27th September 2016. See also
     Australian Survey Response, SM, 16th October 2016.

60   Australian Survey Response, Jannelle Collins, ND, 2016.

61 Australian Survey Response, Janine McMinn, ND, 2016.

62 Australian Survey Response, SM, 16th October 2016.

63 Australian Survey Response, Robyn Tassicker, 11th October 2016.

64 Australian Survey Response, Shane O'Neil, 25th November 2016.

65 Australian Survey Response, Carole Turner, NG, 2016.

66 Canadian Survey Response, Debra McAuslan, 29th September 2016. See also Canadian Survey Response, Gail Benjafield, 2nd September 2016.

67 British Survey Response, Dee Leamey, 28th September 2016.

68 Australian Survey Response, Lilian Magill, ND, 2016.

69 Australian Survey Response, JA, 10th October 2016.

70 British Survey Response, Barbara Hearn, 9th October 2016.

71 Australian Survey Response, Betty O'Neill, 21st August 2016.

72 Australian Survey Response, BL, 22nd September 2016.

73 Australian Survey Response, Stephanie Hume, September 2016.

74 Canadian Survey Response, Alison Madden, 29th August 2016.

75 Canadian Survey Response, Brenda Turner ND, 2016.

76 Australian Survey Response, Harriet Jones, 6th August 2016.

77 Canadian Survey Response, Mary Jane, 27th September 2016.

78 Canadian Survey Response, Brenda Lee, 5th September 2016.

79 British Survey Response, Barbara Hearn, 9th October 2016.

80 British Survey Response, Barbara Hearn, 9th October 2016.

81 British Survey Response, Hannah Frost, 12th September 2016.

82 Wendy Brown, *Undoing the Demos: Neoliberalism's Stealth Revolution* (US: Zone Books, 2017).

83 Julie Rak, *Boom: Manufacturing Memoir for the Popular Market* (Waterloo, Ontario: Wilfrid Laurier University Press, 2013).

84 Retz, *Empathy and History*, Chapter 1, 5.

85 Australian Survey Response, Anonymized, date NG, 2016.

86 Australian Survey Response, AM, 24th September 2016.

87 Canadian Survey Response, Brenda Lee, 5th September 2016.

88 Canadian Survey Response, Glenna Morrison, 1st September 2016.

89 Canadian Survey Response, Deb McAuslan, 29th September 2016.

90 British Survey Response, Barbara Hearn, 9th October 2016.

91 British Survey Response, PC, 22nd September 2016.

92 Including Canadian David Dobson, 25th September 2016.

93 Canadian Survey Response, Gail Lewis, 30th August 2016.

94 Australian Survey Response, Dawn Springett, 21st December 2016.

95 Canadian Survey Response, Brenda Turner, ND, 2016.

96 Australian Survey Response, Peter Keeda, 8th November 2016.

97 Australian Survey Response, AM, 24th September 2016.

98   Australian Survey Response, HB, 26th September 2016.

99   Australian Survey Response, BL, 22nd September 2016.

100 Australian Survey Response, Marilyn Myers, ND.

101 Canadian Survey Response, David Dobson, 25th September 2016.

102 Australian Survey Response, Robyn Dryen, Australian Jewish Genealogical Society 3rd December 2016.

103 Bloom, *Against Empathy,* 11.

104 Pamela Cox, 'Preface', in Sasha Handley, Rohan McWilliam and Lucy Noakes (eds.), *New Directions in Social and Cultural History* (Bloomsbury, 2018), xvi.

105 Bruce Macfarlane, 'Defining and Rewarding Academic Citizenship: The Implications for University Promotions Policy', *Journal of Higher Education Policy and Management* 29, no. 3 (2007): 261–73, DOI:10.1080/13600800701457863, Raewyn Connell, *The Good University: What Universities Actually Do and Why It's Time for Radical Change* (Melbourne: Monash University Press, 2019) and Tom Sperlinger, Josie McLellan and Richard Pettigrew, *Who Are Universities For? Remaking Higher Education* (Bristol: University of Bristol Press, 2019).

106 Retz, *Empathy and History,* chapter 1 'Reforming the Past'.

Chapter 6

1   Australian Survey Response, 19th October 2016.

2   Stephanie Downes, Sally Holloway, and Sarah Randles, *Feeling Things: Objects and Emotions through History* (Oxford University Press, 2018), Introduction. http://blogs.cardiff.ac.uk/familyarchive/ (accessed 6th November 2020).

3   Laura King, 'The Shape of His Knees Bulged in the Cheap Tweed: Clothes and Textiles in Remembrance', Blog post, 16th April 2019, https://livingwithdying.leeds.ac.uk/2019/04/16/the-shape-of-his-knees-bulged-in-the-cheap-tweed-clothes-and-textiles-in-remembrance/. This is the website dedicated to this AHRC funded project https://livingwithdying.leeds.ac.uk/ (accessed 11th December 2020). Laura is currently writing the book based on this project which will be published by Oxford University Press.

4   Tanya Evans, 'The Use of Memory and Material Culture in the History of the Family in Colonial Australia', *Journal of Australian Studies* 36, no. 2: 207–28, DOI:10.1080/14443058.2012.678584.

5   On the many meanings of objects, see John Styles and Amanda Vickery, *Gender, Taste and Material Culture in Britain and North America, 1700–1830* (London: Yale University Press, 2006).

6   For an introduction to how an appreciation of material culture enriches our understanding of the past, see Karen Harvey (ed.), *History and Material Culture: A*

Student's Guide to Approaching Alternative Sources (London: Routledge, 2009). For a warning of the value and danger associated with the use of such sources, see Carolyn Steedman, 'What a Rag Rug Means', *Journal of Material Culture* 3, no. 3 (1998): 259, 81.

7   Much of my thinking on this subject has been informed by some excellent work by cultural historians of colonial America, see Susan Stabile, *Memory's Daughters: The Material Culture of Remembrance in Eighteenth-Century America* (Ithaca: Cornell University Press, 2004) and Margaretta Lovell, *Art in a Season of Revolution: Artisans and Patrons in Early America* (Philadelphia: University of Penn Press, 2005). Thanks to Joanne Begiato for prompting me to read these.

8   On a British early-modern example, see Claire Smith, 'The Governor's Daughter', in Sue Pritchard (ed.), *Quilts 1700–2010, Hidden Histories, Untold Stories* (London: Victoria and Albert Publishing, 2010), 54. For a brief mention of the challenge of some collections to Australian patrilineality, see Chris Healy, *From the Ruins of Colonialism: History as Social Memory* (Cambridge: Cambridge University Press, 1997), 104.

9   Only three in Alan Atkinson's, *Camden: Farm and Village Life in Early New South Wales* (Oxford: Oxford University Press, 1988), 174, 79. See also Patricia Grimshaw and Charles Fahey, 'Family and Community in Nineteenth Century Castlemaine', *Australian Historical Studies* (1982): 88, 125 and John Ferry, 'The Will and the Way: Inheritance Practices and Social Structure', *Journal of Australian Colonial History* 1, no. 2 (1999): 122, 41.

10 Styles and Vickery, *Gender, Taste*, 12, 9. For an excellent account of the use of portraiture as genealogy by British aristocratic women challenging patriarchal representations of family lines which emphasized the contribution of women to aristocratic lineage, see Kate Retford, 'Patrilineal Portraiture? Gender and Genealogy in the C18th English Country House', in Styles and Vickery, *Gender, Taste*, 315–40.

11 Margaretta Lovell uses this phrase in a different context in her discussion of the use of portraiture by colonial American men in her *Art in a Season of Revolution*, 138.

12 Quote from Smith, 'The Governor's Daughter', 54. Those that were passed down the maternal line on the Quilt Register include: 686 NTV, 1041JJ, 79R, 153MR, 203WO, 25NTA, 386CW, 717EGV, 913 AK, 1033 NG and 1114JH. For further evidence on quilts not on the register, see Annette Gero, *The Fabric of Society; Australia's Quilt Heritage from Convict Times to 1960* (Sydney: Beagle Press, 2009). Here is the National Quilt Register of Australia: https://www.nationalquiltregister.org.au/ (accessed 11th December 2020).

13 A mourning sampler is on display in the Powerhouse Discovery Centre at Castle Hill marking the death of a three-week-old infant Edward Quartermain in 1872, 'Not lost but gone before.' Object 2001/45/1.

14 On Erikson, see Charles Slater, 'Generativity versus Stagnation: An Elaboration of Erikson's Adult Stage of Human Development', *Journal of Adult Development* 10, no. 1 (2003): 53–65.

15 Thanks to Celia Harris for informing me about the concept of generativity.

16 Susan Moore et al., *The Psychology of Family History* (Routledge, 2020), Chapter 5, 'Generativity and Altruism', 48–50.

17 Australian Survey Response, 9th September 2019 (this was not part of the original surveys collected for this project in 2016 and not counted in the earlier figures).

18 Margaret Knopp's Scrapbook, Woods Point, 1884, https://collections. museumsvictoria.com.au/items/1479453; https://prov.vic.gov.au/explore-collection/ provenance-journal/provenance-2009/woods-point-my-dwelling-place (accessed 20th December 2020).

19 Louise Blake, 'The Ties that Bind: Investigating the bond between four generations of women in my family', Masters in Biography and Life Writing, Research Project, Semester 1, 2004, Monash University.

20 Australian Survey Response, Verity Morris, 1st May 2017.

21 Australian Survey Response, Dawn Springett, 21st December 2016.

22 Canadian Survey Response, Carole Whelan, 4th September 2016.

23 Canadian Survey Response, Anon., 6th September 2016.

24 Canadian Survey Response, Mary Holland, 25th September 2016.

25 Canadian Survey Response, Walt Crites, 3rd September 2016.

26 British Survey Response, Kate Hurst, 22nd September 2016.

27 Australian Survey Response, 22nd August 2016.

28 Australian Survey Response, Janelle Collins, ND, 2016.

29 Australian Survey Response, MN (anon), 12th July 2016.

30 British Survey Response, Kath Robinson, ND, 2016.

31 Australian Survey Response, Tracey Treloar, 30th September 2016.

32 Email communication with Julie Poulter 2016.

33 Australian Survey Response, JM, 10th October 2016.

34 Australian Survey Response, Patsy Trench, ND, 2016.

35 British Survey Response, Doreen Leamy, 28th September 2016.

36 Australian Survey Response, Janelle Collins, ND, 2016.

37 Canadian Survey Response, Pamela Fane, 8th October 2016.

38 https://www.reliving.co.uk/; https://www.milife.online/about-us; https://www.tota. world/ (all accessed 16th November 2020). Thanks to Nick Barratt for alerting me to these sites.

39 Carolyn Steedman, 'Lord Mansfield's Voices: In the Archive, Hearing Things', in Downes, Hollway, Randles, *Feelings Things*, 217.

40 Australian Survey Response, CA, 20th July 2016.

41 Australian Survey Response, Shane O'Neil, 25th November 2016.

42 Australian Survey Response, Richard Reid, ND, 2017.

43 Australian Survey Response, Dianne Mitchell, 5th September 2016.

44 Australian Survey Response, Greer Gamble, 15th February 2019. This survey was not part of the group of surveys undertaken in 2016 upon which this book is largely based.

45 See http://familybibles.org.uk/ (accessed 6th November 2020); https://www.ebay.com/b/Family-Bible/29223/bn_7023355254 (accessed 6th November 2020).

46 http://midas.sag.org.au/attachments/biblelist.pdf (accessed 16th November 2020).

47 https://familyhistorydaily.com/family-history/the-importance-of-family-bibles/ (accessed 6th November 2020); https://ancestralfindings.com/family-bibles/ (accessed 6th November 2020); https://blog.genealogybank.com/genealogy-101-4-the-family-bible.html (accessed 6th November 2020).

48 https://faithinthetown.wordpress.com/blog-2/ (accessed 16th November 2020). Karin Wulf, 'Bible, King and Common Law: Genealogical Literacies and Family History Practices in British America', *Early American Studies* 10, no. 3 (2012): 467–502.

49 British Survey Response, Doreen Leamey, 28th September 2016.

50 Australian Survey Response, Tracey Treloar, 30th September 2016.

51 Canadian Survey Response, TR, 25th September 2016.

52 British Survey Response, Kath Robertson, ND.

53 British Survey Response, HN, 15th September 2016.

54 British Survey Response, Peggy Beckett, 25th September 2016.

55 Email exchange with Alison Woolf, Society of Australian Genealogists, 22nd December 2018.

56 Australian Survey Response, Shane O'Neil, 25th November 2016.

57 Canadian Survey Response, Alison Madden, 29th August 2016.

58 Canadian Survey Response, Debra McAuslan, 29th September 2016.

59 Meeting with Gemma Beswick 18th December 2020 and Survey Response from Gemma Beswick 15th January 2021 (this survey was not counted as part of the 2016 surveys).

60 https://www.abc.net.au/everyday/australia-can-have-a-racism-problem-and-multicultural-food/11636756 (accessed 21st December 2020); Lara Anderson and Heather Merle Benbow, 'Cultural Indigestion in Multicultural Australia: Fear of "Foreign" Foods in Australian Media', *Gastronomica: The Journal of Food and Culture* 15, no. 1 (2015): 34–43.

61 Oral History Interview undertaken in Balmain Library with Justina Lui, 17th November 2016.

62 Canadian Survey Response, TR, 25th September 2016.

63 Australian Survey Response, JA, 10th October 2016.

64 On Dana Saxon see: http://ancestors-unknown.org/1/previous/2.html, http://www.fastcompany.com/3029871/whos-next/why-researching-our-ancestors-has-the-power-to-change-lives on Sleeter: http://historyandfamily.blogspot.com.au/ (last accessed 26.6.14).

65 Christine Sleeter, 'Critical Family History, Identity, and Historical Memory', *Educational Studies* 43 (2008): 114–24, 114–15, 116, 188. Her blog: http://historyandfamily.blogspot.com.au/.

66 http://www.netherywylie.net/.

67 Nethery Whylie, 'She's not who you thought she was', MFA dissertation, April 2014, 41.

68 http://www.transart.org/summer-events-berlin-2014/2014/06/23/nethery-wylie-booktych-digital-sketches-for-a-family-album/ (accessed 23 July 2014).

69 Australian Survey Response, no specific date given, 2016.

70 Merrill, N., and R. Fivush, 'Intergenerational Narratives and Identity across Development', *Developmental Review* 40 (2016): 72–92. https://doi.org/10.1016/j.dr.2016.03.001.

71 Canadian Survey Response, 6th September 2016.

72 Most public historians endorse Raphael Samuel's plea for history to be understood as a social form of knowledge Raphael Samuel, *Theatres of Memory* (London: Verso, 1994), 8. See Ramos and Taithe (eds.), *The Impact*, 2.

Epilogue

1 Parts of this epilogue have been co-authored with my collaborators in family history scholarship Jerome de Groot and Matthew Stallard. Some of these ideas on the future of family history have been shared in an article submitted to the *History Workshop Journal*.

2 Pedro Ramos Pinto and Bertrand Taithe (eds.), *The Impact of History? Histories at the Beginning of the Twentieth Century* (Abingdon and New York: Routledge, 2015), 11–12.

3 See also Martha Nussbaum, *Not For Profit: Why Democracy Needs the Humanities* (New Haven: Princeton University Press, 2010).

4 Stephane Levesque, *Thinking Historically: Educating Students for the Twenty-First Century* (University of Toronto Press, 2008), 17.

5 Nussbaum, *Not For Profit*, 133.

6 https://www.history.ac.uk/whats/ihr-partnership-seminars (accessed 24th January 2021).

7 Alexander Cook, 'The Use and Abuse of Historical Reenactment: Thoughts on Recent Trends in Public History', *Criticism* 46, no. 3 (2004): 487–96 (accessed 24 Jan 2020).

8 Katie Barclay, 'Falling in Love with the Dead', *Rethinking History* 22, no. 4: 459–73.

9 See Janet Weston, 'History at Large: Oral Histories, Public Engagement and the Making of *Positive in Prison*', *History Workshop Journal* 87 (2019): 211–24.

10 See Charles C. Cole, Jr., 'Public History: What Difference Has it Made?' *The Public Historian* 16, no. 4 (1994): 9–35.

11 Karen Harvey, 'Envisioning the Past: Art, Historiography and Public History', *Cultural and Social History* 12, no. 4: 527–43.

12 For other examples, see also Martine Brennan, 'Democratising access to the past through digital public history: digital archives, digital interpretation and the creation of the *Enslavement to citizenship* project', MA thesis (Public History and Cultural Heritage), University of Limerick, August 2020.

13 https://historianscollaborate.com/ (accessed 29th January 2021) and the earlier version: (accessed 30th January 2020); Nick Barratt, 'Working Together', *Who do you think you are? Magazine,* July 2019. https://nataliepithers.wixsite.com/ historianscollab (accessed 30th January 2020); Nick Barratt, 'Working Together', *Who do you think you are? Magazine,* July 2019.

14 Thomas Cauvin, *Public History: A Textbook of Practice* (London: Routledge, 2016), 205–6.

15 https://history.cass.anu.edu.au/centres/ncb/events/related-histories-studying-family (accessed 17th December 2020). The conference papers will be published by Routledge in 2021.

16 https://ncph.org/history-at-work/hold-for-international-family-history-post-from-jermoe-degroot/; https://ncph.org/history-at-work/author/jerome-de-groot-and-tanya-evans/ (accessed 30th January 2020).

17 https://livingwithdying.leeds.ac.uk/family-history-collaboration/ (accessed 17th December 2020).

18 https://inheritingthefamily.org/ (accessed 17th December 2020).

19 https://thehipsterhistorian.com/about/ (accessed 14th January 2021).

20 *Sydney Morning Herald*, 13th December 2019.

Bibliography

Primary Sources

Oral Histories

Interview with Doreen Leamey, Upminster, Essex, UK, 6th October 2016.
Interview with Maria Linders, Friends Room, State Library of NSW, 14th September 2016.
Interview with Justina Lui, Balmain Library, 17th November 2016.
Interview with Ken McKinlay, Ottawa, October 2016.
Interview with John Reid, Carleton University, Ottawa, Canada, 12th October 2016.
Interview with Gail Roger, Libraries and Archives, Ottawa, Canada, 13th October 2016.
Interview with Michael Williams, Friends Room, State Library of NSW, 30th August 2016.

Communication

Email correspondence with Marg Doherty, Secretary of the Australian Federation of Family History Organizations, 20th August 2020.
Email correspondence with Ruth Graham, Executive Officer of the Society of Australian Genealogists, December 2020.
Email correspondence with Dianne Johnstone, November 2016.
Email correspondence with Justina Lui, 12th September 2016.
Email correspondence with Julie Poulter, 26th April 2016.
Email correspondence with Alison Woolf, Society of Australian Genealogists, 22nd December 2018.

Surveys

Australian Survey Responses, 2016–2017.
British Survey Responses, 2016.
Canadian Survey Responses, 2016.

Secondary Sources

Books and Articles

Lynn Abrams, *Oral History Theory* (London: Routledge, 2016), http://www.auswhn.org.au/blog/oral-history/.

Sara Ahmed, *The Cultural Politics of Emotions* (Edinburgh: Edinburgh University Press, 2004).

Alison Alexander, *Tasmania's Convicts: How Felons Built a Free Society* (Sydney: Allen and Unwin, 2010).

Carla Almeida Santos and Grace Yan, 'Genealogical Tourism: A Phenomenological Examination', *Journal of Travel Research* 49, no. 1 (2010): 56–67.

Lara Anderson and Heather Merle Benbow, 'Cultural Indigestion in Multicultural Australia: Fear of "Foreign" Foods in Australian Media', *Gastronomica: The Journal of Food and Culture* 15, no. 1 (2015): 34–43.

Tracy Arial's plea for more academics to collaborate, 'How Genealogy Improves Historical Study', in Randy Boswell (ed.), *The Personal Past: History, Genealogy and the Personal Impulse*, Spring-Summer 2020, Association of Canadian Studies, 67–70. https://acs-aec.ca/en/publications-en/the-personal-past-history-identity-and-the-genealogical-impulse/.

Paul Ashton and Meg Foster, 'Public Histories', in Sasha Handley, Rohan Mcwilliam and Lucy Noakes (eds.), *New Directions in Social and Cultural History* (London: Bloomsbury, 2018).

Paul Ashton and Paula Hamilton (eds.), 'Australians and the Past', *Australian Cultural History*, Special Issue, 22, 2003.

Paul Ashton and Paula Hamilton, *History at the Crossroads: Australians and the Past* (Ultimo: Halstead Press, 2003).

Paul Ashton and Paula Hamilton, 'At Home with the Past: Initial Findings from the Survey', *Australian Cultural History* 23 (2003).

Alan Atkinson's, *Camden: Farm and Village Life in Early New South Wales* (Oxford: Oxford University Press, 1988).

Jane Badets, 'Who Am I? Reflections on Measuring Ethnic Ancestry in Canada', R. Boswell (ed.), *The Personal Past: History, Identity and the Genealogical Impulse*, Canadian Issues, 2020, 26–32.

Katie Barclay, 'Falling in Love with the Dead', *Rethinking History* 22, no. 4 (2018): 459–73.

Ashley Barnwell, 'From Convict Shame to Convict Chic: Intergenerational Family Memory and Family Histories', *Journal of Family History* 12, no. 4 (2017): 398–411.

Ashley Barnwell, 'Hidden Heirlooms: Keeping Family Secrets across Generations', *Journal of Sociology* 54, no. 3 (2017): 446–60.

Ashley Barnwell, 'Family Secrets and the Slow Violence of Social Stigma', *Sociology* 53, no. 6 (2019): 1111–26.

Ashley Barnwell, 'Keeping it secret: Revealing the secrets in your family history' (ed. K. Hyde) [Blog post]. December 15 2017; https://blogs.ancestry.co.uk/ancestry/2017/12/15/keeping-it-secret-revealing-the-secrets-in-your-family-history/.

Keith Barton, 'History, Humanistic Education and Participatory Democracy' in Ruth Sandwell (ed.), *To the Past: History Education, Public Memory and Citizenship in Canada* (Toronto: University of Toronto Press, 2006), 54–6.

Paul Basu, *Route Metaphors of 'Roots Tourism' in the Scottish Highland Diaspora* (London: Routledge: 2004).

Frank Bongiorno, 'Asa Briggs and the Remaking of Australian Historiography', in Miles Taylor (ed.), *The Age of Asa: Lord Briggs, Public Life and History in Britain since 1945* (Basingstoke: Palgrave, 2016), 90–107.

Frank Bongiorno, '"Real Solemn History" and Its Discontents: Australian Political History and the Challenge of Social History', *Australian Journal of Politics and History* 56, no. 1 (2010): 6–20.

Joanna Bourke, 'Fear and Anxiety: Writing about Emotion in Modern History', *History Workshop Journal* 55 (2003): 111–33.

Alison Baxter, *A Cornish Cargo: The Untold History of a Victorian Seafaring Family* (Self-published, 2020).

Angus Baxter, *In Search of Your Roots: A Guide for Canadians Seeking their Ancestors* (Toronto: Macmillan, 1977).

Judith Bennett and Angela Wanhalla (ed.), *Mother's Darlings of the South Pacific: The Children of Indigenous Women and US Servicemen World War II* (Honolulu: University of Hawaii Press, 2016).

Michael Bennett, *Pathfinders: A History of Aboriginal Trackers in NSW* (Sydney: New South, 2020).

Lauren Berlant, *The Queen of America Goes to Washington City Essays on Recognition and Sexual Difference* (Durham: Duke University Press, 1997).

Paul Bloom, *Against Empathy: The Case for Rational Compassion* (London: Harper Collins, 2016).

Rob Boddice, *The History of Emotions* (Manchester: Manchester University Press, 2018).

Rob Boddice, 'The History of Emotions', in Sasha Handley, Rohan Mcwilliam and Lucy Noakes (eds.), *New Directions in Social and Cultural History* (London: Bloomsbury, 2018).

Tony Boddington, 'Empathy and the teaching of history', *British Journal of Educational Studies* 28, no. 1 (1980): 13–19.

Alan Booth, 'Making Teaching Public: The Scholarship of Teaching and Learning in History in Perspective', in David Ludvigsson (ed.), *Enhancing Student Learning in History: Perspectives on University History Teaching* (Opuscula Historica Upsaliersia, 48, 2012).

Alan Booth, 'Pedagogy and the Practice of Academic History in late-Twentieth-century Britain', *Rethinking History: The Journal of Theory and Practice* 13, no. 3 (2009): 317–44.

Randy Boswell (ed.), *The Personal Past: History, Identity and the Genealogical Impulse* (Canadian Issues, Association of Canadian Studies, Spring-Summer, 2020).

Wendy Bottero, 'Practising Family History: Identity as a Category of Social Practice', *British Journal of Sociology* 66, no. 3 (2015): 534–66, https://doi.org/10.1111/1468-4446.12133.

Wendy Bottero, 'Who Do You Think They Were? How Family Historians Make Sense of Social Position and Inequality in the Past', *British Journal of Sociology* 63, no. 1 (2012): 54–74.

Pierre Bourdieu, 'The Forms of Capital', J.G. Richardson (ed.), *Handbook of Theory and Research for the Sociology of Education* (New York: Greenwood Press, 1986), 241–58.

James Boyce, *Van Diemen's Land: A History* (Melbourne: Black Inc., 2008).

Bettina Bradbury, *Caroline's Dilemma: A Colonial Inheritance Saga* (Sydney: New South Publishing, 2019).

Fritz Breithaupt, *The Dark Sides of Empathy* (Ithaca: Cornell University Press, 2019).

Wendy Brown, *Undoing the Demos: Neoliberalism's Stealth Revolution* (US: Zone Books, 2017).

Rachel Buchanon, *Ko Taranaki Te Maunga* (Wellington: Bridget Williams Books, 2018).

David Burchell, 'The Trouble with Empathy', *Griffith Review* (Winter 2005): 115–32.

Judith Butler, *The Psychic Life of Power: Theories in Subjection* (Redwood City: Stanford, 1997).

John Bynner, 'Whatever Happened to Lifelong Learning? And Does It matter', *Journal of the British Academy*, 2017, https://www.britac.ac.uk/sites/default/files/03%20 Bynner%201836.pdf.

John Cairns, 'Some Reflections on Empathy in History', *Teaching History* (1989): 13–18.

Carmen Calill, *Oh, Happy Day, Those Times and These Times* (London: Penguin, 2020).

Caroline-Isabelle Caron, *Se Creer des Ancestres: Un Parcours Genealogique Nord-American XIX-XX seicles* (Quebec: Septentrion, 2006).

Erica Cervini, *Yizkor for Rose: A Life Lost and Found* (Self-published, 2020).

Nancy Chodorow, *The Reproduction of Mothering: Psychoanalysis and the Sociology of Mothering* (Oakland: University of California Press, 1978).

Anna Clark, 'Inheriting the Past: Exploring Historical Consciousness across Generations', *Historical Encounters: A Journal of Historical Consciousness, Historical Cultures, and History Education* 1, no. 1 (2014): 88–102.

Anna Clark, *Private Lives, Public History* (Melbourne: Melbourne University Press, 2016).

Anna Clark, 'Ordinary People's History', *Journal of Australian Studies* 9, no. 1 (2012): 201–16.

Anna Clark and Tanya Evans, 'Family History and Transnational Historical Consciousness', in Anna Clark, Anne Rees and Alecia Simmonds (eds.), *Transnationalism, Nationalism and Australian History* (Basingstoke: Palgrave Macmillan, 2017), 167–78.

Anna Clark and Carla Peck (eds.), *Contemplating Historical Consciousness: Notes from the Field* (New York and Oxford: Berghan Books, 2020).

Inga Clendinnen, 'The History Question: Who Owns the Past', *Quarterly Essay*, 23, September 2006.

Deborah Cohen, *Family Secrets: Shame and Privacy in Modern Britain* (Oxford: Oxford University Press, 2013).

Raewyn Connell, *The Good University: What Universities Actually Do and Why It's Time for Radical Change* (Melbourne: Monash University Press, 2019).

Margaret Conrad, Dubé, N., Northrup, D. and Owre, K., "'I want to know my bloodline": New Brunswickers and Their Pasts', *Journal of New Brunswick Studies/ Revue d'études Sur Le Nouveau-Brunswick* 1 (2010).

Margaret Conrad, Kadriye Ercikan, Gerald Friesen, Jocelyn Letourneau, Delphin Muise, David Northrup and Peter Seixas, *Canadians and Their Pasts, The Pasts Collective* (Toronto: University of Toronto Press, 2013).

Trudy Cowley, *A Drift of Derwent Ducks: Lives of the 200 Female Irish Convicts Transported on the Australasia from Dublin to Hobart in 1849* (Hobart: New Town, 2005).

Pamela Cox, 'Preface', in Sasha Handley, Rohan McWilliam and Lucy Noakes (eds.), *New Directions in Social and Cultural History* (London: Bloomsbury, 2018).

Ann Curthoys, 'Crossing Over: Academic and Popular History', *Australasian Journal of Popular Culture* 1, no.1 (2012): 7–18.

Graeme Davison, 'Ancestors: The Broken Lineage of Family History', in his *The Use and Abuse of Australian History* (Allen and Unwin: Sydney, 2000).

Graeme Davison, *Lost Relations: Fortunes of my Family in Australia's Golden Age* (Allen and Unwin: Sydney, 2015).

Graeme Davison, 'Paradigms of Public History', *Australian Historical Studies* 24, no. 96 (1991): 4–15.

Graeme Davison, 'Public History' in Graeme Davison, John Hirst and Stuart Macintyre (eds.), *Oxford Companion to Australian History* (South Melbourne: Oxford University Press, 2001), 538.

Graeme Davison, 'Yarning in the Street': The Evolution of Australian Public History', in Stuart Macintyre, Lenore Layman and Jenny Gregory (eds.), *A Historian for All Seasons: Essays for Geoffrey Bolton* (Clayton: Monash University Publishing, 2017), 71–97.

David Dean and John Walsh, 'Some Reflections on Public History in Canada Today', *International Public History*, January 2020, https://www.degruyter.com/view/ journals/iph/2/2/article-20190021.xml.

Jerome de Groot, *Consuming History: Historians and Heritage in Contemporary Popular Culture* (London: Routledge, 2009).

Jerome De Groot, 'Genealogy, Hobby, Politics and Science', in his *Consuming History: Historians and Heritage in Contemporary Popular Culture* (London: Routledge, 2009).

Jerome de Groot, 'On Genealogy', *The Public Historian* 37, no. 3 (2015): 102–27.

Jerome de Groot and Matthew Stallard, "'Things Are Coming Out That Are Questionable, We Never Knew about": DNA and the New Family History', *Journal of Family History* 45, no. 3 (2020): 274–94, https://sites.manchester.ac.uk/double-helix-history/author/mfatsjd2/.

Heather Devine, *The People Who Own Themselves: Aboriginal Ethnogenesis in a Canadian Family, 1660–1900* (Calgary: University of Calgary Press, 2004).

Mark Donnelly, 'Public History in Britain: Repossessing the Past', in Paul Ashton and Alex Trapeznik (eds.), *What Is Public History Globally* (London: Bloomsbury, 2019), 24–35.

Michael Dove and Michelle Hamilton, 'Public History in Canada: Public Service or Public Service?', in Ashton and Trapeznik (eds.), *What Is History Globally?* (London: Bloomsbury, 2019), 37–49.

Stephanie Downes, Sally Holloway and Sarah Randles, *Feeling Things: Objects and Emotions through History* (Oxford: Oxford University Press, 2018), http://blogs.cardiff.ac.uk/familyarchive/ (accessed 6th November 2020).

Christopher Dummitt and Michael Dawson, *Contesting Clio's Craft: New Directions and Debates in Canadian History* (London: Institute for the Study of the Americas, University of London, 2009).

Robyn Eastley, 'Using the Records of the Tasmanian Convict Department', *Tasmanian Historical Studies* 9 (2004): 139–42.

Alice Echols, *Shortfall: Family Secrets, Financial Collapse and a Hidden History of Banking in America* (New Ork: The New Press, 2017).

Silvia Edling, Heather Sharp, Jan Lofstrom and Niklas Ammert, 'The Good Citizen: Revisiting Moral Motivations for Introducing Historical Consciousness in History Education Drawing on the Writings of Gadamer', *Citizenship, Social and Economics Education* 19, no. 2 (2020): 133–50.

Silvia Edling, Heather Sharp, Jan Lofstrom and Niklas Ammert, 'Why Is Ethics Important in History Education? A Dialogue between the Various Ways of Understanding the Relationships between Ethics and Historical Consciousness', *Ethics and Education* 15, no. 3: 336–54.

Delyth Edwards, *Cultural, Autobiographical and Absent Memories of Orphanhood: The Girls of Nazareth House Remember* (Cham, Switzerland: Palgrave, 2017).

Geof Eley, *A Crooked Line: From Cultural History to the History of Society* (Ann Arbor: University of Michigan Press, 2005).

Jason Endacott, 'Reconsidering Affective Engagement in Historical Empathy', *Theory and Research in Social Education* 38, no. 1 (2010): 6–47, DOI:10.1080/00933104.201 0.10473415.

Jason Endacott and Sarah Brooks, 'An Updated Theoretical and Practical Model of Historical Empathy', *Social Studies Research and Practice* 8 (2013): 41–58.

Jason L. Endacott, 'Negotiating the Process of Historical Empathy', *Theory & Research in Social Education* 42, no. 1 (2014): 4–34, DOI:10.1080/00933104.2013.826158.

Jason Endacott and Sarah Brooks, 'Historical Empathy: Perspectives and Responding to the Past', in *Wiley International Handbook of History Teaching and Learning* (Hoboken: Wiley Publishing, 2018).

Asri Erll, 'Locating Family in Cultural Memory Studies', *Journal of Comparative Family Studies*, vol. 42, no. 3, Families and Memories: Continuity and Social Change (May-June 2011): 303–18.

Richard Evans, 'Review of *Who do you think you are?*' *History Australia* 5, no. 3 (December 2008).

Tanya Evans, 'The Use of Memory and Material Culture in the History of the Family in Colonial Australia', *Journal of Australian Studies* 36, no. 2: 207–28, DOI:10.1080/144 43058.2012.678584.

Tanya Evans, 'Secrets and Lies: The Radical Potential of Family History', *History Workshop Journal* 71 (2011): 49–73.

Tanya Evans, *Fractured Families: Life on the Margins in Colonial New South Wales* (Sydney, New South Press, 2015).

Tanya Evans, 'Who Do You Think You Are? Historical Television Consultancy', *Australian Historical Studies* 46, no. 3 (2015): 454–67.

Tanya Evans, 'Enhancing Student Engagement through Flipping: A Case Study in Australian History', *The History Teacher*, Society for History Education affiliate of American Historical Association 51, no. 4 (August, 2018): 611–38.

Tanya Evans, 'Discovering Violence in the Family', in Alana Piper and Ana Stevenson (ed.), *Gender Violence in Australia: Historical Perspectives* (Clayton, VIC: Monash University Publishing, 2019), 20–33.

Tanya Evans and Jerome De Groot, 'Emerging Studies in Family History', in *International Public History* (Berlin: De Gruyter, 2019).

Tanya Evans and Jerome De Groot (eds.) Special Issue on Family History, *International Public History* (Berlin: De Gruyter, 2019).

John Ferry, 'The Will and the Way: Inheritance Practices and Social Structure', *Journal of Australian Colonial History* 1, no. 2 (1999): 122–41.

John Field, *Social Capital*, Second Edition (London: Routledge, 2008).

John Field, 'Good for Your Soul? Adult Learning and Mental Well-Being', *International Journal of Lifelong Education* 28, no. 2 (2009): 175–91.

Ruth Finnegan, 'Family Myths, Memories and Interviewing', in Robert Perks and Alistair Thompson (ed.), *The Oral History Reader*, 2nd ed (New York: Routledge, 2006).

Robyn Fivush, 'Maternal Reminiscing Style and Children's Developing Understanding of Self and Emotion', *Clinical Social Work Journal* 35 (2007): 37–46, https://doi.org/10.1007/s10615-006-0065-1.

Robyn Fivush, 'The Development of Autobiographical Memory', *Annual Review of Psychology* 62 (2011): 559–82.

Robyn Fivush and Catherine A. Haden, *Autobiographical Memory and the Construction of a Narrative Self: Development and Cultural Perspectives* (Mahwah, New Jersey: Psychology Press, Lawrence Erlbaum Associates, 2003).

Ute Frevert, *Emotions in History* (Budapest: Central University Press, 2011).

Michael Frisch, *A Shared Authority: Essays on the Craft and Meaning of Oral and Public History* (New York: State University of New York Press, 1990).

Lucy Frost, 'The Politics of Writing Convict Lives: Academic Research, State Archives and Family History', *Life Writing* 8, no. 1 (2011): 19–33.

Lucy Frost and Hamish Maxwell- Stewart (eds.), *Chain Letters: Narrating Convict Lives* (Melbourne: Melbourne University Press, 2001).

David Gagan and H.E.Turner, 'Social History in Canada: A Report on the State of the Art', *Archivaria*, 14 January (1982): 27–52.

Bernard Gammerl, 'Can You Feel Your Research Results: How Do Deal with and Gain Insights from Emotions Generated during Oral History Interviews', in H. Flam and J. Kleres (eds.), *Methods of Exploring Emotions* (London: Routledge, 2015).

James Gardner, 'Trust, Risk and Public History: A View from the United States', *Public History Review* 17 (2010): 52–61.

Annette Gero, *The Fabric of Society; Australia's Quilt Heritage from Convict Times to 1960* (Sydney: Beagle Press, 2009).

Liz Gloyn, Vicky Crewe and Laura King, 'Ties that Bind: Materiality, Identity, and the Life Course in the "Things" That Families Keep', *Journal of Family History* 43, no. 2 (2018): 157–76.

Anna Green and Kathleen Troup, *Houses of History: A Critical Reader in Twentieth-Century History and Theory* (New York: New York University Press, 1999).

Patricia Grimshaw and Charles Fahey, 'Family and Community in Nineteenth Century Castlemaine', *Australian Historical Studies* (1982): 21, 82, 88–125.

John Gillis, *A World of their Own Making: A History of Myth and Ritual in Family Life* (Oxford: Oxford University Press, 1997).

Alex Haley, *Roots: The Saga of an American Family* (New York: Doubleday, 1976).

Paula Hamilton and Kate Darian Smith, 'Memory and History in Twenty-First Century Australia: A Survey of the Field', *Memory Studies* 5, no. 3 (2013): 370–83.

Kristyn Harman, 'The Transformative Power of Digital Humanities when Teaching Family History Online', *Journal of University Teaching and Learning Practice* 15, no. 3 (2018), https://ro.uow.edu.au/jutlp/vol15/iss3/7/ (accessed 26th Sept 2018).

Richard Harris and L. Foreman-Peck. '"Stepping into other peoples" shoes': Teaching and assessing empathy in the secondary history curriculum', *International Journal of Historical Learning, Teaching and Research* 4, no. 2 (2004): 98–111.

Ruth Harris and Lyndal Roper, 'Introduction to a Special Issue Marking Olwen Hufton's Intellectual Contribution to History', *Past and Present*, Vol. 1, January 1–11, 2006.

Victoria Haskins, 'Beyond Complicity: Questions and Issues for White Women in Aboriginal History', *Australian Humanities Review*, 39, September 2006.

Frigga Haug et al., *Female Sexualisation: A Collective Work of Memory* (E. Carter, Trans) (London: Verso, 1987).

Chris Healy, *From the Ruins of Colonialism: History as Social Memory* (Cambridge: Cambridge University Press, 1997).

Clare Hemmings, 'Invoking Affect: Cultural Theory and the Ontological Turn', *Cultural Studies* 19, 5th September (2005): 548–67.

Steven High, 'Sharing Authority in Writing Canadian History: The Case of Oral History', in Christopher Dummitt and Michael Dawson (eds.), *Contesting Clio's Craft: New Directions and Debates in Canadian History* (London: Institute for the Study of the Americas, University of London, 2009), 21–6.

Peter Hobbins, 'Public History: Exploring Productive Relationships with Partner Practitioners', November 2018, http://www.phansw.org.au/public-history-exploring-productive-relationships-with-partner-practitioners.

Jack Hodgkins, *Broken Ground* (Toronto: Emblem Editions, 1998).

Jules Hudson and Nick Barratt, 'The Rise and Rise of Family History', *History Today* 57, no. 4 (2007): 20–1.

Franca Iacovetta, 'Springsteen's "Working on a Dream" and Remembering Thirty Years of Activist Collaborations in Canadian Labour and Social History', *Left History*, Spring/Summer 2017, The University of Toronto, 5–26.

Christine Ingleton, 'The Use of Memory-Work to Explore the Role of Emotions in Learning', *Research and Development in Higher Education* 16 (1994): 265–71.

Paul Irish, *Hidden in Plain View: The Aboriginal People of Coastal Sydney* (New South, Sydney, 2017).

Ludmilla Jordanova, 'Public History' in her *History in Practice* (London: Arnold, 2000).

Jorma Kalela, 'Making History: The Historian and the Uses of the Past', in Hilda Kean and Paul Martin (eds.), *The Public History Reader* (Oxon: Routledge, 2013).

Michael Kammen, 'Carl Becker Redivivus: Or, Is Everyone Really a Historian?', *History and Theory* 39, no. 2 (2000): 230–42.

Grace Karskens, *The Rocks: Life in Early Sydney* (Melbourne: Melbourne University Press, 1997).

Gregory Kealey, 'The Writing of Social History in English Canada, 1970–1984', *Social History*, Oct 1985, vol. 10, no. 3, North American Issue, 347–65.

Hilda Kean, 'Public History and Raphael Samuel: A Forgotten Radical Pedagogy?' *Public History Review* 11 (2004): 51–6.

Hilda Kean and Paul Ashton, *People and Their Pasts: Public History Today* (Houndmills, Basingstoke: Palgrave Macmillan, 2008).

Hilda Kean, Paul Martin and Sally J. Morgan, (eds.) *Seeing History: Public History in Britain Now* (London: Francis Bootle, 2000).

Christine Kenneally, *The Invisible History of the Human Race: How DNA and History Shape Our Identities and Our Futures* (Melbourne: Black Inc, 2014).

Carol A. Kidron, 'Being There Together: Dark Family Tourism and the Emotive Experience of Co-presence in the Holocaust Past', *Annals of Tourism Research* 41 (2013): 175–94.

Laura King and Jessica Hammett, 'Family Historians and Historians of the Family: The Value of Collaboration', in Paul Ashton, Tanya Evans and Paula Hamilton (eds.) *Making Histories Public* (Berlin: De Gruyter, 2020), 237–51.

Anne-Marie Kramer, 'Kinship, Affinity and Connectedness: Exploring the Role of Genealogy in Personal Lives', *Sociology* 45 (2011): 379–95, https://doi.org/10.1177/0038038511399622.

Noeline Kyle, 'Genealogy', in Graeme Davison, John Hirst and Stuart Macintyre, *The Oxford Companion to Australian History* (Oxford [1998], 2001), 280–1.

Susan Lanzoni, *Empathy: A History* (New Haven: Yale University Press, 2018).

Steph Lawler, 'Rules of Engagement: Habitus, Power and Resistance', *Sociological Review, Special Issue: Feminism after Bourdieu* edited by Lisa Adkins and Beverley Skeggs, volume 52, Issue 2, October, 2004, 110–28.

Peter Lee, 'History Teaching and the Philosophy of History', *History and Theory* XXII, no. 4 (1983): 19–49.

Stephane Levesque, *Thinking Historically* (Toronto: University of Toronto Press, 2008).

Alison Light, *Common People: The History of an English Family* (London: Penguin, 2014).

Alison Light, 'Genealogy Is Not History's Poor Relation', *The Guardian*, accessed October 12, 2020, https://www.theguardian.com/books/2014/oct/11/genealogy-not-historys-poor-relation-family.

Sian Lindley, 'Before I forget: From Personal Memory to Family History', *Human-Computer Interaction* 27, no. 1–2 (2012): 13–36.

Margaretta Lovell, *Art in a Season of Revolution: Artisans and Patrons in Early America* (Philadelphia: University of Penn Press, 2005).

Ann Low-Beer, 'Empathy and History', *Teaching History* (1989): 8–12.

Bruce Macfarlane, 'Defining and Rewarding Academic Citizenship: The Implications for University Promotions Policy', *Journal of Higher Education Policy and Management* 29, no. 3 (2007): 261–73, DOI:10.1080/13600800701457863.

Jane McCabe, Race, *Tea and Colonial Re-Settlement* (London: Bloomsbury, 2017).

Gary McCain and Nina M. Ray, 'Legacy Tourism: The Search for Personal Meaning in Heritage Travel', *Tourism Management* 24, no. 6 (2003): 713–17.

Trevor McClaughlin, *Barefoot and Pregnant? Irish Famine Orphans in Australia* (Melbourne: Genealogical Society of Victoria, 1991).

Bruce Macfarlane, 'Defining and Rewarding Academic Citizenship: The implications for university promotions policy', *Journal of Higher Education Policy and Management* 29, no. 3 (2007): 261–73, DOI:10.1080/13600800701457863.

Kirsten McKenzie, *Scandal in the Colonies* (Melbourne: Melbourne University Press, 2004).

Natalie Merrill and Robyn Fivush, 'Intergenerational Narratives and Identity across Development', *Developmental Review* 40 (2016): 72–92. https://doi.org/10.1016/j.dr.2016.03.001.

Susan Moore, Doreen Rosenthal and Rebecca Robinson, *The Psychology of Family History* (London: Routledge, 2020).

Frank Mort, 'Foreword', in Sasha Handley, Rohan McWilliam and Lucy Noakes (eds.), *New Directions in Social and Cultural History* (London: Bloomsbury, 2018).

Alice Munro, *The Beggar Maid: The Story of Flo and Rose* (Toronto: Vintage, 1991).

Alice Munro, *Open Secrets: Stories* (Toronto: Vintage, 1995).

Lisa Murray and Mark Dunn, 'Public History in Australia', in Paul Ashton and Alex Trapeznik (eds.), *What Is Public History Globally?* (London: Bloomsbury, 2019).

Catherine Nash, 'They're Family!': Cultural Geographies of Relatedness in Popular Genealogy', in Sara Armed, Anne-Marie Fortier and Mimi Sheller (eds.), *Uprootings/Regroundings: Questions of Home and Migration* (Oxford and New York: Berg, 2003), 179–203.

Christine Nash, 'Genealogical Identities', *Environment and Planning D: Society and Space* 20 (2002): 27–52.

Christine Nash, *Genetic Geographies: The Trouble with Ancestry* (Minnesota: Minnesota University Press, 2015).

Leighann Neilson, 'Why Are Canadians Researching Their Family History?', Randy Boswell (ed.), *Personal Past: History, Identity and the Genealogical Impulse* (Canadian Issues, Association of Canadian Studies, Spring-Summer, 2020), 22–5.

Sally Newman, 'The Freshman Malady': Rethinking the Ontology of the "Crush"', *Rethinking History* 16, no. 2 (2012): 279–301.

Martha Nussbaum, 'Compassion: The Basic Social Emotion', *Social Philosophy and Policy* 13, no. 1 (1996): 27–58. doi:10.1017/S0265052500001515

Martha Nussbaum, *Not For Profit: Why Democracy Needs the Humanities* (New Haven: Princeton University Press, 2010).

Adele Nye and Marnie Hughes-Warrington, Jill Roe, Penny Russell, Mark Peel, Desley Deacon, Amanda Laugeson and Paul Kiem, 'Historical Thinking in Higher Education', *History Australia* 6, no. 3 (2016): 73.1–73.16, DOI:10.2104/ha090073.

Betty O'Neil, *The Other Side of Absence: Discovering My Father's Secrets* (Sydney: Ventura Press, 2020).

Jenny Onyx and Jennie Small, 'Memory-Work: The Method', *Qualitative Inquiry* 7, no. 6 (2001): 773–86, https://doi.org/10.1177/107780040100700608.

James Opp and John Walsh (eds.), *Home, Work and Play: Situating Canadian Social History* (Oxford: Oxford University Press, Third Volume 2015).

Jan Plamper, *The History of Emotions: An Introduction* (Oxford: Oxford University Press, 2015).

Jan Plamper, William Reddy, Barbara Rosenwein and Peter Stearns, 'The History of Emotions: An Interview with William Reddy, Barbara Rosenwein and Peter Stearns', *History and Theory*, 49, no. 2 (May 2010): 237–65.

Pedro Ramos Pinto and Bertrand Taithe (eds.), *The Impact of History? Histories at the Beginning of the Twentieth Century* (Abingdon and New York: Routledge, 2015).

Alana Piper and Ana Stevenson (eds.), *Gender Violence in Australia* (Melbourne: Monash University Publishing, 2019).

Cassandra Pybus, 'The Old Commodore: A Transnational Life', in Desley Deacon, Penny Russell and Angela Woollacott (eds.), *Transnational Ties: Australian Lives in the World* (Canberra: Australian National University E PRess, 2008).

Julie Rak, *Boom: Manufacturing Memoir for the Popular Market* (Ontario: Wilfrid Laurier University Press, Waterloo, 2013).

Peter Read, 'Before Rockets and Aeroplanes': Family History', in Paul Ashton and Paula Hamilton (eds.), *At Home with the Past, Australian Cultural History*, no. 23 (2003): 131–42.

Elaine Reese, Catherine Haden and Robyn Fivush, 'Mother-child Conversations about the Past: Relationships of Style and Memory over Time', *Cognitive Development* 8, no. 4 (1993): 403–30. https://doi.org/10.1016/S0885-2014(05)80002-4.

John Reid, 'The Development and Transformation of Canadian Genealogy', in Randy Boswell (ed.), *Personal Past: History, Identity and the Genealogical Impulse* (Canadian Issues, Association of Canadian Studies, Spring-Summer, 2020).

Kate Retford, 'Patrilineal Portraiture? Gender and Genealogy in the C18th English Country House', in John Styles and Amanda Vickery (eds.) *Gender, Taste, and Material Culture in Britain and North* America, *1700–1830* (New Haven, U.S.: Yale University Press for Yale Center for British Art and the Paul Mellon Centre for Studies in British Art, 2007), 323–52.

Tyson Retz, *Empathy and History: Historical Understanding in Re-Enactment, Hermeneutics and Education* (New York and Oxford: Berghahn Books, 2018).

David Roberts quoted in 'Sons and Daughters of the Southern Cross', *Sydney Morning Herald*, 10–11 Oct. 2009, p. 5.

Emily Robinson, 'Touching the Void: Affective History and the Impossible', *Rethinking History* 14, no. 4 (2010): 503–20.

Portia Robinson, *The Hatch and Brood of Time: A Study of the First Generation of Native-Born White Australians 1788–1828*, vol. 1 (Melbourne: Oxford University Press, 1984).

Barbara Rogoff, 'Developing Understanding of the Idea of Communities of Learners', *Mind, Culture and Activity* 1, no. 4 (Fall 1994): 209–29.

Lyndal Roper, *Oedipus and the Devil: Witchcraft, Sexuality and Religion in Early Modern Europe* (Abingdon: Routledge, 1994).

Gillian Rose, *Doing Family Photography: The Domestic, the Public and the Politics of Sentiment* (Farnham, Surrey UK: Ashgate, 2010).

Roy Rosenweig and David Thelan, *The Presence of the Past: Popular Uses of History in American Life* (New York: Columbia University Press, 1998).

Barbara Rosenwein, 'Worrying about Emotions in History', *American Historical Review* 107, no. 3 (June 2002): 821–45.

Barbara Rosenwein and Riccardo Cristiani, *What Is the History of the Emotions?* (Cambridge: Polity Press, 2018).

Henriette Roued Cunlifee, 'Collection Building Amongst Heritage Amateurs', *Collection Building* 36, no. 3 (2017): 108–14.

Henriette Roued-Cunliffe, 'Visualising Historical Networks, Family Trees and Wikipedia', *Academic Quarter*, Volume 15. Autumn, 2017, 40–54, http://akademiskkvarter.hum.aau.dk/AKsamlet/AK_Vol_15_10_2017.pdf.

Henriette Roued Cunliffe and Copeland, *Participatory Heritage* (London: Facet, 2017).

Penny Russell, 'Travelling Steerage: Class, Commerce, Religion and Family in Colonial Sydney', *Journal of Australian Studies* 38, no. 4 (2014): 383–95.

Raphael Samuel, *Theatres of Memory: Past and Present in Contemporary Culture* (London: Verso, 1994).

Raphael Samuel and Paul Thompson (eds.), *The Myths We Live By* (London: Routledge, 1990).

Joan Sangster, 'Telling Our Stories: Feminist Debates and the Use of Oral History', *Women's History Review* 3, no. 1 (1994): 5–28, DOI:10.1080/09612029400200046.

Sophie Scott-Brown, *The Histories of Raphael Samuel: A Portrait of a People's Historian* (Canberra: ANU E Press, 2017).

Martha Sear, 'A Thousand Different Hands: History in Communities', in Anna Clark and Paul Ashton (eds.), *Australian History Now* (Sydney: New South, 2013), 198–214.

Peter Seixas (ed.), *Theorizing Historical Consciousness* (Toronto: University of Toronto Press, 2006).

Peter Seixas, 'Progress, Presence and Historical Consciousness: Confronting the Past, Present and Future in Postmodern Time', *Pedagogica Historica: International Journal of the History of Education*, 2012, 48:6, 859–72.

Peter Seixas and Tom Morton, *The Big Six: Historical Thinking Concepts Student Book* (Toronto: Nelson Education, 2012).

Bernard Shaw, *The Fabian Society: Its Early History* (London: Franklin Classics [1892], 2018).

Charles Slater, Generativity versus Stagnation: An Elaboration of Erikson's Adult Stage of Human Development, *Journal of Adult Development* 10, no. 1 (2003): 53–65.

Christine Sleeter, 'Critical Family History, Identity, and Historical Memory', *Educational Studies* 43, no. 114–124, (2008): 114–15.

Carol Smart, 'Families, Secrets, Memories', *Sociology* 45, no. 4 (2011): 539–53.

Babette Smith, *A Cargo of Women: Susannah Watson and the Convicts of the Princess Royal* (Sydney: Allen and Unwin, 1988).

Babette Smith, *Australia's Birthstain: the Startling Legacy of the Convict Era* (Crows Nest, Sydney: Allen and Unwin, 2008).

Babette Smith, 'Molesworth Lives? A Reply to Some Reviewers of *Australia's Birthstain*', *Journal of Australian Colonial History* 11, (2009): 227.

Bonnie Smith, *The Gender of History: Men, Women and Historical Practice* (Boston: Harvard University Press, 1998).

Claire Smith, 'The Governor's Daughter', in Sue Pritchard (ed.), *Quilts 1700–2010, Hidden Histories, Untold Stories* (London: Victoria and Albert Publishing, 2010).

Tom Sperlinger, Josie McLellan and Richard Pettigrew, *Who Are Universities For? Remaking Higher Education* (Bristol: University of Bristol Press, 2019).

Mary Spongberg, *Writing Women's History since the Renaissance* (New York: Palgrave, 2002).

John Spurway, 'The Growth of Family History', *Push* 27 (1989): 53–112.

Susan Stabile, *Memory's Daughters: The Material Culture of Remembrance in Eighteenth-Century America* (Ithaca: Cornell University Press, 2004).

Peter Stearns, 'History of Emotions', in Michael Lewis, Jeannette Haviland-Jones and Lisa Feldman Barrett (eds.), *Handbook of Emotions* (New York: Guilford Press, 2008, 3rd ed).

Peter Stearns, *Shame: A Brief History* (Champain: University of Illinois Press, 2017).

Robert Stebbins, *Serious Leisure* (London: Transaction Publishers, 2007).

Carolyn Steedman, 'Lord Mansfield's Voices: In the Archive, Hearing Things', in Stephanie Downes, Sally Holloway and Holly Randles, *Feeling Things: Objects and Emotions through History* (Oxford: Oxford University Press), 209–25.

John Styles and Amanda Vickery, *Gender, Taste and Material Culture in Britain and North America, 1700–1830* (London: Yale University Press, 2006).

Shurlee Swain and Nell Musgrove, 'We Are the Stories We Tell about Ourselves: Child Welfare Records and the Construction of Identity Among Australians Who, as

Children, Experienced Out-Of-Home "Care"', *Archives and Manuscripts* 40 (2012): 1, 4–14, https://doi.org/10.1080/01576895.2012.668840.

Penny Summerfield, 'Mass-Observation: Social Research or Social Movement'? *Journal of Contemporary History* 20, no. 3 (1985): 439–52. doi:10.1177/002200948502000306.

Penny Summerfield, *Histories of the Self: Personal Narratives and Historical Practice* (London: Routledge, 2019).

Jean Teillet, 'Indigenization: How Genealogy and DNA Justify Race Shifting in Eastern Canada', Randy Boswell (ed.), *Personal Past: History, Identity and the Genealogical Impulse* (Canadian Issues, Association of Canadian Studies, Spring-Summer, 2020), 40–3.

Pat Thane and Tanya Evans, *Sinners, Scroungers, Saints: Unmarried Motherhood in Twentieth Century England* (Oxford: Oxford University Press, 2012).

Shirley Tillotson, 'The Canadian Historical Review at 100 years', *Canadian Historical Review* 100, no. 3 (September 2019): 315–48.

Penny Tinckler, 'Photo-Interviews: Listening to Talk about Photos', in *Using Photographs in Social and Historical Research* (London: SAGE, 2014), https://dx.doi.org/10.4135/9781446288016.n9.

John Tosh, *Why History Matters* (Houndmills: Palgrave, 2008).

James Vernon, 'Who's Afraid of the Linguistic Turn: The Politics of Social History and Its Discontents', *Social History* 19, no. 1 (1994): 81–97.

Keith Wailoo, Alondra Nelson and Catherine Lee, *Genetics and the Unsettled Past: The Collision of DNA, Race and History* (New Brunswick: Rutgers University Press, 2012).

Penny Walters, *Ethical Dilemmas in Genealogy* (Self Published, San Bernardino, California, 2020).

Francois Weil, *Family Trees: A History of Genealogy in America* (Cambridge: Harvard University Press, 2013).

Sam Wineburg, *Historical Thinking and Other Unnatural Acts* (Philadelphia: Temple University Press, 2001), http://historicalthinkingmatters.org/why/.

Theses

Jennifer Barrera, 'The Millers: Historical Analysis of an Early Australian Colonial Family', PhD thesis, Federation University 2020.

Alison Baxter, 'Debatable Lands: Exploring the Boundaries of Fiction and Nonfiction through Family History', Oxford Brookes PhD thesis, 2019.

Louise Blake, 'The Ties That Bind: Investigating the Bond between Four Generations of Women in My Family', Masters in Biography and Life Writing, Research Project, Semester 1, 2004, Monash University.

Louise Blake, 'Women and Community on the Upper Goulburn Goldfields', Monash University PhD thesis, 2019.

Shauna Bostock Smith, 'From Colonisation to My Generation: An Aboriginal Historian's Family Research from Past to Present', ANU PhD thesis, 2020.

Shaw, Emma, 'Life in the "Past Lane": An Exploration of the Motives and Metahistorical Understanding of Family History Researchers', PhD thesis, University of Newcastle, 2017.

Helen Little, 'Genealogy as a Theatre of Self-Identity: A Study of Genealogy as a Cultural Practice within Britain Since c. 1850', PhD thesis, University of Glasgow, 2010.

Marian Lorrison, 'Love and Other Bruises: Passion and Yearning in a Time of Social Transformation', PhD thesis, Macquarie University, 2020.

Amy Smith, 'Family Webs: The Impact of Women's Genealogy Research on Family Communication', PhD thesis, Graduate College of Bowling Green State University, 2008.

Simon Titley-Bayes, 'Family History in England, c. 1945–2005: Culture, Identity and (Im)mortality', unpublished PhD thesis, University of York, 2006.

Unpublished Articles/Papers

Tanya Evans, Jerome De Groot and Matthew Stallard, 'I don't even trust what I read in the history books': family history and the future of co-production and collaboration' Article under review.

Del Muise, 'Heritage Omnivores: Canadian Baby Boomers at Home and in Public' (unpublished paper).

Emma Shaw, 2017, conference paper 'Family history as public pedagogy: learning to "do" and produce history in public spaces', paper presented at 'Related Histories' conference, National Library of Australia, 28th November.

Peter Sherlock, 'Colonial Memories: the Hungerfords of Farley' (unpublished paper).

Online Articles

Martin Bashforth, nd. 'What is Radical about Family History, Part 1', https://bashforth.wordpress.com/politics/what-is-radical-about-family-history-part-1/.

Mike Esbester, 'Thoughts on Collaboration: The Start of a Manifesto', http://www.railwayaccidents.port.ac.uk/thoughts-on-collaboration-the-start-of-a-manifesto/.

Rebecca Curtin, 'Australian families suffering "silent war" of domestic violence says advocate', *ABC News*, 18 May 2016.

Eric Evans, Social History Society, 2016; http://socialhistory.org.uk/wp-content/uploads/2018/01/Evans-speech.pdf (accessed 17th Sept 2018).

'Fact file: Domestic violence in Australia', *ABC News* 15 April 2016, https://www.abc.net.au/news/2016-04-06/fact-file-domestic-violence-statistics/7147938?nw=0 (accessed 28th January 2021).

'Hear them speak', *The Guardian Labs*, accessed 19 December 2017, https://www.theguardian.com/nab-more-that-matters/ng-interactive/2017/dec/07/hear-them-speak-victims-of-domestic-violence-share-their-stories#/.

https://www.abc.net.au/news/2017-02-21/community-heritage-groups-at-risk-of-becoming-history/8289296.

https://anglo-celtic-connections.blogspot.com/2012/03/counteracting-decline-of-genealogical.html;https://australiascience.tv/community-groups-battle-volunteer-decline/ (accessed 4th Dec 2020).

https://www.theguardian.com/society/2020/dec/01/the-worst-year-domestic-violence-soars-in-australia-during-covid-19 (accessed 4th December 2020).

https://www.familytreemagazine.com/premium/genealogy-insider-genealogy-tourism/.

https://www.businessdestinations.com/relax/an-interest-in-genealogy-is-fuelling-heritage-tourism/.

https://www.historians.org/publications-and-directories/perspectives-on-history/december-2012/the-future-of-local-historical-societies.

https://www.nytimes.com/2020/05/01/us/coronavirus-college-enrollment.htmlhttps://www.theguardian.com/australia-news/2020/jun/19/incredibly-frustrating-australian-year-12-students-express-dismay-at-skyrocketing-fees-for-arts-degrees;https://www.theguardian.com/commentisfree/2020/jun/19/doubling-university-fees-for-the-arts-will-leave-australia-less-equipped-for-our-complex-world (all accessed 4th December 2020).

Laura King, 'The Shape of His Knees Bulged in the Cheap Tweed: Clothes and Textiles in Remembrance', Blog post, 16th April 2019, https://livingwithdying.leeds.ac.uk/2019/04/16/the-shape-of-his-knees-bulged-in-the-cheap-tweed-clothes-and-textiles-in-remembrance/. This is the website dedicated to this AHRC funded project https://livingwithdying.leeds.ac.uk/ (accessed 11th December 2020).

Maggie Loughran, 'History of Genealogy/Family History', *Making History: The Changing Face of the Profession in Britain* (2008) https://archives.history.ac.uk/makinghistory/resources/articles/family_history.html.

Del Muise, 'Heritage Omnivores: Canadian Baby Boomers at Home and in Public' (unpublished paper).

Del Muise, 'Why Start in Family History', *Genealogy in Canada*, http://genealogyincanada.blogspot.ca/search/What%20Makes%20%20A%20Genealogist%20Start (accessed 13th March 2017).

Wendy O'Brien and Kate Fitz-Gibbon, '"Silent victims": Royal Commission recommends better protections for child victims of family violence', *The Conversation*, 1 April 2016.

Barack Obama, https://www.theguardian.com/science/2013/jan/04/barack-obama-empathy-deficit (accessed 30th October 2020). Obama's speech on YouTube: https://www.youtube.com/watch?v=4md_A059JRc (accessed 30th October 2020). The transcript of Obama's speech to students at North Western University: https://www.northwestern.edu/newscenter/stories/2006/06/barack.html (accessed 30th October 2020).

Alana Piper, 'Did they see it coming? How fortune-telling took hold in Australia - with women as clients and criminals', *The Conversation*, 3rd February 2020.

Hanna Roisin, 'The End of Empathy', NPR, April 15th 2019, https://www.npr.org/2019/04/15/712249664/the-end-of-empathy?fbclid=IwAR0p16X-C6-v3U0Ch-kck7ne6ryKwuxPity3o0OxirP2SCvraj-K60VW6o4.

Barbara Taylor, 'History Workshop Journal', *Making History: The Changing Face of the Profession in Britain* (Institute of Historical Research online source, 2008), https://archives.history.ac.uk/makinghistory/resources/articles/HWJ.html.

Sarah Wendt, 'Why don't we speak up when we see signs of domestic violence?' *The Conversation*, 1 October 2014.

Websites

A Criminal Record: http://acriminalrecord.org/about/ (accessed 23rd November 2020).

Acadiensis was established in 1971, https://www.acadiensis.ca/.

Active History: http://activehistory.ca/.

Ancestors in the Attic: https://www.tvguide.com/tvshows/ancestors-in-the-attic/episodes/472273/.

Ancestry.com: https://www.ancestry.com/corporate/blog/using-facebook-to-grow-your-family-tree/;https://www.gsq.org.au/event/using-social-media/.

Bicentennial History Research Project: http://archivescollection.anu.edu.au/index.php/bicentennial-history-project-research-school-of-social-sciences (accessed 27th April 2018).

Canadians and Their Pasts project see: http://www.canadiansandtheirpasts.ca/.

Co.As.It.: www.coasit.org.au (accessed 11th December 2020).

Fabians: https://fabians.org.uk/about-us/our-history/ (accessed 24th November 2020).

Facebook for Canadian Genealogy: https://genealogyalacarte.ca/wp-content/uploads/2019/04/Facebook-for-Canadian-Genealogy-May-2019.pdf (accessed 21st September 2020).

https://www.campop.geog.cam.ac.uk/ (accessed 24th November 2020).

https://findingaway.auctr.edu/AAFHA.asp and https://www.aahgs.org/ (both accessed 23rd November 2020).

Family Bibles: http://familybibles.org.uk/ (accessed 6th November 2020).

Family Search

Christine Sleeter's blog: http://historyandfamily.blogspot.com.au/.

Dana Saxon: http://ancestors-unknown.org/1/previous/2.html,http://www.fastcompany.com/3029871/whos-next/why-researching-our-ancestors-has-the-power-to-change-lives.

Family Tree Magazine: https://www.familytreemagazine.com/resources/online/best-social-media-for-genealogy/ (accessed 7th December 2020).

Federation of Family History Societies: https://www.familyhistoryfederation.com/ about 2016; Australian Federation of Family History Organisations Inc., 2004, https://affho.org/#:~:text=AFFHO%20was%20established%20in%201978,or%20 territory%20and%20New%20Zealand.

Founders and Survivors: http://www.foundersandsurvivors.org/.

Histoire Engagée: http://histoireengagee.ca/.

HistoriansCollaborate: https://historianscollaborate.com/ (accessed 28th January 2021).

https://web.archive.org/web/20111004102343/http://www.ontarioroots.com/index.html ?%2Fcontent%2F01%2Fmenu_01_01.html.

https://www.familysearch.org/blog/en/heritagetourism/; https://familytreetours.com/ (both accessed 21st September 2020).

https://www.theguardian.com/australia-news/2019/mar/06/descended-from-both-sides-of-queenslands-bloody-massacres (accessed 4th September 2020).

https://www.newcastle.edu.au/newsroom/faculty-of-education-and-arts/massacre-map-and-guardian-australia-partnership-project-wins-premiers-history-award (accessed 23rd November 2020).

https://tracesmagazine.com.au/ (accessed 7th January 2020).

Irish Family History Centre: https://www.irishfamilyhistorycentre.com/article/expert-workshop-child-incarceration-in-19th-century-dublin-by-aoife-oconnor (accessed 23rd November 2020).

The Killing Times: https://www.theguardian.com/australia-news/series/the-killing-times (accessed 4th September 2020).

Labour/Letravail was established in 1976: http://www.lltjournal.ca/index.php/llt.

Legacies of British Slave Ownership: https://www.ucl.ac.uk/lbs/; https://www.abc.net. au/religion/australia-and-the-dark-legacy-of-slave-ownership/12744288 (accessed 23rd Nov 2020).

John Reid: https://anglo-celtic-connections.blogspot.com/2020/.

Julie Poulter's website: https://www.quirkycharacters.com.au/about.html.

Miles Taylor, 2016, Social History Society: http://socialhistory.org.uk/wp-content/ uploads/2018/01/Taylor-speech.pdf (accessed 17th September 2018).

MiLife: https://www.milife.online/about-us.

One Name Guild: http://www.one-name.org/guild.html (accessed 23rd November 2020).

Pat Thane, 'Asa Briggs, Baron Briggs of Lewes, 1921–2016' http://socialhistory.org. uk/2017/04/19/pat-thane-on-asa-briggs/.

Random Acts of Genealogical Kindness: https://raogk.org/ (accessed 7th December 2020).

Reliving: https://www.reliving.co.uk/.

Social History: https://socialhistory.org.uk/about/our-history/ (accessed 11th April 2018); https://www.theguardian.com/society/2010/aug/10/keith-nield-obituary (accessed 24th November 2020).

Social History/Histoire Sociale: https://muse.jhu.edu/journal/440 was established in 1968, https://www.hssh.ca/about-us/#anchor-journalhistory (accessed 25th November 2020).

Traditions of the Ancestors: https://www.tota.world/ (all accessed 16th November 2020).

University of New England: https://www.une.edu.au/study/study-options/study-areas/history-and-political-science/local-family-and-applied-history (accessed 8th June 2018).

University of Tasmania: http://www.utas.edu.au/arts-law-education/study/diploma-of-family-history (accessed 8th June 2018).

University of Toronto Press: https://utorontopress.com/us/books/by-series/canadian-social-history-series (accessed 24th November 2020).

Urban History Review was established in 1972: https://www.erudit.org/en/journals/uhr/.

Who do You Think you Are?: https://www.bbc.co.uk/programmes/b007t575/episodes/guide.

Podcasts

Amateur Family History Podcast (UK): https://podcasts.apple.com/gb/podcast/amateur-family-history-podcast-uk/id1448636109.

Britain: BBC4 Tracing your roots: https://www.bbc.co.uk/programmes/b006zbxm/episodes/downloads.

Canada: French-Canadian Legacy Podcast: https://fclpodcast.com/.

Digging Into the Past: Family History in Canada: https://www.bac-lac.gc.ca/eng/news/podcasts/Pages/family-history-canada.aspx.

Maple Stars and Stripes: https://maplestarsandstripes.com/.

Index